Clinical Health Psychology and Primary Care

Clinical Health Psychology and Primary Care

Practical Advice and Clinical Guidance
for Successful Collaboration

———

Robert J. Gatchel and Mark S. Oordt

American Psychological Association
Washington, DC

First printing February 2003
Second printing January 2004

Published by
American Psychological Association
750 First Street, NE
Washington, DC 20002
www.apa.org

To order
APA Order Department
P. O. Box 92984
Washington, DC 20090-2984

Tel: (800) 374-2721, Direct: (202) 336-5510
Fax: (202) 336-5502, TDD/TTY: (202) 336-6123
Online: www.apa.org/books
E-mail: order@apa.org

In the U.K., Europe, Africa, and the Middle East, copies may be ordered from
American Psychological Association
3 Henrietta Street
Covent Garden, London
WC2E 8LU England

Typeset in Goudy by Argosy, Waltham, MA

Printer: United Book Press, Inc., Baltimore, MD
Cover Designer: Ni Design, Baltimore, MD
Project Manager: Argosy, Waltham, MA

The opinions and statements published are the responsibility of the authors, and such opinions and statements do not necessarily represent the policies of the American Psychological Association.

Library of Congress Cataloging-in-Publication Data
Gatchel, Robert J., 1947–
    Clinical health psychology and primary care : practical advice and clinical guidance for successful collaboration / by Robert J. Gatchel and Mark S. Oordt.—1st ed.
      p. cm.
    Includes bibliographical references and index.
    ISBN 1-55798-989-3 (alk. paper)
    1. Clinical health psychology. 2. Primary care (Medicine) I. Oordt, Mark S. II. Title.

R726.7.G375 2003
616'.001'9--dc21

2002043751

British Library Cataloguing-in-Publication Data
A CIP record is available from the British Library.

Printed in the United States of America

To my wife, partner, and
best friend in the world, Anita Jo.—*Robert J. Gatchel*

To my wife, Ruth, and our wonderful children, Andrew,
Martha Rose, Carol, and Ellen.—*Mark S. Oordt*

CONTENTS

ACKNOWLEDGMENTS

We would like to acknowledge the help and support we received from the American Psychological Association's publications staff, particularly Susan Reynolds and Ed Meidenbauer, as well as from Kathleen Byrne. We would like to thank the reviewers of this book, Peter J. Vicente and Robert G. Frank. In addition, we greatly appreciated the outstanding work of Carol Gentry.

INTRODUCTION

The American Psychological Association designated 2001 through 2010 as the Decade of Behavior. Arguably, there are few settings where attention to behavior and its consequences are more relevant than in the primary care physician's office. Lifestyle factors such as tobacco use, inactivity, a high-fat diet, and high-stress careers have been recognized for many years now as key contributors to the ailments for which people commonly seek medical care. In fact, according to the U.S. Centers for Disease Control and Prevention, lifestyle factors contribute strongly to the top 10 causes of death in the United States. Their role, in fact, is greater than that of genetic, biological, or environmental factors.

The primary care physician is the front-line provider who, in addition to medically evaluating and treating the patient, must assess, educate, motivate, and intervene in terms of these lifestyle issues in an effort to provide well-rounded care, promote health, and prevent disease. With the growth of managed care, many physicians are tasked with doing this while faced with greater numbers of impaneled patients and shorter appointment times. It has been estimated that up to 70% of primary care medical appointments are for problems stemming from psychosocial issues. Furthermore, more than 50% of psychotropic medications used in the United States are prescribed by primary care physicians (with only 12% prescribed by psychiatrists). This has led some to the conclusion that primary care is the de facto mental health system in this country.

Given these facts, the increasing interest and support for behavioral health care providers to integrate their practices into the primary care setting are not surprising. Psychologists, psychiatrists, and social workers colocated with primary care clinic physicians can provide a breadth of expertise to address the psychosocial and mental health needs of primary care patients. Behavioral health integration into primary care can also ease physicians' workloads, improve health outcomes, ease access to mental health services for patients, and enhance patient satisfaction with care.

Clinical health psychologists working in primary care are in a unique position; they can go beyond providing assessment and treatment of primary mental health problems by offering expertise to enhance the effectiveness of treatment for the primary *medical problems* presenting in the primary care setting. Specialty trained clinical health psychologists are experienced in the medical culture, tend to be knowledgeable in medical conditions and procedures, and are skilled at assessing, conceptualizing, and intervening, using empirically based treatments with patients struggling with health concerns and their psychosocial sequelae. Research data indicate that health psychology interventions can improve medical treatment outcomes, enhance treatment adherence, decrease long-term complications of disease, and decrease medical overutilization (a matter of increasing importance in today's capitated health care systems). Moreover, as reviewed throughout this book, self-management approaches are often needed to modify maladaptive lifestyle behaviors such as tobacco use and overeating. Such approaches are receiving renewed attention from the American Psychological Association (APA); for example, the *Monitor on Psychology* recently published a series of articles on self-management in the areas of exercise, weight loss, work stress, stress-reduction methods, and wellness models.[1]

Although the body of work on models for integrating clinical psychology and primary care is growing, not much has been written specifically on the practice of clinical health psychology in this setting. The primary care clinic presents unique challenges to even highly experienced health psychologists because it calls on different skills than those used in specialty clinics, treatment programs, or hospital settings. Clinical health psychologists integrating into primary care must adapt their practices to the primary care culture if they are to be successful and accepted. This may include working in 15- to 30-minute appointment slots, making decisions and recommendations with limited data, and making recommendations to physicians that can be conveyed in no more than 2 or 3 minutes.

This text is designed to provide practical guidance to psychologists and psychology students working or considering working in a primary care setting. It combines empirical knowledge with practical advice gleaned from experience, and thus is intended to be a practice handbook that providers can keep handy in their offices and refer to frequently. It is written for clinical psychologists who are interested in transitioning into a primary care setting or those already working in primary care who may be interested in expanding services from a primary focus on mental health issues to assisting

[1] American Psychological Association. (2002). Self-care for you. *Monitor on Psychology, 33*, 48–68.

in the treatment of physical health problems and psychophysiological disorders. It is also relevant to clinical health psychologists who may have been working in specialty settings (e.g., pain clinics or cardiac rehabilitation) and who are seeking a review of key areas before integrating into primary care where a broader range of patient conditions is likely to be encountered. It may also be used as a classroom text for clinical psychology students and medical students. It is applicable to courses in health psychology or those covering models of psychological practice. As a practical handbook, it would be useful as a resource for any clinical practicum or internship rotation involving primary care.

We begin with an overview of clinical health psychology in primary care that includes a review of several models for integrating into a medical practice, a discussion of the differences between specialty health psychology services and primary care health psychology services, and a listing of skills necessary for success in the primary care setting. Chapter 2 is devoted to suggestions for establishing and maintaining a clinical health psychology practice in the primary care setting. It addresses relationship building with colleagues of different disciplines, soliciting of referrals, understanding the primary care culture, availability, ethical concerns, and financial issues. The subsequent chapters are devoted to common health complaints and diseases seen in primary care, and the collaborative role a clinical health psychologist can play in managing these patients within the primary care setting. The chapters on diabetes, hypertension, cardiovascular disease, asthma, acute and chronic pain, insomnia, obesity, and gastrointestinal disorders begin with a description of the conditions and their common medical treatments to help psychologists work collaboratively and in an informed manner with physician colleagues. Each of these chapters also covers the psychosocial and behavioral factors related to the condition and strategies psychologists can use to intervene within the context of a primary care appointment. A glossary of terms related to the medical condition and its treatment as well as recommendations for further reading concludes each chapter.

In addition to the chapters organized around disease states, several chapters are presented to assist psychologists in working with patient issues that cut across diagnoses. These include chapters on modifying health-compromising behaviors (tobacco use, excessive alcohol or drug use, and inactivity), working with high utilizers of medical care, and helping patients cope with chronic or terminal illness. Throughout many of these chapters, case studies are presented to illustrate the practice of health psychology in primary care. These are fictional cases but represent common scenarios seen in actual practice. The book concludes with a discussion of future trends and opportunities in health psychology and integrated primary care. Both of these fields are relatively young, and there is tremendous potential for growth and expansion in these efforts to serve patients and relieve suffering.

The growth of health psychology in the past 30 years is testimony to the field's value within the modern health care system. Our hope is that this book will enhance the application of health psychology research and clinical practice in the primary care setting for the benefit of patients and physicians alike. We both have a wealth of experience working in this setting, and we hope our insights, combined with the empirically based information presented, will provide a pragmatic guide for those interested in transitioning into the primary care setting.

Clinical Health Psychology and Primary Care

1

CLINICAL HEALTH PSYCHOLOGY IN THE PRIMARY CARE SETTING: AN OVERVIEW

Clinical health psychology is the application of psychological knowledge to the "promotion and maintenance of health, the prevention and treatment of illness, and the identification of etiologic and diagnostic correlates of health, illness and related dysfunctions" (Matarazzo, 1980, p. 815). Nevertheless, a commonly held assumption by medical providers is that all clinical psychologists provide care solely within the *mental* health arena. For example, when the junior author, Mark Oordt, and colleagues initially integrated their practice with that of a primary care clinic, they regularly stopped by the offices of each medical provider to remind them of these newly integrated psychological services and to ask if any of the day's patients might benefit from a consultation. "I don't think I have any 'psych' cases for you today" was a common reply. Oordt and his colleagues felt that, despite early efforts to educate these physicians about the skills of clinical health psychologists and their potential contribution to the *health care* of the physicians' patients, the physicians' preconception placed them, as psychologists, into the realm of *mental health* alone.

As medical providers gain more experience working with clinical health psychologists, they are also likely to gain a greater understanding of what a psychologist can do to prevent disease, modify health risk behaviors, reduce disability, bolster the effectiveness of medical treatments, and improve health-related quality of life. Furthermore, the collaborative role of health psychologists for treating medical patients is likely to become increasingly recognized and valued as physicians and other health care workers continue to embrace the biopsychosocial model (Engel, 1977) for understanding their patients and to abandon outdated notions of mind–body dualism.

THE BIOPSYCHOSOCIAL MODEL OF HEALTH AND ILLNESS

The biopsychosocial model is increasingly being shown to be the most heuristic approach to medical illnesses in general (Gatchel, 1999; Turk, 1996). This model focuses on the complex interaction of variables—biological, psychosocial, and medico–legal—that patients encounter when dealing with a persisting, distressing medical condition. It accounts for the likelihood that patients' lives are adversely affected in a variety of ways by their medical condition, thus requiring a comprehensive assessment and treatment approach designed to address all aspects of required care, both biological as well as psychosocial. This is in contrast to alternative, outdated, and purely biomedical approaches designed to seek out the often-elusive "quick-and-easy" treatment plan resulting in a "medical cure."

The integration of a clinical health psychologist into the primary care setting is, almost by definition, the application of the biopsychosocial model. When behavioral health care is provided by referral to a specialty mental health provider, a clear line is being drawn between what is in the physical realm (that which can be treated in the medical setting) and what is in the mental realm (that which must be referred to the mental health setting). The message often received by the patient is "My doctor thinks this is all in my head." In contrast, when behavioral health care is provided by a member of the primary care team (who happens to be a clinical health psychologist), there is more consistency to the message that good health care involves attention to psychological as well as physical aspects of health and illness. In fact, the inclusion of a clinical health psychologist on the primary care team communicates the reality that health and illness are multifactorial concepts. Indeed, all health problems have psychological components.

MODELS OF PRIMARY CARE PSYCHOLOGY

The approaches for providing psychological services in primary care fall on a continuum. The structure selected will depend on the characteristics of the particular health care setting, the "buy-in" from organizational leadership, financial arrangements, the skills and preferences of the medical providers and staff, and the skills and preferences of the psychologists.

Colocated Clinics Model

At one end of a continuum is colocation of a traditional psychological clinic and a primary care clinic. This model does not constitute primary care psychology per se, because the psychologist is not integrated into the primary care clinic. The primary care clinic is likely to be a primary referral source for the psychologists. However, patients may be referred from a variety of other sources as well. The medical and psychological clinics may share appointment and reception services and waiting rooms, but they remain two separate organizations.

Colocation alone, however, can provide several advantages. Referrals between clinics may be easier, especially if one scheduling system is used. Medical and psychological providers will be familiar with each other's work, and communication between physicians and psychologists is likely to be facilitated by physical colocation. This is likely to improve collaboration and enhance patient perception that different aspects of care are well coordinated. Additionally, stigma from seeing a psychologist might be reduced when the patient is able to receive care at the same location where other medical services are provided.

> A 27-year-old female graduate student complains to her physician of abdominal cramping and diarrhea. She is referred to a gastroenterologist for further evaluation that results in no definitive findings. She is diagnosed with irritable bowel syndrome and returns to her primary care physician for management. Her physician recommends dietary changes and fiber supplements, but her symptoms do not improve. After several months, the physician suggests that the stress from her academic program may be exacerbating the symptoms and recommends she see a psychologist who works in the same building and who specializes in treatment of people with medical concerns. The patient contacts the psychologist, who schedules her for an evaluation appointment. At the first session, the psychologist obtains the patient's consent to discuss her treatment with her physician so they can coordinate care. The patient and the psychologist agree on a treatment plan oriented around a cognitive–behavioral approach to managing stress and relaxation training. The physician is informed of the plan, and during routine follow-up appointments, he inquires about her progress and encourages use of relaxation skills.

Psychologist as Primary Care Provider Model

A more integrated model of care involves the psychologist as a provider within the primary care clinic. In this model, the psychologist provides individual and group therapy for a variety of mental health conditions or psychophysiological disorders. The primary care physicians refer patients. The standard of care is that of an outpatient mental health or health psychology clinic. Patients receive comprehensive assessments, they must give informed consent for the psychologist's treatment plan because it is separate from the physician's treatment, and the treatment interventions are standard for what psychologists provide in other settings. In this system, the psychologist collaborates with the physician but is an independent provider who is primarily responsible for that aspect of care. This model of practice is similar to the colocation model discussed earlier, but the patient's care is provided as part of the primary care practice per se.

An advantage of this model is that patients receive comprehensive behavioral health care through the primary care clinic. Because a member of the primary care team is seeing the patients, they are less likely to perceive their care as being "turned out." Furthermore, many patients referred to mental health clinics do not make or keep their initial appointments, whereas our experience shows that approximately 90% of those referred to the primary care psychologist are initially evaluated. The primary limitation is that the demand for services may quickly overwhelm the time the psychologist has available. This may mean that only limited categories of patients can be treated (i.e., the most severe) or, a worst-case scenario, that a backlog develops so patients cannot obtain appointments. This may lead to a perception among colleagues that the psychology service is not available and, therefore, is not of practical utility to the primary care practice.

> A 55-year-old man complains to his primary care physician that he has slept poorly for the past 6 months. The problem was precipitated by a hospitalization following a heart attack, and it has been progressively worsening. His medical recovery has been going well, but he admits to some fear about having another cardiovascular event and some anxiety about dying in his sleep. He has been taking sleep medication when he "really needs it" (approximately three times per week) since the hospitalization. The physician sends the patient to the reception desk to schedule an appointment with the primary care psychologist. The psychologist conducts a comprehensive evaluation of the patient and formulates a treatment plan to address the man's insomnia and anxiety. Treatment is provided through 12 weekly sessions. The psychologist and the physician collaborate by the psychologist providing cognitive–behavioral therapy and the physician setting a schedule for tapering off the medication. They also communicate informally about the patient's progress. Once the insomnia has improved, psychological treatment is terminated, and the patient continues to see the physician for routine medical care.

Behavioral Health Consultant Model

A third model involves the psychologist as a behavioral health consultant. The psychologist is a member of the primary care management team and is called on to provide expertise for behavioral, emotional, and psychosocial aspects of the health care plan. Because all patients have psychosocial factors relevant to their health, the psychologist is likely to see a broad range of the clinic's population. The behavioral health consultant sees patients for evaluation and makes recommendations to the primary care case manager (a physician), who is responsible for providing and coordinating the care. The behavioral health consultant may follow the patient to monitor implementation of the recommendations but, in most cases, will limit contact to one or two sessions. In seeing the patient for follow-up, the behavioral health consultant collaborates by providing psychological and behavioral interventions while maintaining communication about the patient's progress and treatment plan with the physician, who remains the primary decision maker.

In situations in which more definitive mental health care is needed, the behavioral health consultant makes that recommendation to the primary care manager and facilitates the referral. The psychologist maintains the role of consultant, however, and does not provide those services herself or himself. In addition, the behavioral health consultant may provide targeted services to a specific group of primary care patients, often those who are high utilizers of medical care. Care may take the form of a clinical pathway for intervening with a specific disorder (e.g., depression, diabetes) or may involve a psychoeducational group intervention (stress management, chronic pain group, or relaxation skills training). This targeted approach is referred to as *vertical integration*, while the broad-based consultant services approach targeting the clinic's population at large is called *horizontal integration* (Strosahl, 1998).

The advantages of this model include the potential to provide services to a large percentage of the population served by the clinic. The brief consultation approach allows greater access to the psychologist for more patients because appointment slots typically are not filled by ongoing care visits. The potential for consolidated care is also greater because one provider (the primary care case manager) maintains responsibility for the patients' care. A limitation to the model is that patients receive only assessment and treatment at the primary care level. Although this may be sufficient for some patients, others will need to be referred elsewhere for more intensive care.

A 41-year-old woman visits her primary care provider and is diagnosed with diabetes. She is referred to a nurse educator, who provides extensive education on the disease and recommended lifestyle changes for managing it. At a follow-up visit, her physician inquires about her lifestyle changes, and she expresses low confidence that she can lose the recommended weight. She has tried a number of commercial and popular diets and, although she has lost a few pounds, she never has been successful at keeping the weight off. The physician introduces the patient to the clinic's behavioral health consultant, who is able to work the patient into a same-day appointment slot. The psychologist and the patient discuss the patient's barriers to weight loss, devise a plan for targeting change in those areas, and select an initial goal on which to work. Additionally, the psychologist recommends a book that provides a sensible, rational approach to weight loss. The psychologist communicates the recommended plan to the physician and offers to meet with the patient again in 4 weeks to assess progress and address any problems. The physician incorporates the weight loss strategy into the patient's general health care plan and inquires about her progress at future health care visits.

Staff Adviser Model

A fourth model involves the psychologist as expert consultant to the medical providers only. The psychologist does not necessarily maintain an office in the primary care setting but is available by pager at all times. The psychologist has no independent contact with the patient for evaluation or treatment. Rather, the psychologist provides a specialized knowledge base for assisting the physician with diagnosis, treatment planning, resources, or approach to care. The psychologist may sit in during the patient's appointment with the medical provider and then provide advice to the physician, either with the patient present or absent. Alternatively, the medical provider may verbally present the case for the psychologist's consultation in person or over the telephone. Depending on the size of the primary care clinic, the psychologist may also provide consultation/liaison services to other clinics or medical units. Those other responsibilities, however, will need to be flexible to allow time for primary care consultation requests throughout the day.

One advantage of this method is that one provider, with whom the patient has an established relationship, gives all care. Additionally, this is an excellent model for medical training programs, because it provides ongoing education for medical students, interns, and residents in attending to behavioral, emotional, and psychosocial factors. A limitation is that the psychologist is not being utilized to help manage the workload of the primary health care provider.

A second-year family practice resident pages the primary care psychologist and requests assistance in working with a "difficult" patient, a 35-year-old woman with chronic leg pain. She presented to her appointment angry and accusatory in her demeanor, insisting that the doctor increase the dosage of the narcotic she has been using. The patient has been taking the medication on an as-needed basis and has gone through her normal month's supply in 2 weeks. The physician is concerned about abuse of the medication and asks for consultation on managing the patient's chronic pain. The psychologist interviews the patient with the physician present, and then they step out of the exam room to discuss the case. The psychologist presents her conceptualization of the patient's pain problem from a biopsychosocial perspective. She makes specific recommendations for changing to an interval schedule for the medication and for improving the pacing of the patient's activities to prevent exacerbation of the pain. The physician implements the plan and follows the patient as before.

Combining Models

Each of the models just discussed offers opportunity for improving attention to the emotional and behavioral needs of primary care patients. These models are not mutually exclusive, however. A stepped-care approach may be used, whereby the physician initially consults with the psychologist to formulate a behavioral treatment plan. If the patient does not make the desired changes, the psychologist may then interview the patient to further assess the problem and refine the intervention. If again there is not sufficient improvement, the psychologist may decide to engage the patient in a treatment protocol, with weekly therapy sessions, to increase the likelihood of change (Pruitt, Klapow, Epping-Jordan, & Dresselhaus, 1998).

REFERRALS TO PRIMARY CARE HEALTH PSYCHOLOGY

Regardless of the model used to integrate clinical health psychology into primary care, patients must be prepared for these services in a way that will allow them to benefit the most. As Gatchel and Weisberg (2000) have noted in discussing the assessment and treatment of patients with pain, treatment professionals must be astutely aware that many medical patients are very sensitive to the term *psychological treatment*. They perceive it as suggesting that their physicians believe that their medical condition is not real, but merely imaginary. An effort must be made, therefore, to convince patients that the reason they are being requested to undergo any psychological or behavioral treatments is to deal comprehensively with their general psychophysiological functioning. A pervasive misperception about psychological treatments—and about psychology in general—seems to have developed because so many patients in the past have been told that their medical condition is not real.

It is imperative that patients be educated about the role of psychological treatment as a component of their overall health care. Indeed, we often find it useful for referring physicians to describe us as "the member of our health care team with expertise in ... (lifestyle change, stress, depression, etc.)." Additionally, we use the phrase *behavioral medicine evaluation and treatment* rather than *psychological evaluation and treatment* in our first encounters with patients in a primary care setting. These terms help to diffuse some of the misperceptions about the evaluation and treatment process and can help reinforce to patients the medical nature of this assessment/ treatment process.

We emphasize with our patients that one reason for the behavioral medicine evaluation and treatment is that various medical conditions, especially if chronic in nature, can lead to pressures and changes of lifestyle that most people find unpleasant, at the very least. Unplanned and unwanted lifestyles changes can lead to stress, so patients often feel worse than they ever anticipated, and the acute stress can interfere with physical recovery. We explain this in terms of a cycle in which the medical condition—and the changes it brings—leads to stress, which leads to increased medical symptoms, which leads to increased stress, and so on. This *medical symptom–stress cycle* is then pointed out to the patients as important to deal with (see Figure 1.1).

We also explain that the behavioral medicine evaluation and treatment will focus on stress-related issues that are intertwined with the actual medical condition. Of course, for ethical reasons, we clearly state that we are psychologists and that the evaluation/treatment process involves psychological issues that are related to their medical condition. By this time, though, the preparation of patients makes them less resistant to the idea of having psychological evaluation and treatment.

Note also that we try to avoid using terms such as *psychological problems* and *psychopathology* whenever possible. Instead, we use the terms *stress, biopsychosocial disorders, behavioral medicine,* and so on, which have a more neutral connotation. Most patients are relieved when these terms are used and, consequently, are more open to the evaluation and treatment process. Indeed, the lay public in general is quite familiar with the notion of stress and does not interpret it with any negative psychiatric connotations. The evaluation and treatment process is discussed as a means to deal with stress

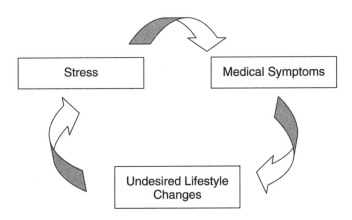

Figure 1.1. The medical symptom–stress cycle.

factors that could be interacting with their medical condition. Patients are frequently quite receptive and understanding of this purpose. Therefore, careful education of the patient before the psychological assessment/treatment process, by both the referring physician and the psychologist, can help reduce resistance to undergoing this process.

Finally, initiating any treatment focusing on the "somatic" aspect of the disorder, such as the use of biofeedback and stress management, as a way of dealing with the role of stress and its physiological counterpart, tension, usually helps patients to engage in the treatment process more easily and in a nonthreatening manner. Moreover, such treatment modalities begin to teach patients that they can indeed control their physiology, which, in turn, increases their confidence that they can actively control their medical condition. Indeed, biofeedback and stress management procedures have been found to be highly efficacious in reducing anxiety and tension in patients. These reductions, in themselves, are very rewarding to patients who immediately begin to feel a sense of relief that their overall functioning is being positively affected. Once patients are "hooked" into the treatment, they become less resistant or threatened by us openly talking about more personal types of stressors or cognitions that are contributing to their medical condition.

DIFFERENCES BETWEEN SPECIALTY CLINIC HEALTH PSYCHOLOGY PRACTICE AND PRIMARY CARE HEALTH PSYCHOLOGY

The first two models of primary care discussed earlier require no specific skills beyond those used by clinical health psychologists practicing in other settings. These models involve application of general clinical health psychology practices into the primary care setting. The last two models discussed, however, require unique skills and a different philosophy of care because the psychologists must function as primary care providers. This means they must adapt their assessment and intervention approaches to the primary care structure, including brief appointment times and short notice access to care. They also must function as a member of a multidisciplinary team. Psychologists who are truly integrated into a primary care team give up some level of autonomy of practice in that the primary "customer" is the primary care manager, not the individual patient. Additionally, integration into primary care requires a shift to a population health model of care, in which the goal is to affect the entire population served by the clinic, rather than limiting behavioral health care only to those who exceed a certain threshold of need.

Because the larger body of clinical health psychology literature can be readily applied to specialty care work (even when done in primary care settings), most of this book addresses primarily health psychologists who are integrated as members of a primary care team. The book includes a discussion of the unique skills required to work as a member of a primary care team, and it also suggests approaches for addressing common diseases and health-related problems within the structure of the primary care setting.

SKILLS REQUIRED FOR CLINICAL HEALTH PSYCHOLOGISTS INTEGRATED INTO PRIMARY CARE

As discussed earlier, the culture of primary care is distinct from other health care settings in which psychologists may work. As such, psychologists who are integrated into a primary care setting will need specific skills to adapt to that setting. The following skills are suggested for optimizing success.

Focused Assessment

One of the most challenging aspects of primary care work for many psychologists is the "unlearning" of assessment skills that have served them well in outpatient mental health or health psychology clinics. Health psychologists are trained to thoroughly assess patients, a process that includes the study of symptom presentation, functional analysis, biopsychosocial factors, psychopathology, history, and health habits. Many psychologists commonly use extensive psychometric testing as well. The time constraints and demands in primary care make this approach to assessment impractical.

To be useful to medical providers, the primary care health psychologist must be able to make quick assessments and practical recommendations. To accomplish that, psychologists must conduct an assessment that focuses primarily on the presenting problem or the referral question. Many areas of importance may thus be de-emphasized, and the clinician new to primary care may struggle with discerning what domains and details can be left out. For example, a health psychologist who is referred a patient with uncontrolled diabetes might explore myriad avenues to uncover factors contributing to nonadherence to medication requirements. Beliefs, social contingencies, past history, side effects, depression, anxiety, relationship with physician, finances, alcohol use, and many other factors may be playing a role, but in-depth analysis of each of these would be impossible in a 15- to 30-minute evaluation.

A helpful strategy is to use broad, closed-ended questions to cover general areas. Those areas that yield significant information can be probed in more depth, whereas those areas that do not can be put aside. Questions that have the greatest predictive power should be used. For example, depression can be screened reasonably well by asking about mood and anhedonia (Spitzer et al., 1994). Areas such as risk for harm to self and others do not need to be evaluated comprehensively in all cases, but can be screened for briefly with patients in distress, with significant loss, or with other notable risk factors. Certainly, some relevant details will not come to light using this approach. For most patients, however, a focused assessment will be sufficient to identify target problems and make genuinely helpful recommendations, or will be adequate to recognize that more definitive care is indicated.

In considering this type of brief assessment, it is important to remember the setting and role in which the psychologist is functioning. At first impression, some people may conclude that we are advocating for a lower standard of care for mental health services. This, however, is not the case. Including a psychologist as a member of the primary care team is, in actuality, exceeding the standard of care for addressing behavioral health concerns in the primary care setting. In such a situation, the primary care team now has access to expertise that is not normally a part of primary heath care. This can increase the level of care for the 50% of patients with mental health needs who receive treatment for those needs from their primary care provider (Narrow, Reiger, Rae, Manderscheid, & Locke, 1993), as well as many more with physical health concerns. Those in need of a higher level of care will receive it by way of referral to specialty-level mental health services.

Time Efficiency

Many clinical psychologists are trained to assess and treat within a standard 50-minute appointment. The primary care setting often does not afford such time. The pace in primary care is rapid, and providers, including those in behavioral health, must be efficient to meet the demands of such a pace. If a psychologist uses an hour for each patient in a busy primary care setting, a backlog will soon develop, patients will not be able to be seen in a timely manner, and the psychologist will cease to be useful to the physicians in the practice.

Time efficiency involves making maximal use of the brief time available with each client. As mentioned earlier, primary care psychologists must focus quickly on the presenting problem in the assessment phase and avoid spending too much time gathering information that is "nice to know" but not essential. A session must be well planned so that appropriate amounts of time are spent in introduction, assessment, education, selection of interventions, recommendations, contact with referring physician (when necessary for medication issues), homework, and developing a follow-up plan. Doing all this in a brief 15- or 30-minute time frame requires strong organizational and time management skills. Psychologists are likely to struggle in this environment if they do not adapt to the pace of primary care.

Decisiveness With Limited Data

The brief time available for each patient limits the amount of data available to the psychologist. Therefore, primary care psychologists must be able to draw conclusions and make decisions based on limited information. Those who are uncomfortable in pressing ahead without a thorough exploration of every aspect of a patient's life, past and present, will not be well suited for primary care work.

This does not mean, however, that providers can make unsupported conclusions or use a "cookie-cutter" approach, treating all patients the same without regard for their individual situations and needs. On the contrary, primary care psychologists must develop highly tuned skills for eliciting *key* information on which to base decisions without spending time going down blind alleyways. Primary care providers must have expert knowledge on what are the best indicators, risk factors, and predictors of a particular disorder or problem area. They should also use well-constructed and validated psychometric instruments to increase the predictive power of the data obtained. This will ensure that, although many aspects of a patient's life remain unexplored, the data available are those necessary for making correct decisions.

Cognitive–Behavioral Expertise

Psychologists will benefit from having a broad range of brief interventions to apply to the variety of problems encountered in the primary care clinic. Although no studies are available to date showing one theoretical orientation to psychotherapy to be more effective than others within the primary care setting, some practical considerations apply. Depending on the model of primary care psychology used, therapy that is relationship focused may be more or less practical. When the psychologist is integrated into the clinic as a team member, interventions are generally behaviorally focused and brief. For this, a solid foundation in behavioral and cognitive–behavioral theory and practice is likely to be useful.

Skills for Enhancing Motivation to Change

Many patients are referred to the primary care psychologist for assistance with changing health-related habits and behavior. Common targets are tobacco use, exercise, diet, alcohol, and medication adherence. The stages-of-change model (Prochaska, DiClemente, & Norcross, 1992) is a helpful heuristic for conceptualizing a patient's readiness to make the necessary changes. A psychologist in primary care can be a particularly useful resource for physicians, not only in formulating effective behavior change plans but also in helping patients find the motivation to make the necessary changes.

Motivational interviewing, originally developed by Miller and Rollnick (2002) for working with patients with alcohol dependencies, has been applied to a variety of health behaviors (Botelho & Skinner, 1995; Rollnick, Mason, & Butler, 1999) and is a highly useful skill set for application in the primary care setting. Physicians will attest to the fact that many action-oriented behavior change recommendations meet with significant resistance because the patient is not yet personally invested in making the change. Even one brief motivational interviewing session can enhance readiness and increase success. This service can be invaluable to primary care physicians and to the health of their patients.

Appreciation for a Population Health Focus

Primary health care is different from specialty health care in many ways. One important distinction is that primary care is focused on maximizing the health of the impaneled population as a whole, whereas specialty care focuses in-depth on the disease of each individual. With this as a framework, the primary care psychologist will need to maintain a population health perspective to succeed in that setting. Primary care should involve prevention of disease and illness as well as treatment. Psychologists in primary care should be willing to accept *all referrals*, not just those who meet criteria for a *DSM-IV* diagnosis or severe health behavior problems. For example, psychologists might be referred every newly diagnosed person with diabetes to address the psychosocial and behavioral aspects of the disease at the forefront, before they become problematic.

Patients who need to stop smoking, change diet, reduce alcohol intake, or learn to manage stress might be referred to create a plan for success and to prevent relapse. This should not occur only after patients have failed in their initial efforts but rather on initial recommendation to maximize self-efficacy and improve the chance of success on the first effort. As a member of the primary care team, the psychologist's role is to provide the behavioral and psychosocial components of primary health care; this is a much broader role than that of working only with the mental health issues that present to the clinic.

Good Communication With Physician Colleagues

The value of psychologists' work in primary care settings will depend largely on the degree with which they can communicate clearly and efficiently with referring physicians. A few recommendations for communicating with medical colleagues in primary care are as follows:

- *Avoid psychology lingo:* Explain yourself in common terms that are easy to understand.

- *Get to the point:* Physicians are busy and often do not have time to linger in conversation. Aim toward giving verbal feedback to referring physicians in about 30 seconds. If they have further questions or are interested in further information, they can initiate further inquiry.
- *Stand behind your perspective:* Psychologists are trained differently than physicians, but this is where our value lies. Do not be a fanatic, but also do not give in to opposing opinion too easily.
- *Keep written consult reports brief and neat:* Recommendations should be concrete and specific.
- *Do not take it personally if physicians do not take your advice:* The people they refer remain their patients, and they are ultimately responsible for treatment decisions.

Ability to Function as a Team Member

Primary care clinics rely on smooth-running teamwork. Physicians, nurses, medical technicians, other health care providers, office managers/administrators, receptionists, billing staff, and cleaning staff all perform interacting duties to ensure quality care for patients. Primary care psychologists must be able to maintain good working relationships with all members of the team and work collaboratively in the best interests of the patients and the practice. Psychologists have skills that may be applied toward ensuring maximum team effectiveness, resolving conflicts between primary care team members, and recommending organizational changes to enhance job satisfaction and performance.

Tolerance for Position in a Hierarchical System

In primary care, the physician is at the "top of the ladder." Medical doctors are likely to have higher status, have access to more perks, and make more money than other providers in the clinic (e.g., physician assistants, nurse practitioners, psychologists). A highly trained senior psychologist may have more years of formal education and experience than some physician colleagues but is still likely to be lower in the hierarchy. Psychologists who have difficulty tolerating that status are likely to find greater satisfaction working in another setting in which they can be more independent in their practice.

Flexible Hours/Availability

Primary care psychologists should try to be flexible in their hours so as to be accessible to primary care managers for consultation when needed. This may mean staying late to assist with a difficult clinical situation or to research the answer to a colleague's question. Primary care psychologists should also establish a means for being contacted (pager or cell phone) during clinic hours when not in the office and should be willing to answer calls promptly.

Understand Medical Conditions, Procedures, and Medications

Working in a medical clinic requires knowledge of medical terminology, a basic understanding of the common diseases and their treatments, and a familiarity with medications. Obviously, clinical health psychologists are a step ahead of generalist psychologists in this area due to their specialized training working with medical patients and their frequent collaboration with medical colleagues. Collecting a well-selected library of reference materials can be essential for maintaining this knowledge. It should include a medical dictionary, a current medication handbook (e.g., *Physicians Desk Reference*), an anatomy text (e.g., *Gray's Anatomy*), and an encyclopedia of diseases (e.g., *The Merck Manual of Diagnosis and Therapy*). Reliable Web sites on the Internet can also be a source of information (e.g., MD Consult at www.mdconsult.com and Web MD at www.webMD.com). This current volume is intended to be useful in this regard as well. Psychologists will also benefit from reading primary care journals and newsletters to be aware of current issues.

SUMMARY

Integrated primary care settings offer psychologists and primary care medical providers a unique opportunity to work closely together to meet the biopsychosocial needs of patients. A number of models have been used for integrated care, with varying levels of medical–behavioral collaboration. Each offers potential benefits and drawbacks. The primary care setting has its own "rules of engagement," and not all clinical psychologists adapt well or enjoy working in this setting. For those with the skills and interests outlined in this chapter, it can be a highly rewarding environment with tremendous potential to have a positive effect on the lives of patients.

RECOMMENDED READING

Blount, A. (Ed.). (1998). *Integrated primary care: The future of medical and mental health collaboration*. New York: W. W. Norton.

GLOSSARY

biopsychosocial model A model for understanding disease and illness that accounts for the complex interaction of variables (biological, psychosocial, and medico–legal) that patients encounter when dealing with a persisting, distressing medical condition.

horizontal integration A form of integrated behavioral health care that is broad in scope and attempts to affect a wide array of people within a clinic's population.

psychophysiological disorders Health disorders characterized by dysfunctions in various bodily organs and systems that are intimately linked with psychosocial factors.

vertical integration Behavioral health care targeted at addressing the needs of a specific group.

REFERENCES

Botelho, R. J., & Skinner, H. (1995). Motivating change in health behavior: Implications for health promotion and disease prevention. *Primary Care, 22,* 565–589.

Engel, G. L. (1977). The need for a new medical model: A challenge for biomedicine. *Science, 196,* 129–136.

Gatchel, R. J. (1999). Perspectives on pain: A historical overview. In R. J. Gatchel & D. C. Turk (Eds.), *Psychosocial factors in pain: Critical perspectives* (pp. 3–17). New York: Guilford Press.

Gatchel, R. J., & Weisberg, J. N. (2000). *Personality characteristics of patients with pain.* Washington, DC: American Psychological Association.

Matarazzo, J. D. (1980). Behavioral health and behavioral medicine. *American Psychologist, 35,* 807–817.

Miller, W. S., & Rollnick, S. (2002). *Motivational interviewing* (2nd ed.). New York: Guilford Press.

Narrow, W., Reiger, D., Rae, D., Manderscheid, R., & Locke, B. (1993). Use of services by persons with mental and addictive disorders: Findings from the National Institute of Mental Health Epidemiologic Catchment Area Program. *Archives of General Psychology, 50,* 95–107.

Prochaska, J. O., DiClemente, C. C., & Norcross, J. C. (1992). In search of how people change: Applications to addictive behavior. *American Psychologist, 47,* 1102–1114.

Pruitt, S. D., Klapow, J. C., Epping-Jordon, J. E., & Dresselhaus, T. R. (1998). Moving behavioral medicine to the front line: A model for the integration of behavioral and medical sciences in primary care. *Professional Psychology: Research and Practice, 29,* 230–236.

Rollnick, S., Mason, P., & Butler, C. (1999). *Health behavior change: A guide for practitioners.* Edinburgh, Scotland: Churchill Livingstone.

Spitzer, R. L., Williams, J. B. W., Kroenke, K., Linzer, M., de Gruy, F. V., III, Hahn, S. R., et al. (1994). Utility of a new procedure for diagnosing mental disorders in primary care: The PRIME-MD 1000 study. *Journal of the American Medical Association, 272,* 1749–1756.

Strosahl, K. (1998). Integrating behavioral health and primary care services: The primary care mental health care model. In A. Blount (Ed.), *Integrated primary care: The future of medical and mental health collaboration* (pp. 139–202). New York: W. W. Norton.

Turk, D. C. (1996). Biopsychosocial perspective on chronic pain. In R. J. Gatchel & D. C. Turk (Eds.), *Psychological approaches to pain management* (pp. 3–32). New York: Guilford Press.

2

ESTABLISHING A PRIMARY CARE
PSYCHOLOGY SERVICE

Throughout this book, we review clinical approaches to working with primary care patients, including theoretical and practical perspectives. This chapter sets the stage for application of that material by discussing some of the key issues psychologists should attend to in establishing a primary care service. Although each health care environment presents unique challenges, the issues presented here apply to most settings and serve to build a foundation for addressing clinic-specific concerns and obstacles. We believe that diligent attention to the factors discussed in this chapter will help create a behavioral health service that can surmount these obstacles and one that will be responsive to both providers' needs and to the health concerns of patients.

The integrated primary care movement is experiencing growing interest (Rabasca, 1999). However, many health care organizations and individual physicians are still unfamiliar with the concept. Even among those who are oriented to the idea of psychological services being integrated into a primary care team, a variety of reactions can be expected. In our experience, the vast majority of primary care physicians, nurse managers, and clinic administrators are highly enthusiastic about integrated services. Certainly, this is echoed nationally by the increasing numbers of health systems that are integrating care. Because patients with psychosocial and behavioral needs are prevalent in primary care (Kroenke & Mangelsdorff, 1989), most clinic personnel seem to recognize and welcome the potential gain from adding behavioral expertise and resources into the staffing mix. A few, however, may resist integration of a behavioral health provider for a variety of reasons. Some providers believe psychological services are stigmatizing and, therefore, would hesitate to refer any patient who does not have a severe mental illness. Others may resist integration because they prefer to manage the behavioral and psychological aspects of care themselves. In some systems, competition for fees between physicians and psychologists also may be a barrier to acceptance in primary care.

Once a psychologist becomes fully integrated, however, many of the providers who were resistant are likely to learn to value the in-house services offered. Good service and satisfied patients are likely to yield more referrals to psychologists, as well as a greater commitment to integrated practice within the clinic as an indispensable way of providing health care. Nevertheless, careful planning and a deliberate strategy are essential for success and for obtaining a buy-in from medical colleagues. The key issues discussed next are intended to provide a road map to achieve that success.

KEY FACTORS IN ESTABLISHING A PSYCHOLOGY SERVICE IN PRIMARY CARE

Get Your Foot in the Door

As with any new endeavor, a thriving primary care psychology service will not just suddenly appear. Its establishment requires patience and perseverance while the psychologist "proves" his or her worth to the rest of the clinic staff. Because most primary care staff are not accustomed to having psychologists as part of the team, acceptance must be earned. The services a clinical health psychologist can provide, however, are greatly needed in the primary care setting, so odds are good that providers, nurses, and other staff will quickly embrace the new model. Because patients tend to be highly receptive to behavioral health services in primary care (Talcott, Russ, & Dobmeyer, 2001) if appropriate steps are taken to minimize stigma and obstacles, patients' comments to their physicians regarding integrated care will also tend to increase the psychologist's acceptance among colleagues.

The first steps for integrating a psychology service into the primary care clinic are to establish basic support from clinic management and to gain access to the infrastructure to do the work. Necessary resources include office space, scheduling, reception, chart management, coding and billing services, and so on. That said, it is important, at least in the early stages, that the psychologist be willing to accept minimal support, if necessary. This may mean tolerating inconveniences, such as having a different office to work in every day, but will lead to the psychologist getting a foot in the door. At the beginning, the best course of action may be to avoid requesting that procedures be altered to accommodate the clinic's new nonmedical provider. For example, some psychologists working in primary care prefer that patients' vital signs not be taken when care is focused primarily on psychosocial or behavioral needs. Psychologists may also want medical technicians or nurses to score psychometric instruments for them. Although these special considerations may be arranged once the psychologists are more fully integrated, they are likely to do best, at least in the early stages, if they do not expect much in return from the clinic. Once the psychologists have proven what they have to offer, they will find it easier to obtain support for changes to the system.

Additionally, primary care psychologists should initially focus on establishing services that meet the priorities and needs of the clinic. Interviews with the clinic's director, medical providers, and nursing staff can shed light on what these priorities are. (This will also help illuminate where the real power structure lies in the clinic, which is essential information.) For example, if the clinic is establishing a new clinical pathway for hypertension, the psychologist can offer to contribute by running a relaxation or stress management group. If staff express frustration with a few demanding, high-utilization patients, the psychologist might offer to see these patients as soon as possible. Demonstrating responsiveness to the clinic's priorities, rather than first marketing one's own interest or specialty area, will pay off with greater enthusiasm for the behavioral health program among clinic staff and will lead to "word-of-mouth" advertising, more referrals, and growth of the service.

Be a Team Member

By virtue of their training in medical settings, clinical health psychologists may be more accustomed to working as part of a health care team than are other clinical psychologists. Nevertheless, we cannot overemphasize the importance of being a team player within the primary care setting. Psychologists who try to function outside the team mentality will soon find their referrals drying up, and they may experience a decided lack of respect from clinic colleagues. A number of suggestions are provided here for being an effective team member.

See All Patients Referred

Physicians will refer patients when they believe the psychologist has something to offer or when they have run out of options from their own skills set. If psychologists accept these referrals, and do their best to help, they will be seen as valuable assets to the clinic. On the other hand, psychologists who see only certain types of patients, or only patients whose acuity exceeds a specific threshold, are not likely to be highly utilized. For example, a health psychologist may have specialized training and interest in chronic pain management or cardiovascular disease and have less interest in seeing common depression or anxiety cases. Likewise, a psychologist may hesitate to see patients with mild "problems in living" who do not display significant psychopathology. Being a member of the primary care team, however, means seeing whichever patients the referring physicians believe are in need of behavioral heath services.

View Referring Physicians as Your Primary Customers

For a team to function well, all members must work toward the same goals. Therefore, primary care psychologists must ensure that their work is "in sync" with the care being provided by the referring physician. The potential exists for patients to become significantly confused if the psychologist and physician are giving contradictory messages or working toward different goals. For example, a physician may refer a woman to the primary care psychologist to learn relaxation skills that will help her better manage her chronic pelvic pain. During the evaluation, the psychologist learns of significant experiences of abuse when the patient was a child and, believing this is a factor in the woman's pain, proceeds with a treatment plan centered around resolving abuse issues. In this example, the physician and the psychologist are working with different agendas. As a primary care team member, the psychologist in this example should provide the services requested by the referring physician (assuming, of course, that the patient consents). When the psychologist identifies additional factors that may be contributing to the patient's condition or distress, recommendations should be made to the physician directing the patient's care, and the patient's overall treatment plan must be adapted so that all health care providers are working together. This type of coordination may be unfamiliar to psychologists who are accustomed to practicing as independent providers. It is essential, however, for primary care.

Communicate Well

To coordinate in the manner just discussed, clear communication must be established between all members of the primary care team. One of the primary complaints by physicians who refer patients to external mental health clinics is that they typically receive little or no feedback about the status of patients or the care they are receiving. This is largely due to confidentiality standards that prohibit psychologists from discussing their cases. Patients can, of course, provide consent for their mental health and medical providers to communicate with each other. However, this consent is often not requested.

For true integration of behavioral health services into primary care, communication among providers must occur. This is actually one of the key benefits, for both patients and providers, of integrating psychologists into primary care. Feedback from the psychologist's evaluation should include significant findings, impressions, and recommendations. Special effort should be made to provide this feedback on the same day the patient is seen. Given the rapid pace and busy schedules within primary care, the feedback is best kept brief and should be focused on the referring physician's primary concerns.

Build Key Relationships

Success in building a primary care psychology practice and in being accepted as a team member will largely depend on strong relationships with colleagues. Buy-in from all levels of clinic staff will not only lead to utilization of behavioral health services but will also ensure that the psychologist gets the support needed to do the job. In virtually every organization (including primary care clinics), there are people in formal leadership jobs, and there are people who actually influence the organization and whom people follow. Sometimes these true leaders are the people in the formal positions, but sometimes they are not. Psychologists must quickly learn who has influence in the clinic and form a good working relationship with these people. This may be the clinic director or the office manager, but it could also be a particularly charismatic physician or a nurse who has been with the practice for the past 20 years. If the "movers and shakers" in the organization are enthusiastic about integrated care, that enthusiasm is likely to rub off on others.

Psychologists should also make a point of getting to know support personnel in the clinic. This includes medical technicians, receptionists, schedulers, billing staff, and medical coders. These people are unlikely to be familiar with the role and abilities of a clinical health psychologist. If they understand the value of the psychologist in comprehensive health care, they will be more likely to accurately represent the psychological services to patients and will have more motivation to provide support.

Certainly, each psychologist will have his or her own preferred style of building relationships with colleagues. The following strategies, based on our experience, are offered to assist in the process.

Sit in With Physician Colleagues

When first setting up a primary care practice, a psychologist may benefit in several ways from seeking an invitation to sit in for several hours with each of the medical providers. First, sitting in with each provider guarantees that everyone will know the psychologist by name and face early on. This is particularly important in a large, busy practice, where a new member of the staff may go unnoticed by some providers for a significant period of time. Second, this will allow the psychologists to learn the practice styles of their particular referring providers. Knowing the manner in which colleagues work can pay off in better collaborative treatment efforts. Third, brief discussions after each patient visit may allow the psychologists an opportunity to provide input on the case and to suggest ways in which they may be able to contribute to the care of similar patients in the future. This type of "applied education" about what services the psychologist has to offer can have much more impact than the commonly used 15-minute presentation at a staff meeting and may go far in building positive perceptions of the psychologist's professionalism and credibility. Finally, for psychologists who have never worked in a primary care clinic, sitting in on patient visits can provide a "crash course" in the primary care culture.

We should note that physicians and patients are likely to vary in their receptiveness to this arrangement. Those in medical education settings are likely to be accustomed to students observing during medical visits and may not object to a psychologist colleague doing the same. In other settings, more resistance may initially be seen, although our experience is that a discussion of potential benefits often makes the idea more appealing to medical providers.

Act Like a Primary Care Provider

For psychologists to be accepted as part of the primary care team, they must act as if they are part of it. In other words, psychologists must do the things that the other providers do. This may mean attending lunches or presentations by pharmaceutical company representatives. They should attend holiday parties and other social functions. Participation in these informal activities communicates commitment to be part of the organization rather than to remain an outsider. Psychologists should also stay current on the major medical journals relevant to primary care (see the Recommended Readings section at the end of this chapter) and should apply for affilliations or memberships with professional organizations, such as state or regional primary care associations. Being able to speak knowledgeably about the issues facing primary care providers, as well as the latest medical findings, will facilitate acceptance.

Assist Coworkers

Psychologists have unique skills that can be useful to the nursing or support staff. Offering classes to clinic personnel on stress management, conflict management, or assertive communication can not only help coworkers experience healthy, effective living but can also help them quickly come to value having a psychologist in the clinic. Likewise, psychologists can offer in-service workshops to help both providers and support staff better perform their jobs. Topics might include motivational interviewing (Miller & Rollnick, 1991), strategies for working with dissatisfied or demanding patients, and approaches to screening for mental health disorders. The time expended in building staff relationships by offering staff something of value to assist them in accomplishing their own roles in the clinic is likely to be paid back many times over with attentive support for the psychologist.

Persist in Marketing Psychology Services

Until the medical providers in the clinic become accustomed to having an in-house psychologist, they should be consistently reminded of the newly available services. We have used a variety of strategies for marketing, some of which are discussed below.

Designate a "Problem of the Week"

A weekly flyer can be distributed to all providers notifying them of a "Problem of the Week," that is, a specific clinical condition that the psychologist is highlighting and seeking referrals for. The flyer should *very briefly* outline what services the psychologist can provide. The weekly "problem" may include such issues as depression, treatment adherence, and weight control. Flyers should be readable in a few seconds, or they are likely to be discarded without being read. An example of a flyer is presented in Figure 2.1. Providers are encouraged to be alert for each particular

---

Behavioral Health Consultant Update

Do any of your patients need to lose weight?

The behavioral health consultant can help by:

- Setting realistic, individualized goals for weight loss
- Identifying triggers for overeating
- Establishing a plan for systematically increasing exercise duration
- Providing referring providers with progress reports and patient status updates.

Patients can be scheduled with the BHC at the reception desk, or I can be contacted by pager at 555-3309.

Figure 2.1. Example of a weekly flyer.

"problem" and make an effort to refer patients with such problems to the psychologist. The overarching goals are to increase providers' knowledge of the services provided by the psychologist and to continuously remind them of the service. Many physicians tend to refer only patients with primary mental health problems to a psychologist, because they are not aware of the contribution a clinical health psychologist can provide to nondistressed patients with physical health problems. Such a flyer may be a practical means for educating colleagues about services discussed throughout this book.

Conduct Daily Check-Ins

Strosahl (personal communication, September 2000) suggested going to each provider's office at the start of each day to ask if they have any patients on their daily roster that might benefit from behavioral services. To accommodate patients identified through this method, psychologists should arrange their schedules in such a way that some patients can be seen as walk-ins shortly after their scheduled medical appointment, when needed.

Be Available

As discussed earlier, medical providers are likely to use a behavioral health service that is responsive to their needs and to the needs of their patients. For this reason, it is important that psychologists make themselves highly accessible to their colleagues. For instance, providers should be encouraged to contact the psychologist by pager or cell phone *any time* a question arises, even if the psychologist is in the midst of a therapy session or is otherwise engaged. Although many psychologists are trained to avoid all interruptions during treatment sessions, this is not the norm within primary care settings. Furthermore, psychologists who work in primary care on a part-time basis should try to maintain accessibility even when they are not working in the clinic. Providers typically will not misuse the pager or cell phone for insignificant matters and, often, questions can be addressed in a minute or two. If more time is needed, arrangements can usually be made for the psychologist to recontact the physician at a more convenient time. Psychologists need to reinforce the efforts of providers to use the psychologist's services by responding rapidly. An initially positive experience will increase the likelihood of physicians referring patients or requesting a consultation the next time a need arises.

Arrange your schedule to make consultation convenient. If possible, psychologists should leave time available during the day for physicians to drop in for informal consultation or for seeing patients on a walk-in basis. If the psychologist is out of sight all day seeing patients, physicians will be less likely to perceive the psychologist's services as being available to them. We have had success in leaving one out of every three appointment slots unscheduled to maintain availability. (Note, however, that this is certainly easier to accomplish in settings where the psychologist does not work on a fee-for-service basis.)

Psychologists should also make a point to be available at times when the physicians are available. Often, the only unscheduled time providers have is before the first patient appointment, during the lunch hour, and at the end of the day. Psychologists may benefit from arriving at the clinic at least 30 minutes before the first patient appointment, staying around the clinic during lunch (or having lunch where the other providers are eating), and staying around the office for awhile after the last patient is seen.

Learn the Primary Care Culture

The primary care culture is radically different from that of specialty mental health. The differences between the two, in fact, have the potential to interfere with smooth integration of a psychologist into primary care. Bray (1996) noted that

> collaboration between psychologists and physicians is hampered by factors such as differences in theoretical orientations (biomedical vs. psychosocial), lack of a common language (medical jargon vs. psychological jargon), different practice styles, lack of accessibility to the different providers, and varying expectations for assessment and treatment. (p. 93)

Because it is the psychologist who is moving into the medical setting, it is incumbent on the psychologist to learn the cultural norms of the primary care setting and to do whatever possible to adapt to it. Some recommended steps for doing so are discussed next.

Adopt the Primary Care Pace

Many mental health providers, including clinical health psychologists, are trained to see patients in standard 50-minute sessions. Primary care providers typically work in 15-minute appointment slots. Psychologists working in primary care should adapt their schedule and, thus, their practice style, to that of their medical colleagues. We have found that two back-to-back appointments can be combined for initial appointments, with follow-up care being provided in 15-minute visits.

This schedule is likely to accomplish two goals. First, it will allow sufficient appointment slots for patients to have quick access to psychological services. If patients cannot be seen for a couple of weeks after referral due to scheduling backlogs, physicians will be less likely to refer distressed patients and will be less satisfied with the service. Second, mimicking the work pace of medical colleagues demonstrates a commitment to function as a member of the primary care team. Psychologists who work like a primary care provider are less likely to be treated as outsiders and more readily embraced as a peer.

Adopt a "Population Health" Perspective

As discussed in chapter 1, the goal of primary medical care is to meet the broad health care needs of as many patients in the clinic's population as possible. This is different from specialty care, in which in-depth care is provided for selected patients who meet certain criteria. Primary care patients with routine needs are assessed and treated in accord with protocols to which the majority of people respond well. Patients who need specialized care are referred to specialists who can provide the higher level of care.

Primary care psychologists should parallel this model by providing targeted assistance to large numbers of patients rather than devoting extensive resources to the few with the greatest need. Within this population-oriented perspective, assessment should generally be focused on the presenting problem, as opposed to conducting a comprehensive psychological evaluation, and recommendations should entail brief interventions that have a good chance of moving the patient toward better health and well-being. Patients with more severe problems who cannot be appropriately managed in primary care or who do not respond to primary care treatment should be referred to traditional mental health services. If primary care psychologists attempt to treat every patient in the same manner that is used by mental health clinics, the system will become overwhelmed and is likely to fail.

Give Feedback Promptly and Succinctly

In the primary care environment, communication about patients should typically be brief and to the point. Verbal feedback should be given to referring providers as soon as possible after their patients have been seen. Initial feedback, however, should take no more than 30 to 60 seconds. If providers want more details, let them ask for it. Brevity is necessary because the feedback is often given in the hallway or office between patient visits, which means little time is available for extraneous details. When more extended discussion is needed between the psychologist and physician to coordinate care, it can be useful to establish a time to meet when both providers are available (such as at the end of the day). Primary care physicians are typically very willing to engage in more extended discussions when necessary, but doing so with every patient referred will be too demanding on their limited time.

Likewise, written documentation in primary care should be brief. In contrast to the training of many psychologists, primary care physicians keep focused case notes that only briefly document significant findings, diagnostic impressions, procedures performed, and treatment plan. Rarely do they use full sentences. To fit into the primary care culture, psychologists should adapt their note writing to be similar to that of medical colleagues. Referring physicians will be more likely to read psychologists' documentation and incorporate it into their own care if notes are similar in style and length to their own.

Additionally, documentation will be most helpful to medical colleagues when the recommendations back to the referring provider are clearly spelled out. Primary care physicians will appreciate and benefit most from recommendations that are practical, because the culture of primary care is very action oriented. Recommendations that the psychologist wants the physician to act on should be *specific*. For example, a psychologist may request that, during monthly follow-up visits, the physician ask patients with hypertension about their adherence to recommendations of daily relaxation exercises. The psychologist might also recommend that the physician consider tapering sleep medications 2 weeks after beginning a behavioral treatment program for insomnia. Vague recommendations, such as "ask about self-management" or "the patient shouldn't use sleep medications long term," will be less helpful.

Although we have emphasized the importance of psychologists fitting into the primary care culture, the new skills and services that psychologists bring with them can augment the existing norms. For example, groups and classes (several of which are discussed in later chapters of this book) can enhance traditional primary care services. Additionally, motivational interviewing strategies can be introduced to enhance promotion of healthy lifestyles and adherence to medical regimens.

Attend to Ethical Issues

The American Psychological Association's *Ethical Principles of Psychologists and Code of Conduct* (2002) is the accepted code psychologists must abide by in their practice. Clinicians must carefully consider how the code applies to their particular practice setting to protect the welfare of clients. A comprehensive review of the code is beyond the scope of this chapter. However, some specific issues that are particularly important or that have unique aspects for practice in the primary care setting are discussed.

Ethical Standard 2.01, *Boundaries of Competence*, states that "psychologists provide services, teach, and conduct research with populations and in areas only within the boundaries of their competence based on their education, training, supervised experience, consultation, study, or professional experience." Psychologists working in primary care must be extraordinarily diligent not to practice beyond the services that they are qualified to provide. In our experience, some patients will not distinguish between a medical provider and a psychologist working in primary care. For example, they will sometimes ask for medication and refills. Because most psychologists do not have prescribing privileges, this boundary is easy to maintain. Patients, however, will also ask psychologists for medical advice on a broad range of topics, some of which a psychologist might be fairly well informed about. Issues that are clearly of a medical nature, such as the best medications for a particular condition or the appropriate level of activity following a heart attack, should be deferred to, and coordinated with, a physician. Even if a psychologist has extensive medical knowledge based on experience, issues related to medication and medical status are outside the scope of clinical psychology.

Principle B, *Fidelity and Responsibility*, states that psychologists "cooperate with other professionals and institutions to the extent needed to serve the best interests of those with whom they work." This issue points to the ethical responsibility of primary care psychologists to consider whether each patient seen is best served in the primary care setting or referred to a mental health clinic. Clearly, not all mental health needs are appropriate for treatment in primary care. In our opinion, certain groups of patients should be referred to traditional mental health. These groups include patients at high risk for committing suicide, those who need frequent contact for support and stability, patients needing specialized treatment programs (e.g., patients with substance dependence or eating disorders), patients with active psychoses, and patients who have not responded to an initial trial of treatment in primary care.

Another ethical issue that is particularly relevant to primary care has to do with clarification of roles. Principle C, *Integrity*, states that psychologists "strive to keep their promises and to avoid unwise or unclear commitments." Because, at this point in time, integrated behavioral health care is an unfamiliar concept for many patients, psychologists must clearly articulate the roles they will be performing with respect to patients' overall care. For example, if a psychologist is functioning within a consultancy model, he or she should clearly inform patients that the referring provider is still in charge of their care and that the psychologist's role will be restricted to advising that provider and assisting in initiating a treatment plan. The psychologist should also clarify any differences between primary care psychology, which is often less intensive and may involve limited provider contact, and specialty mental health care. This information will allow patients to make a fully informed choice regarding the type of care they want to receive.

A final issue that we believe presents unique concerns within the primary care setting is confidentiality. Principle E, *Respect for People's Rights and Dignity*, states that psychologists "respect ... the rights of individuals to privacy, confidentiality, and self-determination" and are "aware that special safeguards may be necessary to protect the rights and welfare of persons or communities whose vulnerabilities impair autonomous decision-making." In primary care settings, it is essential that team members communicate with each other to meet the needs of patients collaboratively. Psychologists in primary care, however, still have an obligation to protect confidentiality. The way around this dilemma is to obtain consent from each patient allowing team members to communicate with each other about their care. Most patients understand the benefits of having their various providers working together in a coordinated fashion and, therefore, will allow this communication. If they do not, however, care will need to be provided within the constraints of confidentiality. Furthermore, even when consent is given, psychologists must only discuss patient information that is pertinent to other team members, and only with those people (e.g., the primary physician) who need to know the information. Along the same lines, psychologists should be discreet about what they write in the medical record. Because all primary care staff typically use the same medical chart, the psychologist should take care to avoid documenting details of a patient's life that are not essential for other providers to know.

Plan Around Financial Issues

A number of models were presented in chapter 1 describing how psychologists can integrate their practices into a primary care practice, including colocation of separate clinics, psychologists as providers in primary care, and two models in which psychologists are consultants. The model chosen may depend largely on financial issues related to different types of practice, because different systems of health care will support integrated psychologists differently.

Some practices are based on fee for service. In these settings, providers bill patients or insurance companies for the services provided. Third-party payers typically exclude certain services from reimbursement. Medicare, for example, specifically excludes "consultation" services, psychophysiological therapy (e.g., biofeedback training for headaches or anxiety), as well as the majority of preventive services and across-the-board screenings (APA, 2001). Furthermore, in the past few years, many insurance plans changed their policies so they now only reimburse psychologists for *mental health* care (using psychiatric codes). As a result, clinical health psychologists who want to work with medical disorders have encountered more difficulty with third-party payment. Primary care psychologists working in a fee-for-service practice have sometimes had to limit their practice to treatment of primary or comorbid mental health disorders (e.g., treating major depression in a patient with cardiac problems or adjustment disorders in newly diagnosed patients with diabetes) to get reimbursed. In January 2002, six new current procedural terminology (CPT) codes became available for behavioral assessment and interventions with physical health patients (see Table 2.1). This allows psychologists to bill for services directed at physical health and eliminates the need for a mental health diagnosis for psychological services to be reimbursed (Smith, 2002). Unfortunately, these codes are reimbursed at significantly lower levels than would be paid if psychologists were reimbursed for using medical CPT codes. Even though payers have begun refusing payment on claims in which psychologists have used medical codes, health psychologists should continue to advocate for reimbursement on these higher

TABLE 2.1
New Current Procedural Terminology (CPT) Codes

CPT Code	Service Provided	Approx. Medicare Payment per 15-Minute Unit
96150	Assessment, initial	$26
96151	Reassessment	$26
96152	Intervention, individual	$25
96153	Intervention, group (per person)	$ 5
96154	Intervention, family with patient	$24
96155	Intervention, family without patient	$23

Note. These CPT codes are for behavioral, social, and psychophysiological assessment and interventions for the prevention, treatment, or management of physical health problems.

paying codes. Facts that justify the use of these codes, suggested by Deardorff (personal communication, January 2002), include the following:

- Within the scope of their license, psychologists can provide treatment for physical problems. This treatment is not "psychotherapy," and it does not address mental health problems. (*Note:* When the nature of treatment is psychotherapy, it is then more appropriate to bill as such.)
- Laws are in effect in most states that prohibit discrimination of reimbursement based on the degree the provider holds (e.g., PhD vs. MD) as long as the treatment provided is within the scope of the provider's training and expertise.
- It is not appropriate to bill using a psychiatric diagnosis and treatment code, if this not the situation.
- Given what is known about the benefits and cost effectiveness of many health psychology assessment and intervention services, a payer's unwillingness to reimburse psychologists for these services represents a lack of commitment to quality, cost-effective care.

Psychologists attempting to integrate their practices into multidisciplinary private group practices may have an advantage over those in independent practice in terms of contracting with third-party payers. Some health management companies, in forming their provider networks, may be more willing to contract with a relatively small number of group practices than with a large number of individual providers, thus making the integrated practice more attractive (American Psychological Association Practice Directorate [APAPD], 1996). Laws differ in each state regarding how psychologists and physicians can associate in practice (i.e., partnerships, professional corporations, limited liability companies). Psychologists interested in these arrangements are referred to the publication *Models of Multidisciplinary Arrangements: A State-by-State Review of Options* (APAPD, 1996) and should seek legal counsel.

Providers involved will also need to work out overhead cost issues related to integrated practice. For some, colocated clinics may prove to be the simplest arrangement in these settings, because overhead can be split in an equitable way based on space and staff services used. Some psychologists prefer to hire their own staff for scheduling and billing. This can ensure that the psychologist's accounts, which will require specific knowledge of mental health insurance and coding procedures, get adequate attention. Collaborative models of care, in which physicians and psychologists see patients together in group or individual sessions, may be more complicated. Some third-party payers, such as Medicare, do not pay for similar services by more than one provider during the same time period, nor do they pay for more than one visit in a day (APA, 2001). Practices that are committed to providing the best quality care to their patients can probably make collaborative care work; financial issues, however, may present significant obstacles.

Psychologists must also attend to ethical concerns related to the financial aspects of practice. For example, psychologists must avoid splitting fees with physicians or other heath care providers with whom they work collaboratively or from whom they receive referrals. They also must not provide financial "kickbacks" to providers who refer patients for psychological evaluation or treatment.

One obstacle psychologists will encounter is that insurance companies often contract the management of mental and behavioral services to a management mental health care company, often referred to as a mental health "carve-out." Patients maintain maximum benefit by using a psychologist who is in on the panel of the preferred provider network (PPN) rather than paying higher out-of-pocket costs for an out-of-network psychologist. For most psychologists, it is probably quite important to try to get on as many of these provider panels as possible. Psychologists will need to verify coverage and obtain precertification before seeing patients, both to ensure benefits for their patients, as well as to protect themselves financially. Unfortunately, this may prevent patients from being seen on a same-day basis. Typically, the patient's insurance card has the contact information if a different company manages mental and behavioral services.

Staff model systems are likely to provide more options for clinical health psychologists than fee-for-service systems. A staff model system is one in which providers are salaried by a health care organization, which is responsible for the total health care of a specified population of patients. Examples include health maintenance organizations (HMOs), such as Kaiser Permanente and Group Health Cooperative, and federal systems such as the Veterans Administration and the military health care system. Integrated care was spawned in this type of system and has blossomed within several of them. The financial structure of these systems reinforces health care initiatives that help maintain optimal health in their populations and minimizes the occurrence of chronic and severe disease that often result in costly care. The integration of psychology in primary care is one such initiative. Fortunately, preliminary data are available to support the potential for health care organizations to save money in the long run (cost offset) by effectively meeting the psychosocial needs of patients. Reviews of this literature have been presented by Strosahl (1998), who concluded that "properly done, integrated care and behavioral health services can achieve significant medical cost offsets and improve the quality of mental health care delivered by primary care providers" (pp. 143–144). Psychologists seeking to integrate behavioral health care into primary care clinics within HMOs should be able to articulate this literature with system administrators to sell them on the benefits of adding psychological services.

Furthermore, in today's competitive health care environment, integrated care may be attractive to HMOs because it improves the scope and quality of care provided within a health care plan. Patients and providers alike report high satisfaction with psychological services integrated into primary care (Talcott et al., 2001). Thus, integrated clinics can be used as a marketing feature that distinguishes a health care organization from its competitors in their effort to attract new enrollees.

SUMMARY

Integrated primary care presents a tremendous opportunity for psychologists to collaborate with medical professionals in providing high-quality health care. The primary care culture, however, is unique from other health care settings where psychologists may work, and successful integration of psychology services will require more than just colocation of services. This chapter has detailed practical tips for psychologists working in primary care clinics and has focused on several key elements: being a true member of the primary care team, establishing strong relationships at all levels within the practice, understanding and working within the culture of primary care, and maintaining consistent availability to respond to the needs of the health care team and the patients.

As discussed in the remainder of this book, psychologists have skills that are highly relevant and valuable to the needs of the primary care population. Successful integration into the primary care practice will allow these skills to be used fully and will produce a work environment that is likely to be rewarding for psychologists and physicians alike.

RECOMMENDED READINGS

Select medical journals relevant to primary care include the following:

- *Annals of Internal Medicine*
- *Archives of Family Medicine*

- *Journal of the American Medical Association*
- *New England Journal of Medicine*
- *Preventive Medicine*
- *Primary Care*

American Psychological Assocation. (2002). Ethical principles of psychologists and code of conduct. *American Psychologist, 57*(12).

American Psychological Association, Practice Directorate. (1996). *Models for multidisciplinary arrangements: A state-by-state review of options.* Washington, DC: Author.

GLOSSARY

clinical pathway   An established set of procedures that is implemented for every patient in a given category, such as patients newly diagnosed with diabetes, patients with hypertension, or patients with depression.

cost offset   Net financial savings in the cost of providing medical care after accounting for the added expenditure from adding a specific service. For example, cost offset would be achieved from adding a primary care psychologist if the psychologist's salary and overhead costs are offset by money saved as a result of patients using less overall medical care.

fee for service   A system of health care in which patients, or their insurance companies, are billed for medical services provided. This system is commonly used by private practitioners who are not affiliated with a health care organization (such as an HMO or PPN).

health maintenance organization (HMO)   A type of health care organization in which patients (or their employers) prepay for medical care that is provided through specific clinics operated by the HMO.

mental health carve-out   A separate provision within a health insurance plan for mental health care.

motivational interviewing   A strategy for helping people recognize problems and resolve ambivalence toward health behavior change.

preferred provider network (PPN)   A health care system in which patients (or their employers) join a health care organization that pays for care provided by a network of approved, independently practicing medical providers.

staff model system   A system of health care in which providers are salaried by a health care organization; in capitated staff model systems, customers prepay for medical care and the organization attempts to manage the health of its enrolled population within this budget. The staff model system is also common in federal health care systems, such as the Veterans Administration and the military health care system.

REFERENCES

American Psychological Association, Practice Directorate. (1996). *Models for multidisciplinary arrangements: A state-by-state review of options*. Washington, DC: Author.

American Psychological Association. (2001). *Medicare Handbook: A guide for psychologists*. Washington, DC: Author.

American Psychological Association. (2002). Ethical principles of psychologists and code of conduct. *American Psychologist, 57*(12).

Bray, J. H. (1996). Psychologists as primary care practitioners. In R. J. Resnick & R. H. Rozensky (Eds.), *Health psychology through the life span: Practice and research opportunities* (pp. 89–100). Washington, DC: American Psychological Association.

Kroenke, K., & Manglesdorff, A. D. (1989). Common symptoms in ambulatory care: Incidence, evaluation, therapy, and outcome. *American Journal of Medicine, 86*, 262–266.

Miller, W. S., & Rollnick, S. (1991). *Motivational interviewing*. New York: Guilford Press.

Rabasca, L. (1999, April). More psychologists are building up their practices by partnering with primary care physicians. *APA Monitor Online, 30*. Retrieved from http://www.apa.org/monitor/apr99/doc.html

Smith, D. (2002, January). Psychologists now eligible for reimbursement under six new health and behavior codes. *Monitor on Psychology, 33*, 19.

Strosahl, K. (1998). Integrating behavioral health and primary care services: The primary mental health care model. In A. Blount (Ed.), *Integrated primary care: The future of medical and mental health collaboration* (pp. 139–166). New York: W. W. Norton.

Talcott, G. W., Russ, C. R., & Dobmeyer, A. (2001, October). *Integrating behavioral health providers into primary care in the USAF: The behavioral health optimization project*. Paper presented at Behavioral Healthcare Tomorrow Conference, Washington, DC.

3

DIABETES MELLITUS

The role of psychosocial factors and behavior in people with diabetes has long been recognized by both physicians and psychologists. Diabetes is among those chronic diseases whose course is clearly affected by the patient's behavior. Lifestyle modification is a primary means for managing diabetes and for preventing or delaying its advancement (American Diabetes Association [ADA], 1999). Some individuals, in fact, can successfully manage the disease by attending to diet and exercise alone. For many people, however, changing lifestyle habits is a struggle, and the demands of the complex diabetic regimen are an overwhelming burden both emotionally and behaviorally. Adherence to recommendations for self-monitoring, insulin, exercise, and diet is often relatively poor (Glasgow, 1991; Kurtz, 1990). Furthermore, people with diabetes are faced with the emotional challenges of living with a chronic disease as well as the possibility of severe long-term complications (Polonsky, 1993). Clinical health psychologists within the primary care setting can play a valuable role in helping individuals manage this difficult condition and learn to adapt to its impact on their lives.

Due to increasing prevalence (Centers for Disease Control [CDC], 1999), diabetes is fast becoming one of the most common chronic diseases managed in primary care clinics. Approximately 15.7 million Americans, or 5.9% of the population (CDC, 1998), are estimated to have diabetes. Of these, 10.3 million are diagnosed cases, and 5.4 million are undiagnosed.

These numbers represent a 19% increase in the number of diagnosed cases between 1980 and 1996, and less than 30% of this increase was due to the aging of the U.S. population. In the 1990s, an average of 760,000 new cases were diagnosed each year (CDC, 1999).

The number of people with diabetes encountered in a primary care practice may depend on the population served within a given facility. Minority populations are disproportionately affected by diabetes (CDC, 1998). African American men showed the greatest jump in prevalence, with a more than 50% increase during the 1980s and 1990s as compared to a 10% increase among White women. Non-Hispanic Black people are 1.7 times as likely to have diabetes as non-Hispanic White people of similar age. Hispanic/Latino Americans are almost twice as likely to have diabetes as non-Hispanic White Americans. Native Americans and Alaskan natives are even more at risk; they are 2.8 times as likely to have diabetes as are non-Hispanic White Americans. In fact, 9% of the Native American and Alaskan native populations has been diagnosed with diabetes.

The age distribution within a primary care clinic will also affect the rates at which diabetes is encountered. For individuals older than age 20, the prevalence rate is 8.2%. Older adults have diabetes at over twice this rate, with 18.4% of people older than age 65 having the condition. Therefore, geriatric clinics and practices are likely to see higher rates. Pediatric clinics are likely to see fewer cases because only 1.6% of children and teenagers are affected (CDC, 1998).

WHAT IS DIABETES?

More than 3,000 years ago, a fatal disease causing humans to "urinate honey" was first recognized. In the early second century, Aretaeus of Cappadocia designated the disease *diabetes*, a term meaning "to run through a siphon," and documented its primary symptoms (Chessler & Lernmark, 2000). The term *mellitus*, meaning "honey," was added by Cullen in the 1700s (Hazlett, 2000).

Diabetes mellitus is a chronic disease in which the body is unable to produce or effectively use insulin. The disease is divided into three types. *Insulin-dependent diabetes mellitus* (IDDM), also known as Type I, accounts for 5% of cases. Onset is typically during youth, with peak incidence occurring between the ages of 11 and 14 (Chessler & Lernmark, 2000). IDDM is caused by destruction of the pancreatic islet beta cells. This results in insufficient production of insulin, a protein hormone that is essential for metabolizing carbohydrates. The etiology of IDDM is likely to be multifactorial and may include genetics, viral infections, chemicals and pharmaceuticals, nutritional factors, and *in utero* environment (Chessler & Lernmark, 2000). *Non-insulin-dependent diabetes mellitus* (NIDDM) is also known as Type II diabetes. It is the far more common type of diabetes, accounting for 90% to 95% of cases. NIDDM is caused by a combination of beta-cell dysfunction and insulin resistance stemming from obesity. Approximately 80% of people with Type II diabetes are obese (although only a small percentage of individuals who are obese have diabetes; Davidson & DiGirolamo, 2000). The third type of diabetes is *gestational diabetes*, which develops in 2% to 5% of all pregnancies but disappears after the pregnancy is over. A history of gestational diabetes increases the risk for women later developing NIDDM (CDC, 1999).

Diagnostic criteria for diabetes were revised in 1997 by the ADA Expert Committee (ADA, 1997). Nongestational diabetes mellitus requires an impaired fasting plasma glucose level of 126 mg/dl or greater, or a random plasma glucose level of 200 mg/dl or greater. Abnormal results must be confirmed by repeat testing on a different day. Additionally, the person must be experiencing symptoms such as excessive urination (polyuria), excessive thirst (polydipsia), ketone bodies in the urine (ketonuria), and rapid weight loss.

Mortality and morbidity from diabetes are primary related to complications from the disease rather than from diabetes per se. Heart disease is the leading cause of diabetes-related deaths. Approximately 60% to 65% of people with diabetes have high blood pressure, which is often a manifestation of diabetic nephropathy, and the risk of both stroke and heart disease is two to four times higher among people with diabetes than those without the disease. Contributing risk factors to this include obesity, sedentary lifestyle, and dyslipidemia. Diabetes is also the leading cause of end-stage renal disease, accounting for approximately 40% of all new cases. In 1995, 27,851 people with diabetes developed end-stage renal disease, and almost 100,000 people with diabetes underwent dialysis or kidney transplantation. Diabetes is also the leading cause of new cases of blindness in adults, and diabetic neuropathy accounts for more than half of lower limb amputations in the United States (CDC, 1999). Finally, Type I diabetes can result in an increased production of ketones, leading to ketoacidosis, coma, and sometimes death. Type II diabetes can lead to hyperosmolar hyperglycemic nonketotic syndrome, which is also life threatening.

COMMON MEDICAL TREATMENTS AND RECOMMENDATIONS

Treatment guidelines for people with diabetes are provided by the ADA (2000). The guidelines state that those with diabetes should receive care from a physician-coordinated team that includes physician, nurses, dietitians, and mental health professionals. The primary goal of treatment for all forms of diabetes is to lower blood glucose levels to normal or near-normal levels to eliminate symptoms and to reduce the risk of complications. The guidelines indicate that the components discussed next should be part of treatment.

Appropriate Frequency of Self-Monitoring of Blood Glucose

Self-monitoring of blood glucose is recommended anywhere from one to seven times per day, depending on the type and frequency of insulin taken and the stability of glucose levels. A minimal level of therapy involves monitoring zero to one time per day; an average level of therapy involves monitoring one to three times per day (fasting and before supper or bed); and intensive therapy requires monitoring four to seven times per day (before meals and at bed, at 3:00 a.m. once a week, postprandial as needed; Nathan, 1997).

Individuals obtain a blood sample through a fingertip prick and test blood glucose levels using a home testing monitor. A normal whole blood glucose level is 100 mg/dl. The goal of self-monitoring is to maintain blood glucose values before meals between 80 and 120 mg/dl and bedtime blood glucose levels between 100 and 140 mg/dl. Some blood glucose monitors convert blood glucose levels to plasma values, which are 10% to 15% higher than whole blood values (goals are 90–130 mg/dl before meals and 110–150 mg/dl bedtime). It is imperative that individuals know whether their monitor and test strips give readings for whole blood or plasma. These goals can be adjusted upward for people with a history of recurrent severe or unrecognized hypoglycemia.

Medical Nutritional Therapy

Recommendations for changing eating habits aim to maintain a balance between insulin dose and the intake of calories and carbohydrates. Because approximately 75% of people with Type II diabetes struggle with obesity, diet changes may also target excess weight, which can interfere with the body's ability to use insulin (called *insulin resistance*). Proper diet also reduces diabetes-associated risk of atherosclerotic vascular disease (AVD) and coronary heart disease (CHD). Patients are instructed to reduce total calorie level and fat intake, as well as sodium if they have hypertension.

Regular Exercise

Exercise can potentially lower blood glucose levels (Type II only) and improve insulin sensitivity (Vranic, Rodgers, Davidson, & Marliss, 2000). It also reduces risks associated with AVD and CHD and contributes to weight loss and cardiovascular fitness. Exercise should be approached with caution, however, because it may lead to hyperglycemia in people with Type I diabetes. (Hyperglycemia is discussed further later in this chapter.) Walking is the exercise of choice for many people because it presents low risk to previously sedentary individuals and is typically convenient and inexpensive.

Insulin Therapy

Multiple injections of insulin are required each day for Type I diabetics and some Type II diabetics. Frequency of insulin depends on the intensity of therapy needed. Minimal therapy involves one to two injections per day of intermediate-acting insulin; average therapy involves two injections per day of intermediate-acting and rapid-acting insulin; intensive therapy requires more than three injections of intermediate-acting or ultralente insulin plus rapid-acting insulin or continuous infusion (Nathan, 1997).

Injections should be given approximately 45 minutes prior to mealtime to allow the insulin to reach the bloodstream before the food causes blood glucose levels to rise. Rapid-acting insulin analogs (e.g., Lispro) reach the bloodstream within minutes and can be taken as soon as 15 minutes prior to eating. Intermediate-acting insulin (neural protamine hagedorn) reaches the blood more slowly, but maximum duration times can be 16 to 20 hours, meaning fewer injections. Less complex insulin regimens or oral medications are used with some Type II diabetics. Injections are usually self-administered using syringes, automatic injectors, infusers, jet injectors, or pen injectors. As noted earlier, insulin therapy can also be administered by way of continuous subcutaneous insulin infusion (CSII). CSII requires an insulin pump, which is worn on the belt, to deliver insulin by way of a small tube inserted under the skin.

Instruction in Prevention and Treatment of Hypoglycemia

Multiple factors can lead to hypoglycemia, including inadequate carbohydrate intake, vigorous exercise, excess insulin dose, or other substances that lower plasma glucose level. Additionally, reduced insulin doses may be necessary when body weight decreases, when certain endocrine deficiencies exist, when doses of corticosteroids are reduced, with liver or kidney failure, after recovery from stressful situations, and at termination of pregnancy. Failure to modulate insulin doses given these factors can result in hypoglycemia (Davidson, Anderson, & Chance, 2000).

Symptoms of hypoglycemia include palpitation tremor, anxiety, perspiration, irritability, a neuroglycopenic state, headache, dizziness, tingling, hunger, blurred vision, difficulty thinking, and faintness. The release of catecholamines generally alerts the patient to take measures to prevent coma from low blood sugar. The absence of these warning signs can occur, however, leading to a dangerous condition know as *hypoglycemic unawareness*. Hypoglycemia can trigger a reactive hyperglycemic episode, ketoacidosis, permanent brain damage, coma, or death, so episodes should be minimized through attentive avoidance of hypoglycemia and, when it occurs, less stringent control of glucose (Vinik & Glass, 2000). If severe hypoglycemia occurs and is recognized, the patient should eat or drink fast-acting sugars such as raisins, soda, orange juice, candy, or milk. Alternatively, glucose tablets or gel can be consumed (ADA, 1999).

Continuing Education and Reinforcement

The diabetic self-care regimen is difficult for many patients, and non-adherence to prescribed medication and lifestyle recommendations is common (Kurtz, 1990). Education for newly diagnosed patients can help them understand the disease and its complications, as well as increase knowledge in self-care recommendations aimed at minimizing complications. Many primary care practices make use of certified diabetes educators and formal diabetes education programs that meet the *National Standards for Diabetes Self-Management Education Programs* (ADA, 2002) to provide teaching to patients. The reader should note, however, that level of glycemic control is not highly correlated with diabetes knowledge (Jacobson, Adler, Wolfsdorf, Anderson, & Derby, 1990).

Periodic Assessment of Treatment Goals

The general aim of diabetic treatment is to maintain the patient's near-normal blood glucose levels and reduce risk factors through lifestyle modification so as to minimize complications. Specific behavioral and physiological goals should be tailored to the individual, however. The ADA guidelines (2000) have stated that "individual treatment goals should take into account the patient's capacity to understand and carry out the treatment regimen, the patient's risk for severe hypoglycemia, and other patient factors that may increase risk or decrease benefit" (p. 533). Additionally, the guidelines list as considerations in formulating a management plan the following factors: the patient's age, school or work schedule, level of physical activity, eating patterns, social situation and personality, cultural factors, and presence of complications or other medical conditions. Because many of these factors can change, periodic reassessment of goals and plans is essential.

BARRIERS TO EFFECTIVE MANAGEMENT OF DIABETES

To manage diabetes well, individuals often must make multiple life changes. On one hand, the fact that behavior change can stem the development of complications adds a level of personal control that is not possible with many other chronic diseases. On the other hand, however, the diabetic regimen can be so complex that it becomes overwhelming for patients, and adherence is often poor (Christensen, Terry, Wyatt, Pichert, & Lorenz, 1983; Kurtz, 1990).

Multiple factors can contribute to adherence difficulties (Polonsky, 1993). Some patients may have inadequate knowledge about diabetes and its management, or they may lack skills necessary for approximating normal glucose levels. For instance, individuals may estimate their blood glucose level based on how they feel (an unreliable measure), rather than from self-monitoring, and therefore maintain higher than optimal blood glucose levels (Polonsky, 1993). Unfortunately, health care providers tend to comply less with ADA guidelines regarding behavioral and patient-focused aspects of care than they do with laboratory tests and other physiologic components (Glasgow, Boles, Calder, Dreyer, & Bagdade, 1999), and this may contribute to knowledge or skill deficits on the part of their patients.

A high percentage of people with diabetes may struggle with the belief that following the recommended regimen cannot be realistically accomplished. Polonsky, Anderson, and Lohrer (1991) found that 83% of women with diabetes surveyed endorsed the following statement: "I am supposed to follow a certain meal plan, but it is impossible." Low self-efficacy (Bandura, 1982) regarding self-management of diabetes may be reinforced when, despite diligent efforts, glycemic control remains poor (a common occurrence). This low self-efficacy, in turn, may contribute to difficulty with adherence to medical recommendations, continued poor glycemic control, and so on, thus creating a self-defeating cycle.

Social support is another dimension that affects glycemic control and adherence. Social factors that have been linked to diabetic regimen adherence include family cohesiveness (Hauser et al., 1990), family conflict (Anderson, 1990), feelings of being alone with one's diabetes (Polonsky et al., 1991), and frequency of supportive and nonsupportive behaviors (Glasgow & Toobert, 1988; Hanson, Henggeler, & Gurghen, 1987). Support from others can assist patients in making difficult behavior changes and maintaining a lifestyle consistent with good diabetes management. Social influences can also serve as a barrier to adherence, especially if friends or family are encouraging deviations from diet, encouraging the use of alcohol or tobacco, or discouraging exercise. Some evidence suggests that men who are satisfied with their level of social support have poorer glycemic control than women who are satisfied with their social support precisely for the reason that men's social contacts promote more nonadherence (Kaplan & Hartwell, 1987).

The inconvenience of monitoring blood glucose levels, injecting insulin several times a day, monitoring calories, taking time to exercise, maintaining current knowledge, attending to foot care, and arranging regular health care appointments can also be an obstacle to adherence. Life activities of work, family, socializing, community involvement, and recreation may take priority and interfere with maintaining health-promoting behaviors. Managing diabetes takes time and money away from other things that may be of more immediate concern to the individual.

Maintaining lifestyle changes can also be difficult because the benefits do not offer immediate reinforcement. People with diabetes must make changes based on the knowledge that exercise, diet modifications, and insulin regimens will prevent or delay long-term complications without actually noticing any tangible benefits. Individuals actually may not feel their best when their blood glucose level is in the normal range and this may, in fact, reduce attempts at adherence. Furthermore, a less than perfect correlation exists between behavioral changes and glucose control and, therefore, even patients who successfully adhere to their regimen may face frustration as they encounter uncontrolled glucose levels. This may lead to discouragement, and even learned helplessness, which can interfere with continued efforts to control blood glucose.

Finally, factors related to the patient's relationship with the physician and health care team can interfere with adherence. The health care team needs to work collaboratively with the patient to set realistic goals and to ensure that these goals are clearly understood. The complexity of the diabetic regimen can leave some patients confused or overwhelmed, and nonspecific instructions can contribute to this. Health care providers should attend to the emotional consequences of diabetes and quality-of-life issues as well as the medical aspects. Patients who feel that the medical team is attending only to their physical well-being but not to other concerns of importance to them may be less effective as a member of their own health care team (Jacobson, Hauser, Anderson, & Polonsky, 1994).

THE CLINICAL HEALTH PSYCHOLOGIST AND PRIMARY CARE DIABETES MANAGEMENT

A clinical health psychologist in the primary care clinic possesses unique skills for helping with the management of patients who have diabetes. ADA guidelines (2000) contain multiple behavioral and psychological components for both the initial visit and continuing care. These include attention to the following:

- Problem solving
- Setting appropriate and attainable goals
- Lifestyle, cultural, psychosocial, educational, and economic factors that might influence the management of diabetes
- Tobacco and alcohol use
- Improving exercise regularity
- Problems with adherence

- Psychosocial issues
- Lifestyle changes.

The true challenges for the health psychologist are, first, to integrate into the primary care practice sufficiently to be considered a member of the team and, second, to adapt clinical skills and knowledge of what works into the structure and culture of primary care practice. This means performing assessments and interventions in 15- to 30-minute sessions, keeping treatment duration to a limited number of visits or using widely spaced appointments for longer term care, and developing strategies that can be carried out by the patients' primary physician.

THE HEALTH PSYCHOLOGIST AS A CONSULTANT TO PHYSICIANS

Health psychologists will have the greatest impact on the diabetic population if they can integrate into the clinic's clinical pathway for management of diabetes. This means that every patient diagnosed with Type I or Type II diabetes should be scheduled with the psychologist shortly following diagnosis. This practice has several advantages over that of limiting consultations to patients who are having difficulty with behavior change or adaptation. First, every patient with diabetes will be given a behavioral risk assessment to identify and address potential problem areas early. Targeting problems early on may prevent difficulties before they develop into serious risks. Second, the stigma of seeing a psychologist can be significantly reduced if it is framed as part of the standard care. Finally, expanding the standard of care to involve the psychologist for consultation will provide every patient with expertise in changing behavior and adaptation to a diabetic lifestyle that can optimize the patient's success. In our experience, patients who later develop psychosocial or behavior change problems are often more receptive to a psychology referral if they have had previous contact with—and we hope a good experience with—the health psychologist.

Assessment

A primary care behavioral risk assessment of a patient with diabetes should cover major areas in which management of the illness may be compromised. The psychologist conducting the evaluation must have a thorough knowledge of factors that are known to predict poor adherence. Additionally, he or she must possess skills for gathering information on a broad range of relevant areas in a short period of time because the pace within the primary care setting necessitates brief evaluations. Use of specialty care assessment modalities (hour-long interviews, traditional psychometric instruments, etc.) is impractical in most primary care settings and may quickly result in the psychologist being overtaxed by just trying to see all of the patients with diabetes, let alone the myriad other patients needing to be seen.

The first goal of the assessment is to quickly identify risk behaviors that may need to be addressed. These include tobacco use, alcohol and drug use, binge eating or overeating, lack of exercise, and stressful lifestyle (including family, work, and recreational activities). Poor dental hygiene should also be assessed because poor glucose control can increase vulnerability to gum infections, and, in turn, gum infections can make it more difficult to control diabetes.

Second, the evaluation should include assessment of intrapersonal, interpersonal, and environmental obstacles to the recommended regimen and behavior change. Intrapersonally, psychologists should address motivation to adhere and self-efficacy about self-management. An understanding of patients' beliefs about the illness and its meaning for their life can shed light on potential barriers. For example, an adolescent's perception of invulnerability to illness or a military member's fears that he or she will be separated from the service may be factors in the degree of motivation each person has for making lifestyle changes. Perceptions that illness represents a personal flaw or a punishment from God can lead to depression, which, in turn, can interfere with adaptation and self-management.

Cognitive functioning should be evaluated as well. Interpersonally, one should assess for family and peer support, occupational conditions and support, and the quality of the patient's relationship with health care providers and the health care system in general. The potential impact of diabetes on the patient's job, school, social life, recreation, and financial status should be covered as well as the impact of these factors on diabetes self-management. Will the job or school schedule accommodate blood glucose monitoring, regular meals, and medication use? Will hobbies or recreational activities need to be adapted? Can the patient afford the supplies and medication required?

Finally, any psychopathology that exists must be identified, because these conditions, particularly affective disorder and eating disorders, predict poor adherence (Lustman, Griffith, & Clouse, 1988; Lustman, Griffith, Clouse, & Cryer, 1986; Marcus & Wing, 1990; Polonsky et al., 1991). It is notable that subclinical depressed mood has not been associated with reduced adherence or blood glucose control (Jacobson et al., 1990). Once identified, the psychologist can make recommendations for the primary physician to consider, including psychopharmacological treatment or referral for psychotherapy. In many cases, however, the psychologist, as a member of the primary health care team, can treat the psychopathology with a short-term, focused intervention.

Behavior Modification Interventions

Behavior modification interventions have been shown to be effective in the primary care setting (Ridgeway, Harvill, Harvill, Falin, Forester, &

Gose, 1999). As the team member with behavioral expertise, the health psychologist can serve a valuable role by developing behavior change strategies for specific patients who continue to struggle after receiving initial diabetes education and general behavior change advice. The psychologist should hand over the change plan to the primary health care provider for implementation. This preserves the medical provider's role as primary care manager, while allowing for individual tailoring to the patient's needs to a degree that otherwise would be unlikely given the vast number of areas a primary care provider has to cover during a patient's visit. Examples of interventions that can be handed over to a physician are as follows:

- The psychologist assesses high-risk situations for a patient who struggles with binge eating. A plan is developed for avoiding these situations or for alternative responses when they are encountered.
- A behavior modification plan is created to help a sedentary patient begin exercising regularly. The plan includes establishing a baseline, setting realistic goals, scheduling small incremental steps toward achieving the goals, a system of self-reinforcement for meeting intermediate goals, and a lapse response plan. The psychologist works with the patient until the plan is implemented, at which time the physician takes over to monitor progress.
- A method for using environmental cues is implemented to help a busy executive increase self-monitoring of blood glucose during the workday.
- A behavioral intervention for smoking cessation is formulated to augment nicotine substitution (prescribed by the physician).
- A patient who is frustrated by difficulties encountered with trying to be perfectly compliant with the physician's numerous recommendations for lifestyle change is assisted by resetting goals to be more realistic and achievable (i.e., less than perfect is okay) and to attempt one change at a time.

In addition to consulting on the formulation of a behavior change plan, health psychologists' skills may be applied to those patients with severe complications of diabetes such as blindness, amputation, or kidney failure. These difficulties can, in many cases, tax patients' coping resources as their quality of life drops dramatically. Their acuity often increases the need for more frequent and intensive medical care, as well.

The health psychologist can serve as a physician-extender by attending to psychosocial and psychological needs while the physician focuses on physiological needs. In some cases, a brief cognitive–behavioral intervention might suffice, targeting patients' maladaptive beliefs about their self-worth, their potential to enjoy life in the future, or their perceived loss of control in life. Contact may be limited to three or four 15- to 30-minute weekly or bimonthly visits. People likely to benefit from these types of services are those with previously good coping skills and no history of serious psychopathology. Generally, these patients will respond to initial interventions within a short period of time. Other patients, however, will require more intensive treatment to avoid further deterioration of their condition. Many of these patients can be managed in primary care, however, with the support and stabilization of more frequent visits. These individuals might best be seen by the psychologist in synchronized appointments with their physician, either on the same day or on alternating weeks. Patients who present with severe psychopathology or acute suicidal risk should be considered for referral to a specialty mental health provider.

Motivational Interviewing

Another useful contribution by the health psychologist is in the area of motivation enhancement for behavior change. Poor adherence to the diabetic regimen often is attributed to negative characteristics, such as insufficient concern for one's health, laziness, or low intelligence. The truth is, however, that patients' low motivation for adherence may be quite reasonable given the contingencies in their environment. The well-intentioned efforts of health care providers to further educate, reason with, convince, induce fear in, and even scold the individual with diabetes are sometimes met with either active or passive resistance. This resistance, however, is an expected reaction from a person when encountering certain kinds of counseling, particularly those that are more directive, coercive, or confrontational (Miller & Rollnick, 2002). Some evidence suggests that people with diabetes who have a higher fear of complications do poorer than those with a low fear (Polonsky, 1993), indicating that those counseling or educational approaches that attempt to motivate by fear of complications may be counterproductive.

Motivational interviewing is a strategy for helping people recognize problems and resolve ambivalence toward change (Miller & Rollnick, 2002) that can be readily applied to people with diabetes. Originally conceived as an approach to alcohol abuse treatment, the principles of motivational interviewing have been applied to a variety of health risk behaviors (Botelho & Skinner, 1995; Rollnick, Mason, & Butler, 1999). The motivational interviewer attempts to draw out "self-motivational statements" so that eventually the patient, rather than the provider, is the one who is presenting the argument for change. The provider builds motivation by asking open-ended questions, listening reflectively, directly affirming the patient, and summarizing to help the person examine both positives and negatives associated with change (Miller & Rollnick, 2002). Self-motivational statements fall into four general categories: problem recognition, expression of concern, direct or implicit intention to change, and optimism about change. These statements can be reinforced and affirmed by the provider to further enhance the patients' motivation to make necessary changes to control blood glucose levels and prevent diabetic complications (see Exhibit 3.1).

While engaging in this process, motivational interviewers are perceptive to signs of resistance to change by the patient. When resistance is recognized, the therapeutic tactics should be altered to attempt to roll with the resistance rather than confronting it head on. A working assumption of motivational interviewing is that client resistance is a therapist problem (Miller & Rollnick, 2002). If resistance is encountered, providers should consider what they may be doing to elicit the resistance and then change strategies, so as not to strengthen patients' resistance as a result of the office visit. Signs that providers may be eliciting resistance include the patient arguing, interrupting, denying, and ignoring the providers. Strategies for handling resistance, adapted from Miller and Rollnick (2002), are presented in Exhibit 3.2.

Motivational interviewing does not replace educational, cognitive, or behavioral interventions. Rather, it is best seen as an approach that precedes these other interventions and helps the patient become ready to benefit from the interventions before they are implemented. For example, it is better for patients with diabetes to come to the conclusion themselves that their inactivity is a risk factor that they want to change than it is for the health care provider to be pushing a plan on patients who do not believe they have time to exercise. The scope of this book does not include providing a thorough overview of motivational interviewing, so interested readers

EXHIBIT 3.1
Examples of Self-Motivational Statements With Diabetic Patients

Problem Recognition	"Perhaps I'm neglecting my health more than I realized." "I can see that over the years, my inconsistency in monitoring blood glucose is going to lead to serious problems." "Maybe I have been foolishly taking risks with my eating."
Expression of Concern	"I'm really worried about this." "How could I let myself go like this?" "I don't know how people do this."
Intention to Change	"How do people check their glucose levels during a busy day? I've got to figure this out." "I want to control this better. What can I do?" "I don't know how I'm going to do it but I've got to lose weight."
Optimism About Change	"I know I can be more regular with the injections if I just put my mind to it." "Other people control their eating; I know I can, too." "I think I can give up alcohol; it'll be worth it in the long run."

EXHIBIT 3.2
Strategies for Handing Resistance

SIMPLE REFLECTION

Definition: Acknowledgment of the patient's disagreement, emotion, or perception
Example:
Patient: All you doctors are trying to tell me how to live my life. I'm sick of it.
Provider: You're tired of people telling you what you should do and not do.

AMPLIFIED REFLECTION

Definition: Reflecting back what the patient said in an amplified or exaggerated form
Example:
Patient: I can't do all these things to keep my blood sugars controlled. It's just too hard.
Provider: So you don't feel you can make changes in any area of your life right now.

DOUBLE-SIDED REFLECTION

Definition: Acknowledging what the patient said and adding to it the other side of the ambivalence
Example:
Patient: Almost every one of my siblings has diabetes and they all drink now and then. I don't see what the big deal is. They're doing fine.
Provider: It sounds like, on one hand, you see the importance of sticking to the recommendations to try to control your blood glucose and prevent long-term complications. On the other hand, however, you see others with diabetes drinking alcohol and not having any problems. That's hard to figure out.

SHIFTING FOCUS

Definition: Shifting the patient's attention away from what seems to be a stumbling block standing in the way of progress
Example:
Patient: I know you want me to check my glucose levels several times a day, but I'm not going to do a blood test at school. It's embarrassing. I'm just not going to do it!
Provider: Okay, let's not get ahead of ourselves. The most important thing is that we keep you healthy and active … doing the things you want to do. How we best do that is something we need to figure out as we go along. So let's not get stuck in the details yet. What I think we should do first is give you some information about what diabetes is and look for some of the things you might feel you can do it keep it in check. Okay?

AGREEMENT WITH A TWIST

Definition: Offering initial agreement, but with a slight twist or change of direction
Example:
Patient: You tell me I may be able to get off the medication if I lose weight, but you don't understand how hard that is. My whole family is heavy. It's in my genes.
Provider: You've got a good point there. Genetics do play a role in a person's weight, and it's important to acknowledge that so we don't have unrealistic expectations. Like we've discussed, exercise and reducing calorie intake can make a difference, but it's certainly not as simple as that. I agree with you on that.

EXHIBIT 3.2
Strategies for Handing Resistance *(continued)*

EMPHASIZING PERSONAL CHOICE

Definition: Reassuring patients that, in the end, they will determine what happens

Example:

Patient: All of these changes you are telling me I need to make ... it's like I'm not going to be allowed to have fun anymore. I really don't know about all of this.

Provider: We've discussed some of the pros and cons of making some lifestyle changes. I can't decide for you what you are going to do, however. It's really up to you to decide.

REFRAMING

Definition: Acknowledging the validity of the patient's observations, but offering a new interpretation for them

Example:

Patient: My wife is always nagging me about my eating. She never gives me a break. I get so angry I want to eat junk food just to get back at her.

Provider: It sounds like she really cares about you and wants you to be healthy. I guess she expresses it in a way that you're angry about. Maybe we can help her find a more helpful way of expressing her concern about you.

---

are directed to in-depth discussions found elsewhere (Botelho & Skinner, 1995; Miller & Rollnick, 2002; Rollnick et al., 1999).

Improving Social Support

Family interactions and social support can either assist or interfere with diabetes management (Cox & Gonder-Frederick, 1992; Schwartz, Coulson, Toovy, Lyons, & Flaherty, 1991). Children, adolescents, and adults belonging to families that are supportive have been found to have better control of their diabetes (Anderson & Auslander, 1980; Anderson, Miller, Auslander, & Santiago, 1981; Hauser et al., 1990). Interventions involving families of those with diabetes can be helpful for improving family relationships, reducing diabetes-specific conflict, and promoting earlier acceptance of diabetes and self-management. There is less evidence, however, that family therapy can impact blood glucose control (Tattersall, McCulloch, & Avelin, 1985; Wysocki, Greco, Harris, Bubb, & White, 2001).

One avenue for enhancing family support is to include family members in all education and treatment planning provided to the patient. This allows family members who will be affected by changes in meal preparation, family schedules, and patient activities to understand the reasons for these changes and be supportive of the family member with diabetes. Family members can also be included in behavior change plans either as coparticipants (e.g., exercise partner) or as "coaches" (e.g., reminding the family member with diabetes to take medications, encouraging healthy eating).

Finally, including family members can help the psychologist and the patient identify potential family barriers to adherence (e.g., the spouse refusing to change to lower fat meals) and address them early in the process.

Individuals with diabetes also need to be able to communicate effectively with family members about what type of "help" is and is not beneficial to them. For example, comments reminding the person with diabetes to exercise may be perceived as helpful or they may be perceived as nagging. The psychologist can work with the family to identify responses that actually do increase health-promoting behavior and to implement them. Some patients may benefit from assertiveness training to help them decrease responses from family or friends that impede good self-management.

Stress Management Training

In a comprehensive review of the literature on stress and diabetes, Jacobson et al. (1994) conclude that that results are mixed as to the influence of stress on metabolic control in patients with diabetes. Some evidence suggests that certain subtypes of individuals with diabetes (e.g., children with Type A behavior pattern) may be at special risk for the direct psychological impact on metabolic control. The strongest findings, however, relate to the clear impact of stress on patients' compliance behaviors that, in turn, affect glycemic control.

Stress is a highly individualistic phenomenon that is related to external demands, cognitive interpretation, coping skills and resources, and a variety of other factors. For example, the experience of managing diabetes itself may be highly stressful for some ("This is ruining my life"), but not for others ("I've had to change some habits and I take medication twice a day but otherwise I live a pretty normal life"). Primary care stress management training with patients who have diabetes should involve an assessment of individuals' situational stressors, their cognitive, emotional, and behavioral reactions to the situations, and the roles these reactions are playing in their health behaviors. Interventions within the primary care setting will typically be focused on specific problem areas or potential difficulties. Identifying and targeting stress reactions early may, for some individuals, prevent adherence difficulties that could interfere with glucose control.

Interventions can address the stressful situations directly by helping patients to change those situational stressors that are within their scope of control. Training for problem-solving skills can be applied to help patients find and implement appropriate and effective solutions. Cognitive behavioral interventions can help patients recognize unhealthy self-talk that may be contributing to emotional distress, low self-efficacy, or unhealthy behavior. Additionally, relaxation exercises may be useful for modulating tension and physiological stress arousal (Surwit & Feinglos, 1983).

Coping With Medical Complications

The potentially severe complications from uncontrolled diabetes can be devastating to individuals and families and can dramatically impact quality of life. Life-changing complications include blindness, lower limb amputation, and end-stage renal disease requiring regular dialysis. Individuals encountering these difficulties face loss of physical function, occupational disability, decreased independence, and increased financial burden. These challenges may contribute to depression, despair, anxiety, fear, guilt, low self-esteem, and feelings of uselessness.

These medical complications and the psychological sequelae present an additional challenge to the primary care physician who must attend to both the physical and emotional aspects of health care. A health psychologist can be the team member who primarily addresses the psychosocial aspects of care to allow the physician to focus on medical factors. This should not be conceptualized as a mind–body dualism, however, whereby one provider cares for the physical illness and another cares for the mental illness. Rather, it is two team members collaborating to provide comprehensive health care for the physical and psychological aspects of diabetes, with each provider applying his or her unique skills to the care of the whole person.

The health psychologist may be useful for assessing the nature and severity of the psychological reaction and for making recommendations. Is it a normal reaction to stress and loss that is likely to respond to normalization, emotional support, and the passage of time? Is it an adjustment disorder that may require brief cognitive therapy and coping skills training? Or is it major depression that might benefit from an antidepressant medication and a referral to specialty mental health care?

During the initial development of complications, the psychologist might schedule appointments that coincide with those of the physician to address psychological and psychosocial needs on a regular basis. Alternatively, the patient may benefit from seeing the psychologist in between physician visits to increase the frequency of contact and support. The appointment schedule used should be decided on collaboratively, based on the psychologist's assessment of needs, the physician's preference, and the desires of the patient.

Adjunctive referral to a diabetes support group may be helpful for some patients when complications arise. Establishing group involvement may be difficult at the stage when serious complications have set in, however, because healthier members sometimes have difficulty accepting patients with complications because those patients' amputations or blindness, for example, represents an uncomfortable picture of their own future. This illustrates the potential benefits of patients seeking support networks early so they are in place when they may be most needed.

Treatment of Comorbid Depression

Depression is common among patients with chronic diseases. People with diabetes who also have higher levels of depression have been found to have poorer adherence to their regimen and generally poorer physical health (Ciechanowski, Katon, & Russo, 2000) than those whose levels of depression are not as severe. Health psychologists should screen for depression as part of their standard diabetes assessment and offer treatment within the primary care setting, if appropriate. Treatment appropriate to the primary care setting may include brief cognitive-behavior therapy or recommendations to the treating physician for antidepressant medication. Patients who are at high risk for self-harm or suicide, or who present with severe neurovegetative signs, are often best referred out of primary care for specialty mental health care.

Collaboration With Certified Diabetes Educators

We advocate that health psychologists in primary care integrate themselves into the clinical pathway for diabetes care. This should be done, however, in a way that augments other available resources rather than replaces them. Many health care systems have certified diabetes educators, who are often nurses with specialized training in diabetes education. The potential for unhelpful conflict and "turf battles" arises when psychologists attempt to integrate into a diabetes care pathway without taking stock of what is already being provided in the system to avoid duplication of services.

The assessment and intervention services discussed earlier offer potential expansion of the care provided to patients with diabetes. Clinical health psychologists are likely to benefit from discussing with certified diabetes educators, as well as physicians, where they believe a psychologist's services would be most useful. Presenting a "menu" of skills and offerings, and asking how they might use those skills, may lead to nurse colleagues asking you to collaborate, rather than feeling challenged by a psychologist's presence. This will certainly pay off for the success of the psychologist's primary care practice in the long run.

Clinical health psychologists are often welcomed as speakers for diabetes education programs. Our involvement in the diabetes education program at several major medical centers and hospitals has been to present one of eight 60- to 90-minute sessions that make up the program. The class is entitled "Coping With Diabetes," and it is adapted from a curriculum designed by William Kelleher at Wilford Hall Medical Center in San Antonio, Texas. The class consists of the components discussed next.

Identifying the Challenge

Introduce the class by its title, "Coping With Diabetes." Ask "Is diabetes something that needs to be coped with?" Ask the participants to list the changes they have been advised to make in order to manage the diabetes. List responses on a large whiteboard. If general responses are given, such as "change how I eat," inquire about the specific changes that need to be made (i.e., smaller portion sizes, less fat, regularly scheduled mealtimes).

Motivational Enhancement

During the preceding discussion, and throughout the class period, people will generally make comments about their personal experiences. The class facilitator should listen for self-motivational statements and offer reflective responses, summaries, or highlights of these statements to reinforce them. Two examples are as follows:

Class member: Yes, eating sweets. That's one I really need to work on.

Facilitator: For you, that would be an especially beneficial change.

Class member: I'm not doing great on the exercise, but I keep working at it. I'm going to stick with it.

Facilitator: Good for you. It sounds like you are motivated to keep trying.

Reinforcement of Effort and Changes Already Made

Referring to the list of recommended behavior changes, ask "Which one of these is the hardest one to change?" Reinforce answers indicating that some behavior changes may be more difficult than others for individual people, but all of them can be hard to change. Conclude that people deserve credit for whatever changes they have been successful at making.

Stress Management

Because the group has concluded that diabetes is something to be coped with, the next stage is to discuss some of the skills that can be useful for coping with something stressful like diabetes. Some of the key skills for coping can be presented as the "Four Rs of Managing Diabetes." The first R is *recognizing the signs of stress*. Discuss how stress can potentially interfere with adherence to diabetes recommendations. People with diabetes must learn to recognize the signs of stress (preferably early) to do something about it. The second R is *relaxation*. Participants are taught a brief diaphragmatic breathing exercise to use for controlling the tension and physiological arousal from stress. The third R is *reassuring thinking*. Present a common stressor, such as a move to a new community, and ask patients if there are things one might think about in reference to the relocation that might contribute to increased distress (e.g., What if we don't like it there? What if my kids do not adjust well to the new school?). What are some things a person could think about that would help them to feel calmer (e.g., We're pretty flexible. It may take some time but we'll adjust.). Next suggest that the same principles may apply to being diagnosed with diabetes. What might a person think about diabetes that might contribute to increased distress? What thoughts might help them control their emotional reactions? The fourth R is *relating assertively*. Generate discussion about situations in which they may need to practice assertive communication to help management of their diabetes (e.g., with a family member who is pushing them to eat, a friend who buys them a beer, a physician who is not answering questions sufficiently).

Each of the four Rs is covered in 5 to 10 minutes, so participants are given only an exposure to the concepts and encouraged to practice them. Patients who feel they need assistance in learning or implementing these skills are invited to make an appointment with the psychologist in the primary care clinic for further assistance.

Behavioral Strategies

The class is concluded by presenting and reviewing a handout that outlines suggestions for successfully making changes in lifestyle habits:

- Select a goal that is realistic.
- Select a goal that is meaningful.
- Set a target date for completion.
- Keep track of progress.
- Break the goal down into small, realistic parts.
- Once accomplished, reward yourself for meeting the goal.
- Establish a relapse plan.

SUMMARY

Clinical health psychologists have valuable skills for working with people in the primary care setting who have diabetes mellitus. Research has shown that behavior modification interventions and attention to the psychosocial aspects of the disease can help patients maintain healthy blood glucose levels and adapt better to life with diabetes. The ADA (2002) treatment guidelines incorporate these findings by strongly emphasizing behavioral factors. Psychologists can be involved by providing routine behavioral risk assessments for all newly diagnosed diabetic patients and assisting with the design of behavior change interventions. Motivational interviewing may be a particularly helpful skill for encouraging change. Psychologists can also help patients better manage diabetes by enhancing social support, providing stress management skills training, and assisting patients in their efforts to cope when medical complications occur. These interventions can be provided one on one and as collaborative efforts with diabetes educators. Diabetes is best managed as a team (ADA, 1999), and a health psychologist can be a key player for maintaining patients' health and quality of life in the face of this difficult condition.

RECOMMENDED READINGS

American Diabetes Association. (2000). Standards of medical care for patients with diabetes mellitus. *Diabetes Care, 23*(Suppl. 1), S32–S42.

Miller, W. S., & Rollnick, S. (2002). *Motivational interviewing* (2nd ed.). New York: Guilford Press.

Polonsky, W. H. (1993). Psychosocial issues in diabetes mellitus. In R. J. Gatchel & E. B. Blanchard (Eds.), *Psychophysiological disorders: Research and clinical applications* (pp. 357–381). Washington, DC: American Psychological Association.

GLOSSARY

beta cells Cells in the pancreas that make insulin.

blood glucose level The amount of glucose in the blood.

blood glucose meter A home measurement device for blood glucose levels. See also *test strip*.

diabetic coma A severe condition that can be a complication of Type I diabetes. It occurs when blood glucose levels rise to extremely high levels and ketones develop. Symptoms include difficulty breathing, coma, and shock, and it can be life threatening. Also called *ketoacidosis*.

fasting plasma glucose test The preferred method for diagnosing diabetes. Blood is drawn after fasting for 8 to 10 hours, and glucose levels are measured. Diabetes is suspected with fasting blood glucose levels greater than 126 mg/dl. A firm diagnosis of diabetes can be made with two positive fasting plasma glucose tests done on different days.

gestational diabetes A type of diabetes that develops when blood glucose levels rise in response to hormones secreted during pregnancy. The pregnant woman is unable to produce enough insulin to use the higher blood glucose levels. This condition usually disappears after pregnancy.

glucose A simple form of sugar obtained from food that the body uses as fuel.

glycohemoglobin (HbA1c) The attachment of glucose to red blood cells. Tests of HbA1c are used to evaluate average blood glucose control over 3 to 4 months.

hyperglycemia A condition in which the blood has too much glucose. Levels of 140 mg/dl or above are considered hyperglycemic.

hyperglycemic hyperosmolar nonketotic syndrome A condition that can be a complication of Type II diabetes in which blood glucose levels markedly increase and the body becomes dehydrated. Symptoms can include confusion, seizures, coma, and death.

hypoglycemia A condition in which there is too little glucose in the blood. Levels below 70 mg/dl are considered hypoglycemic.

impaired fasting glucose tolerance A condition in which a person's blood glucose is tested to be above normal but below diabetic levels. This condition indicates an increased risk for developing diabetes.

insulin   A hormone that the body uses to process glucose.

insulin resistance   A condition in which cells are less responsive to insulin than normal. This is the most common cause of Type II diabetes.

intensive diabetes management   An approach to treatment that involves multiple daily insulin injections, frequent blood glucose monitoring, and active manipulation of exercise and diet in an effort to achieve blood glucose levels similar to what would be produced by a normal pancreas.

ketoacidosis   A severe condition that can be a complication of Type I diabetes. It occurs when blood glucose levels rise to extremely high levels and ketones develop. Symptoms include difficulty breathing, coma, and shock, and it can be life threatening. It is also called a *diabetic coma.*

ketones   Acids that are formed when the body uses fat.

lancets   Devices used for finger-sticking to obtain blood samples for glucose self-monitoring.

mg/dl   Milligrams per deciliter. The unit of measure for blood glucose levels.

nephropathy   Kidney damage.

neuropathy   Nerve damage.

random plasma glucose test   A test that measures the amount of glucose in the blood at any given time, without fasting. It is the simplest way to detect diabetes. A diagnosis of diabetes is given when blood glucose is 200 mg/dl or higher and obvious symptoms of diabetes are present.

retinopathy   Damage to the retina of the eye. This can cause vision problems including blindness.

test strips   Plastic strip that is inserted into a blood glucose meter to measure blood glucose. Some strips change colors when a drop of blood is placed on them depending on the amount of glucose in the blood. The blood glucose meter then analyzes the color intensity and produces a reading of blood glucose level. Other strips use a special enzyme to transfer electrons from the glucose to a chemical on the strip. The meter then measures this flow of electrons and converts it to a blood glucose reading.

Type I diabetes mellitus   A form of diabetes in which the person can no longer produce insulin because beta cells do not function properly. Insulin must be taken from an external source and must be taken in order to survive.

Type II diabetes mellitus   A form of diabetes in which the person is unable to secrete enough insulin to meet the body's needs. Many people with Type II diabetes can control it with diet and exercise, although some need medications or insulin.

REFERENCES

American Diabetes Association. (1997). Report of the expert committee on the diagnosis and classification of diabetes mellitus. *Diabetes Care, 20,* 1183–1197.

American Diabetes Association. (1999). *American Diabetes Association complete guide to diabetes* (2nd ed.). Alexandria, VA: Author.

American Diabetes Association. (2000). Standards of medical care for patients with diabetes mellitus. *Diabetes Care, 23*(Suppl. 1), S32–S42.

American Diabetes Association. (2002). National standards for diabetes self-management education programs and American Diabetes Association review criteria. *Diabetes Care, 25*, S140–S147.

Anderson, B. J. (1990). Diabetes and adaptation in family systems. In C. S. Holmes (Ed.), *Neuropsychological and behavioral aspects of diabetes* (pp. 85–101). New York: Springer-Verlag.

Anderson, B. J., & Auslander, W. F. (1980). Research on diabetes management and the family: A critique. *Diabetes Care, 3*, 696–702.

Anderson, B. J., Miller, J. P., Auslander, W. F., & Santiago, J. V. (1981). Family characteristic of diabetic adolescents: Relationship to metabolic control. *Diabetes, 4*, 580–594.

Bandura, A. (1982). Self-efficacy mechanism in human agency. *American Psychologist, 37*, 122–147.

Botelho, R. J., & Skinner, H. (1995). Motivating change in health behavior: Implications for health promotion and disease prevention. *Primary Care, 22*, 565–589.

Centers for Disease Control. (1998). *National diabetes fact sheet.* Atlanta, GA: Author.

Centers for Disease Control. (1999). *Diabetic surveillance.* Atlanta, GA: Author.

Chessler, S. D., & Lernmark, A. (2000). Type I (insulin-dependent) diabetes mellitus. In J. K. Davidson (Ed.), *Clinical diabetes mellitus: A problem-oriented approach* (3rd ed., pp. 37–58). New York: Thieme.

Christensen, N. K., Terry, R. D., Wyatt, S., Pichert, J. W., & Lorenz, R. A. (1983). Qualitative assessment of dietary adherence in patients with insulin-dependent diabetes mellitus. *Diabetes Care, 6*, 245–250.

Ciechanowski, P. S., Katon, W. J., & Russo, J. E. (2000). Depression and diabetes: Impact of depressive symptoms on adherence, function, and costs. *Archives of Internal Medicine, 160*, 3278–3285.

Cox, D. J., & Gonder-Frederick, L. A. (1992). Major developments in behavioral diabetes research. *Journal of Clinical and Consulting Psychology, 60*, 628–638.

Davidson, J. K., Anderson, J. H. J., Jr., & Chance, R. E. (2000). Insulin therapy. In J. K. Davidson (Ed.), *Clinical diabetes mellitus: A problem-oriented approach* (3rd ed., pp. 329–403). New York: Thieme.

Davidson, J. K., & DiGirolamo, M. (2000). Non-insulin dependent (Type I) diabetes mellitus and obesity. In J. K. Davidson (Ed.), *Clinical diabetes mellitus: A problem-oriented approach* (3rd ed., pp. 13–36). New York: Thieme.

Glasgow, R. E. (1991). Compliance to diabetes regimens: Conceptualization, complexity, and determinants. In J. A. Cramer & B. Spiker (Eds.), *Patient compliance in medical practice and clinical trials* (pp. 209–224). New York: Raven Press.

Glasgow, R. E., Boles, S. M., Calder, D., Dreyer, L., & Bagdade, J. (1999). Diabetes care practices in primary care: Results from two samples and three measurement sets. *Diabetes Educator, 25*, 755–763.

Glasgow, R. E., & Toolbert, D. J. (1988). Social environment and regimen adherence among Type II diabetic patients. *Diabetes Care, 11*, 377–386.

Hanson, C. L., Henggeler, S. W., & Gurghen, G. A. (1987). Social competence and parental support as mediators of the link between stress and metabolic control in adolescents with insulin-dependent diabetes mellitus. *Journal of Consulting and Clinical Psychology, 55*, 529–533.

Hauser, S. T., Jacobson, A. M., Lavori, P., Wolfsdorf, J. I., Herskowitz, R. D., Milley, J. E., & Bliss, R. (1990). Adherence among children and adolescents with insulin-dependent diabetes mellitus over a four-year longitudinal follow-up: II. Immediate and long-term linkages with the family milieu. *Journal of Pediatric Psychology, 15*, 527–542.

Hazlett, B. E. (2000). Historical perspective: The discovery of insulin. In J. K. Davidson (Ed.), *Clinical diabetes mellitus: A problem-oriented approach* (3rd ed., pp. 3–11). New York: Thieme.

Jacobson, A. M., Adler, A. G., Wolfsdorf, J. I., Anderson, B. J., & Derby, L. (1990). Psychological characteristics of adults with IDDM: Comparison of patients in poor and good glycemic control. *Diabetes Care, 13*, 375–381.

Jacobson, A. M., Hauser, S. T., Anderson, B. J., & Polonsky, W. (1994). Psychosocial aspects of diabetes. In C. R. Kahn & G. C. Weir (Eds.), *Joslin's diabetes* (13th ed., pp. 431–450). Philadelphia: Lea & Febiger.

Kaplan, R. M., & Hartwell, S. L. (1987). Differential effects of social support and social network on physiological and social outcomes in men and women with Type II diabetes mellitus. *Health Psychology, 6*, 387–398.

Kurtz, S. M. S. (1990). Adherence to diabetes regimens: Empirical status and clinical applications. *Diabetes Educator, 16*, 50–56.

Lustman, P. J., Griffith, L. S., & Clouse, R. E. (1988). Depression in adults with diabetes: Results of 5 year follow-up study. *Diabetes Care, 11*, 605–612.

Lustman, P. J., Griffith, L. S., Clouse, R. E., & Cryer, P. E. (1986). Psychiatric illness in diabetes mellitus: Relationship to symptoms and glucose control. *Journal of Nervous and Mental Disease, 174*, 736–742.

Marcus, M. D., & Wing, R. R. (1990). Eating disorders and diabetes. In C. S. Holmes (Ed.), *Neuropsychological and behavioral aspects of diabetes* (pp. 102–121). New York: Springer-Verlag.

Miller, W. S., & Rollnick, S. (2002). *Motivational interviewing* (2nd ed.). New York: Guilford Press.

Nathan, D. M. (1997). The treatment of diabetes mellitus to prevent and delay long-term complications: The diabetes control and complications trial. In D. LeRoith, S. I. Taylor, & J. M. Olefsky (Eds.), *Diabetes mellitus: A fundamental and clinical textbook* (2nd ed., pp. 456–461). Philadelphia: Lippincott, Williams & Wilkins.

Polonsky, W. H. (1993). Psychosocial issues in diabetes mellitus. In R. J. Gatchel & E. B. Blanchard (Eds.), *Psychophysiological disorders: Research and clinical applications* (pp. 357–381). Washington, DC: American Psychological Association.

Polonsky, W. H., Anderson, B. J., & Lohrer, P. A. (1991). Disordered eating and regimen manipulation in women with diabetes: Relationships to glycemic control. *Diabetes, 40*(Suppl. 1), 540A.

Ridgeway, N. A., Harvill, D. R., Harvill, L. M., Falin, T. M., Forester, G. M., & Gose, O. D. (1999). Improved control of type 2 diabetes mellitus: A practical education/behavior modification program in a primary care clinic. *Southern Medical Journal, 92*, 667–672.

Rollnick, S., Mason, P., & Butler, C. (1999). *Health behavior change: A guide for practitioners*. Edinburgh, Scotland: Churchill Livingstone.

Schwartz, L. S., Coulson, L. R., Toovy, D., Lyons, J. S., & Flaherty, J. A. (1991). A biopsychosocial treatment approach to the management of diabetes mellitus. *General Hospital Psychiatry, 13*, 19–26.

Surwit, R. S., & Feinglos, M. N. (1983). The effects of relaxation in glucose tolerance in non-insulin dependent diabetes. *Diabetes Care, 6*, 176–179.

Tattersall, R. B., McCulloch, D. K., & Avelin, M. (1985). Group therapy in the treatment of diabetes. *Diabetes Care, 8*, 180–188.

Vinik, A. I., & Glass, L. C. (2000). Diabetic autonomic neuropathy. In J. K. Davidson (Ed.), *Clinical diabetes mellitus: A problem-oriented approach* (3rd ed., pp. 637–659). New York: Thieme.

Vranic, M., Rodgers, C., Davidson, J. K., & Marliss, E. (2000). Exercise and stress in diabetes mellitus. In J. K. Davidson (Ed.), *Clinical diabetes mellitus: A problem-oriented approach* (3rd ed., pp. 267–328). New York: Thieme.

Wysocki, T., Greco, P., Harris, M. A., Bubb, J., & White, N. H. (2001). Behavior therapy for families of adolescents with diabetes. *Diabetes Care, 24*, 441–447.

4

HYPERTENSION

Blood pressure is related to heart muscle activity and to the remaining parts of the cardiovascular system, that is, the blood vessels. Arteries, with the exception of the pulmonary artery, carry oxygenated blood from the heart to other organs and tissues. The capillaries are tiny vessels that carry blood to individual cells, and the veins return blood to the heart after its oxygen has been used. These blood vessels are responsible for peripheral circulation and may dilate or contract at times. When arteries narrow, their resistance to blood flow increases. Another factor that can affect arterial pressure is the phase of the cardiac cycle (resistance is the greatest during expulsion of blood from the heart). Blood pressure is a measure of this resistance, actually measuring the force built up to overcome resistance in the arteries. As peripheral resistance increases, the force that is necessary to overcome resistance also increases. During systole, this force is at its highest point; during diastole, it falls to its lowest point. Therefore, systolic blood pressure is higher than diastolic blood pressure. The condition called *hypertension* occurs when blood pressure becomes chronically elevated. Hypertension is defined as systolic blood pressure (SBP) of 140 mm Hg or greater, or diastolic blood pressure (DBP) of 90 mm Hg or greater. Table 4.1 lists the classification categories of blood pressure for adults age 18 years and older (Joint Committee on Detection, Evaluation and Treatment of High Blood Pressure [JNC VI], 1997).

TABLE 4.1

Classification of Blood Pressure for Adults Ages 18 Years and Older

Category	Systolic (mm Hg)	Diastolic (mm Hg)
Normal	<130	<85
High normal	130–139	85–89
Hypertension		
Stage 1	140–159	90–99
Stage 2	160–179	100–109
Stage 3	>180	>110

Note. From "The Sixth Report of the Joint National Committee on Detection, Evaluation, and Treatment of High Blood Pressure (JNC VI)," by Joint National Committee on Detection, Evaluation, and Treatment of High Blood Pressure, 1997, *Archives of Internal Medicine, 157,* p. 2417. Copyright 1997 by the American Medical Association. Adapted with permission.

Approximately 50 million adult Americans have hypertension. This number is significant because a positive relationship exists between SBP and risk for cardiovascular disease (CVD). Indeed, hypertension is a significant risk factor for stroke, myocardial infarction (MI), and congestive heart failure (CHF). Together, these diseases account for more than 50% of deaths in the United States. Other facts, as listed next, should also be kept in mind when considering hypertension. These were reported in the National Health and Nutrition Examination Survey III, Phase 1, or NHANES III (JNC VI, 1997):

- The prevalence of hypertension increases with age (the risk generally increases between ages 55 and 65).
- Hypertension is about twice as prevalent among African Americans relative to White Americans.
- Hypertension is negatively related to socioeconomic status.
- Prevalence of hypertension increases markedly in women following menopause.
- The percentage of individuals with hypertension who are receiving treatment for it is approximately 55%.
- The percentage of people with high blood pressure controlled to below 140/90 mm Hg is about 29%.
- Nearly three fourths of adult Americans with hypertension are not controlling their blood pressure to below 140/90 mm Hg.
- Hypertension is extremely common in older Americans, with a prevalence of 60% for non-Hispanic White Americans, 71% for non-Hispanic African Americans, and 61% for Hispanics.
- Particularly among older individuals, SPB is a better predictor of events, such as coronary heart disease, heart failure, and stroke, than is DBP.

DETECTION AND CONFIRMATION OF HYPERTENSION

Proper blood pressure measurements are essential for hypertension detection. Repeated blood pressure measurements are needed to determine whether any initial elevations persist and, hence, require prompt attention, or whether they have returned to normal levels and need only periodic monitoring. The American Heart Association has presented guidelines to ensure that blood pressure is measured in a standardized manner using equipment that meets certification criteria (Kaplan, 1998). Note also that measurement of blood pressure outside the clinician's office might prove useful during an initial evaluation of some patients with hypertension and while monitoring their response to treatment. Sometimes, it may be difficult to distinguish sustained hypertension from so-called "white-coat hypertension," which is a condition noted in patients whose blood pressure is consistently elevated in the physician's office or clinic but is normal at other times. Indeed, the blood pressure of people with hypertension has a tendency to be higher when measured in the clinic than outside of the office. Although no universal upper limit for normal home blood pressure has been agreed on, readings of 135/85 mm Hg or greater should be considered elevated.

Many commercially available blood pressure monitors are available. These monitors can be programmed to take readings every 15 to 30 minutes throughout the day and night while patients go about their normal daily activities. These readings can subsequently be downloaded into a personal computer for analysis. Research has demonstrated that normal blood pressure values taken by ambulatory measurement are usually lower than clinic readings while patients are awake (below 135/85 mm Hg), and they are even lower while patients are asleep (below 120/75 mm Hg; Pickering, 1995). In passing, we should also point out that blood pressure falls by 10% to 20% during the night in the majority of individuals. This change appears to be more closely related to patterns of sleep and wakefulness than to time of day.

EVALUATION OF PATIENTS WITH HYPERTENSION

The evaluation of patients with documented hypertension should focus on three major factors:

1. identification of any known causes of high blood pressure
2. assessment of any possible target organ damage and CVD, as well as extent of the disease and response to therapy
3. identification of other cardiovascular risk factors or comorbid disorders that may help to improve prognosis and guide treatment.

The data required for such an evaluation are collected through the patient's medical history, a physical examination, laboratory tests, and other diagnostic procedures as needed. Note that high blood pressure appears to be a multifactorial disorder, consisting of an interaction of several genes with one another, as well as with the environment and lifestyle characteristics of the person. The genetic link is readily apparent by the observation of the fact that blood pressure levels are correlated among family members.

As much as 95% of all hypertension is of unknown cause. Different names have been used for labeling this form of hypertension, such as *essential*, *benign*, *idiopathic*, and *primary*. Currently, the preferred name is *primary hypertension* and is used to distinguish it from all of the remaining types, which are simply "secondary" to known causes such as renal disease or endocrine system dysfunction.

As noted earlier, *white-coat hypertension* refers to the fact that the actual measurement of blood pressure may precipitate an erroneous reaction on the part of the patient, which is only transient in nature but is persistent in some. This reaction is often related to the environment but is mostly related to the measurer. Indeed, most patients have higher blood pressure levels when taken in the office than when taken out of the office. Important questions that have plagued clinicians are "What is the natural history of white-coat hypertension, and does it represent some intermediate stage between normotension and sustained hypertension?" The best conclusion, according to Kaplan (1998), comes from a summary statement made by Verdecchia, Schillaci, Borgioni, Ciucci, and Porcellati (1996):

> White coat hypertension is neither a separate nor a harmful clinical entity: it represents a low-risk stratum of patients with essential hypertension who should be identified by a low threshold of ambulatory blood pressure (daytime below 130/80 mm Hg) or self-measured blood pressure…. A reasonable recommendation could be to seek frequent BP checks, postponing treatment, regardless of clinic measurements, if one is certain of the absence of target organ damage. (p. 1444)

Before leaving this topic, however, we should point out that the debate about whether white-coat hypertension is dangerous and should be treated is an ongoing one. For example, Grande and colleagues (2001) used heart-imaging technology when comparing patients with white-coat hypertension; patients with true, sustained hypertension; and people with normal blood pressure. Results revealed that images of the heart's left-ventricle's functioning and size suggested early signs of CVD, including enlargement and thicker walls, in patients with hypertension or white-coat hypertension, relative to those with normal blood pressure. Although the changes in the patients with white-coat hypertension were not as significant as those in patients with true, sustained hypertension, they suggest that some additional strain is being put on the heart, possibly increasing the risk for future development of CVD. In light of these findings, Moser (2001) suggested treating people with white-coat hypertension.

Risk of CVD in Patients With Hypertension

For patients with hypertension, the risk of CVD is determined by a number of factors besides just the level of blood pressure. These factors include the following: age older than 60 years, diabetes mellitus, dyslipidemia (i.e., disturbance of fat metabolism), family history of CVD (women younger than age 65 or men age 55), gender (men and postmenopausal women), smoking, and physical inactivity. In addition, the presence of target organ damage or clinical CVD also contributes to this risk. All of these factors can independently modify the risk for subsequent CVD, and their presence or absence should be determined during the routine evaluation of patients with hypertension. Based on the evaluation of these risk factors, along with the medical history, physical examination, and laboratory tests, the patient's risk group can be determined, as shown in Exhibit 4.1.

GENERAL TREATMENT ISSUES TO CONSIDER WHEN MANAGING PATIENTS WITH PRIMARY HYPERTENSION

The treatment of hypertension is among the leading reasons for the use of drugs in the United States (Woodwell, 1997). Kaplan (1998) has provided an excellent general overview for the drug management of hypertension, with an emphasis on achieving adherence to such therapy, as well as a comprehensive review of the various classes of drugs currently available. He also reviewed the reasons lifestyle modification is necessary to lower blood pressure. As he noted,

EXHIBIT 4.1
Patients With Hypertension Risk Group Categorization

Risk Group A:	No risk factors; no target organ disease/clinical cardiovascular disease
Risk Group B:	At least one risk factor, not including diabetes; no target organ disease/clinical cardiovascular disease
Risk Group C:	Target organ disease/clinical cardiovascular disease and/or diabetes, with or without other risk factors

Note. From "The Sixth Report of the Joint National Committee on Detection, Evaluation, and Treatment of High Blood Pressure (JNC VI)," by Joint National Committee on Detection, Evaluation, and Treatment of High Blood Pressure, 1997, *Archives of Internal Medicine, 157*, p. 2421. Copyright 1997 by the American Medical Association. Adapted with permission.

Lifestyle modifications should always be offered to those patients who need them because of their past unhealthy habits and their current increased risk for premature cardiovascular disease. For some, they may be the only therapy needed. For others, however, immediate hypertensive therapy is indicated, because delaying the adoption of life-style changes could interfere with achieving control of hypertension. (p. 159)

In terms of medication use, JNC VI (1997) guidelines recommend the use of a low dose of the prescribed drug initially, and then a slow titration of the dose upward on a schedule, dictated by the patient's age, needs, and responses. These guidelines further suggest that the optimal regimen should provide 24-hour coverage, with a once-daily dose. A 24-hour formulation is preferred over shorter acting agents because of greater adherence and more persistent and smooth (rather than intermittent) control of hypertension. Note also that, often, a very low dose of a diuretic (e.g., 6.25 mg of hydrochlorothiazide) can potentiate the effect of other antihypertensive agents without producing adverse metabolic effects.

As of 2002, more than 70 medications had been approved by the Food and Drug Administration for the treatment of hypertension (Victor, in press). Table 4.2 lists the most common of these, as well as their possible side effects. Note that one traditional question has always been "What drug should be used for which patient?" Unfortunately, we still have no precise scientific answer to this question. In the absence of an ideal method, two types of profiling techniques have been advocated, as described in the following sections (Victor, in press). However, in the absence of more precise information, the guiding principle for prescription should always be stringent blood pressure control goals, comorbidity, and optimization of cardiorenal protection.

Renin Profiling

This profiling approach is based on the assumption that the measurement of plasma renin activity (PRA) allows one to categorize all hypertension into two broad pathophysiological subsets: (a) PRA < 0.65, which implies volume-dependent hypertension that requires diuretics as the first-line therapy ("V" drugs), and (b) PRN ≤ 0.65, which implies renin-dependent hypertension that requires first-line therapy with one or more drugs that can block the renin-angiotensin system ("R" drugs), such as beta blockers, angiotensin-converting enzyme (ACE) inhibitors, or angiotensin receptor blockers (see Table 4.2).

Pharmacogenetic Profiling

As Victor (in press) has noted, some nucleotide polymorphisms have been shown to be associated with greater blood pressure reductions with specific drugs. A nucleotide is one of the compounds into which nucleic

TABLE 4.2
Commonly Prescribed Antihypertensive Medications and Possible Associated Side Effects

Drug	Trade Name	Possible Side Effects
ADRENERGIC INHIBITORS		
Guanadrel	*Hylorel*	Postural hypotension; diarrhea[a]
Reserpine (G)	*Serpasil*	Nasal congestion; sedation; depression
Clonidine hydrochloride (G)	*Catapres*	Withdrawal effects
Metoprolol tartrate (G)	*Lopressor*	Insomnia; fatigue; decreased exercise tolerance
Nadolol (G)	*Corgard*	Insomnia; fatigue; decreased exercise tolerance
Propranolol hydrochloride (G)	*Inderol*	Insomnia; fatigue; decreased exercise tolerance
Carvedilol	*Coreg*	Postural hypotension
ACE INHIBITORS		
Benazepril hydrochloride	*Lotensin*	Cough
Captopril (G)	*Capoten*	Cough
Enalapril maleate	*Vasotec*	Cough
DIURETICS		
Hydrochlorothiazide	*Hydrodiuril, Microzide, Esidrix*	May increase cholesterol and glucose levels; biochemical abnormalities
Furosemide (G)	*Lasix*	—

Note. From "The Sixth Report of the Joint National Committee on Detection, Evaluation, and Treatment of High Blood Pressure (JNC VI)," by Joint National Committee on Detection, Evaluation and Treatment of High Blood Pressure, 1997, *Archives of Internal Medicine, 157,* p. 2425–2426. Copyright 1997 by the American Medical Association. Adapted with permission.
[a]Refers to an abnormally low blood pressure when rising to an erect position.

acid is split by the action of nuclease (an enzyme or group of enzymes that splits nucleic acid into mononucleotides and other products). The nucleotides are composed of a base (purine or pyrimidine), a phosphate group, and a sugar (ribose or deoxyribose). Overall, the clinical research on this type of profiling is still in its infancy stage, and primary care physicians who do not specialize in treatment of hypertension may not know about it.

Other Drug Therapy Considerations

Kaplan (1998) also pointed out that, once a good response to drug therapy has occurred, and it has been maintained for at least a year or longer, medications can be reduced or discontinued. In many studies of patients whose medications were discontinued, a great many had their hypertension reappear in 6 to 12 months. In some other studies, though, a significant percentage remained normotensive for 4 years or longer (Schmeider, Rockstroh, & Messerli, 1991). Schmeider and colleagues went on to categorize patients who appear to remain normotensive as having the following characteristics: mild hypertension with low pretreatment blood pressure to begin with, younger age, normal body weight, little known target organ damage, successful treatment with only one drug, low salt intake, and no alcohol consumption.

The decision to stop drug therapy completely is still debatable. However, a reasonable approach in well-controlled patients would be to initially decrease the dose of whatever drug is being used. Finnerty (1990) has found that this approach is quite feasible, without any loss of blood pressure control, in a significant number of patients who have been well controlled on a single drug. If this partial decrease in medication is successful, complete withdrawal can then be attempted with continual surveillance of the patient's blood pressure.

Lifestyle Modifications

Turning now to the issue of lifestyle modifications and their effect on blood pressure control, multiple benefits accrue from such nondrug therapies, including decreasing the overall risk of CVD and other chronic diseases associated with maladaptive lifestyles. Moreover, lifestyle modifications help patients with hypertension for whom drug therapy cannot be completely stopped; combinations of nondrug therapies will often allow for a reduction in the amount of hypertensive drugs needed to control the hypertension. As a consequence, such nondrug therapies should be enthusiastically presented to patients and vigorously pursued, preferably before, and perhaps instead of, drug therapy (Kaplan, 1998). The major lifestyle modifications for patients with hypertension are listed in Exhibit 4.2.

Even though these combined drug–nondrug therapies have been shown to be effective, problems with adherence to them arise because of the lack of high motivation of patients to alter their diets and activity levels. Indeed, nonadherence is a major problem for patients with hypertension; only about

EXHIBIT 4.2
Recommended Lifestyle Modifications for Patients With Hypertension

- Exercise (aerobically) on a regular basis.
- Lose weight if overweight.
- Limit alcohol intake to ≤ 1 ounce/day of ethanol (e.g., 2 ounces of 100-proof whiskey, 8 ounces of wine, 24 ounces of beer).
- Maintain adequate amounts of dietary calcium, magnesium, and potassium.
- Reduce saturated fats and cholesterol in diets for overall cardiovascular health.
- Reduce sodium intake to approximately 110 mmol/day (2.4 g of sodium or 6 g sodium chloride).

one half of patients prescribed any antihypertensive therapy remain on such therapy, and then only for a few months (Kaplan, 1998). Moreover, many patients take therapy only intermittently, which causes three potential hazards: (a) rebound effects when antihypertensive drugs are suddenly stopped, (b) excessive drug effects when drug therapy is restarted and, most importantly, (c) periods without adequate antihypertensive coverage. Kaplan has provided some general guidelines to improve patient adherence to therapy.

Adherence Issues With Patients With Hypertension

Hyman and Pavliak (2001) have noted that, even though hypertension treatment is one of the most common clinical responsibilities of U.S. physicians, only one fourth of patients with hypertension have their blood pressures adequately controlled. Moreover, they found that most of these cases of uncontrolled hypertension consist of isolated, mild systolic hypertension in older adults, the majority of them having adequate access to health care and relatively frequent contact with their physicians.

Over the years, a great deal of research has been directed at ways to prompt patients to follow a physician's advice and prescribed medical regimen. This research was stimulated by the fact that studies of a wide variety of diseases, including hypertension, found that only 40% to 70% of patients adhere to physicians' prescriptions or advice (Baum, Gatchel, & Krantz, 1997). A number of general suggestions have emerged for ways of increasing adherence. Exhibit 4.3 delineates these suggestions as they relate specifically to patients with hypertension.

EXHIBIT 4.3
General Suggestions for Improving Adherence
by Patients With Hypertension

- Always be aware of the potential problem, and be alert to possible signs of no adherence (e.g., BP elevations, weight gain).
- Maintain and encourage regular contact with patients, and follow up with patients who do not return for visits.
- Involve patients in the treatment process by discussing the disease in understandable terms, the rationale for the treatment, and any potential barriers to adherence. Encourage their input in the decision-making process.
- Relatedly, make patients aware of any anticipated side effects, and ensure patients that such side effects can be dealt with if they occur.
- Try to keep the care inexpensive. Discuss cost issues with patients. Use non-drug, low-cost therapies whenever possible.
- Keep care simple, and be sensitive to possible difficulties in adherence to prescribed lifestyle changes. Discuss these issues with patients.
- Use once-daily doses of long-acting drugs whenever possible. Whenever possible, use combination tablets.
- If multiple medications are needed, start with small doses and add effective and tolerated drugs in a stepwise fashion.
- Encourage family support and involvement for the treatment.

AN EXAMPLE OF A BIOPSYCHOSOCIAL TREATMENT PROGRAM FOR PATIENTS WITH HYPERTENSION

We now recognize that the most comprehensive approach to the management of hypertension is a multiple-model approach in which a combination of nondrug and drug therapies is considered for patients (Kaplan, 1998). Rosen, Brondolo, and Kostis (1993) originally developed such a program, which they called the "Heart Saver Lifestyle Program." This program could be used as either primary or adjunctive therapy for hypertension. It was based on the biopsychosocial model of hypertension, which emphasizes assessment/treatment directed at biological, psychological, and social factors. Because it is illustrative of the type of comprehensive program that can successfully manage hypertension, we use the Heart Saver program as an example of how it can be utilized in a primary care setting with the help of a clinical health psychologist. It is broken into two basic components: an assessment phase and a treatment phase.

Assessment

Initially, all patients are systematically screened for a history of CVD and other contraindications for regular exercise or dietary change. Moreover, a systematic assessment of blood pressure is obtained, using standardized procedures as referred to earlier in this chapter, including methods for evaluating white-coat hypertension. In addition, blood chemistry and urine analysis are performed on all patients at baseline. Serum cholesterol (LDL, HDL, and total cholesterol) and triglyceride levels are evaluated to determine patients' overall risk for CVD. This provides important information because patients with elevated cholesterol or triglyceride levels may need additional dietary interventions or adjunctive therapy with cholesterol-lowering agents. Moreover, blood sugar levels may be an indice of adult-onset diabetes, which may require additional dietary interventions. Finally, for those patients who may require an exercise training program, exercise stress testing is obtained for all patients on the basis of this evaluation. The physician or an exercise physiologist will be able to screen for patients who are at risk for cardiovascular complications when exercising. Specific recommendations can then be made regarding the optimal level and intensity of exercise for each patient. Rosen and colleagues (1993) have also pointed out that this stress testing serves an important psychological function in that it can significantly reduce exercise anxiety and serve as a reassurance to patients of the relative safety of a structured exercise program.

Rosen and colleagues (1993) recommended the exclusion from the program of patients with a recent history of alcohol or drug abuse, serious psychiatric illness, or symptoms of dementia. These significant issues would need to be initially dealt with before any expectation of adherence to the program could be expected. A number of other psychosocial variables are also evaluated at baseline because they may be important to deal with in the comprehensive program. Some of the key variables evaluated are mood state, anger and hostility, and current life stressors, which can be evaluated by means of interview or pencil-and-paper tests. Information obtained from such an assessment is used to tailor the stress management intervention that is needed for certain patients. For example, patients with high levels of hostility would be provided with specific cognitive–behavioral interventions for anger management. Moreover, it may be important to evaluate the patient's major style of coping with stress or anger situations and then to come up with a more effective style. Social support is also evaluated because, many times, the involvement of spouses or significant others in the intervention program is an important aspect. In addition, a detailed behavioral history of information about past dieting, exercise, stress management, and so on is obtained because it is well known that past behaviors, such as exercise, are the most reliable predictors of future behavior (such as exercise adherence). Many patients who do not have a past involvement in a regular exercise program may require additional support or encouragement to become fully engaged in one. Any physical limitations to exercise, such as orthopedic problems or chronic pain conditions, as well as barriers to engaging in regular exercise, because of job and social commitments, also need to be carefully evaluated. Often, with special attention to time management techniques, most individuals are surprised that they can find the time for exercise if it is "built into" their schedule rather than assuming that they will exercise "when they find the time to do it."

Finally, because a patient's expectations for treatment success and adherence play a significant role in determining treatment outcome, a number of areas are also addressed by either a questionnaire or interview, including (a) expectations for compliance and any likely compliance difficulties; (b) any previous experiences with hypertension therapy approaches, including past successes or failures; (c) current expectations regarding potential outcome of nondrug treatment; (d) expectations regarding likely effectiveness of the treatment program in lowering blood pressure; and (e) the patient's overall self-efficacy for behavior change.

The preceding psychosocial screening can be accomplished in a very nonthreatening manner by means of a simple intake interview that is integrated with the typical medical evaluation interview and process. In this manner, patients realize that many factors are involved in contributing to heightened blood pressure. This is also a great educational opportunity because it addresses important issues contributing to hypertension that the patients may not have been aware of in the past.

Comprehensive Primary Care Treatment Interventions

Again, following a biopsychosocial model, a multidisciplinary approach is generally recommended for this combined therapeutic approach to hypertension. As a consequence, health professionals from several disciplines, including a nutritionist, exercise physiologist, internist, cardiologist, and clinical health psychologist, will usually be involved in each case. In the Heart Savers Lifestyle Program, clinical health psychologists serve as both treatment providers and as case managers and health care coordinators, helping to identify key patient needs, establish appropriate referral sources, and facilitate compliance with recommended treatment. Patients then are provided a comprehensive training manual and cassette tapes for home practice of relaxation. The treatment manual includes information about "heart-healthy" recipes, calorie-counting and food substitution tables, stress management guidelines, and exercise training schedules. Patients are also carefully instructed in the use of home self-monitoring evaluations forms, which are to be completed weekly throughout the treatment period. This helps the psychologist to track adherence to the prescribed treatment components.

The specific treatment components of this program are listed below (interested readers are referred to Rosen et al., 1993, for more details concerning the program):

- All patients are required to attend weekly group meetings. These meetings serve several purposes, including patient education, training in specific interventional skills (such as calorie counting, specific food preparation, and meal planning), how to seek support for adherence from significant others, and developing strategies for long-term behavior change. These group meetings involve patients and their spouses or significant others. Indeed, the program emphasizes family involvement and social support in helping all aspects of behavior change. The group meetings themselves involve a combination of dietetic instruction, behavioral modeling, weight and blood pressure assessment, and discussion of the weekly self-monitoring data. Specific target goals for caloric intake and sodium consumption are set at this time.

- The weekly group meetings are supplemented with individual or couples counseling sessions whenever needed. This occurs in cases in which important psychosocial issues or concerns about confidentiality issues need to be addressed.

- The exercise training component of the treatment involves encouraging patients to exercise for at least 20 minutes per day for a minimum of 3 days per week. The training levels are established at approximately 50% to 70% of maximum heart rate, which is determined during the initial exercise stress testing. Exercise self-monitoring is required, including the number of days per week that the patient exercises, the duration of the exercise, pulse rates at 10-minute intervals, and any adverse symptoms experienced. Patients are encouraged to develop an individual exercise plan to practice at home or work, after consultation with an exercise physiologist whenever possible.

- A 6-week stress management component of the program is divided into two specific phases: group instruction and then individual application. In the group instruction format, patients are provided instructions on the relationship between stress and hypertension. This is followed by a demonstration in guided practice of specific relaxation techniques. Patients are taught a brief yoga abdominal breathing technique, a modified progressive muscle relaxation technique, and mantra meditation. Patients also are provided with two 30-minute relaxation tapes with detailed instructions for home practice use. These tape instructions are supplemented with in vivo training in the first three sessions of relaxation. This usually produces an overall reduction of about 50% in patients' subjective tension levels following treatment.

  For the second phase of training, patients and their spouses are administered individually tailored stress reduction strategies and thermal biofeedback training as required. In addition, anger management techniques are emphasized during this phase. The final group session focuses on relapse prevention and behavioral maintenance techniques.

- Adherence to this program is evaluated in a number of ways: keeping track of attendance at the intervention meetings; patient recording of home assessment data; regular monitoring by staff members of blood pressure, weight, lipid levels, and food records; and stress management practice. Rosen and colleagues (1993) also suggested using 24-hour ambulatory blood pressure monitoring to assess generalization of treatment efficacy.

Using the preceding program, once patients are able to achieve target blood pressure levels, then it may be possible to reduce the dose level of a hypertensive medication to evaluate whether blood pressure levels will remain the same at the lower dose. If this can be achieved, then an attempt can also be made to eliminate medication completely; of course, regular follow-up will need to be conducted to ensure no insidious increase in blood pressure levels results. Regardless of the program results, however, all patients in the program need to be constantly encouraged to use diet, exercise, and stress management techniques on a regular bases to maintain the lifestyle changes that were produced by the program.

Rosen et al. (1993) found that the overall effectiveness of these lifestyle modifications in the treatment of hypertension is related to the initial health of the particular patient, his or her motivation for change, and the involvement of spouses or significant others in the treatment process. All of these factors can be evaluated and modified if needed by the clinical health psychologist. Cooperation between the primary care physician and the clinical health psychologist is also essential to ensure compliance with such a program. This has to become an active component of treatment for hypertension because, even patients who have access to health care and frequent contact with physicians often experience uncontrolled hypertension (Hyman & Pavliak, 2001). The clinical health psychologist can help monitor this and prevent it from happening in a busy primary care practice.

Brief Primary Care Treatment Interventions

Often, a behavioral health consultant model (one of the models of primary care reviewed in chapter 1) can be used to simply make an initial recommendation to the primary care case manager, provide a couple of treatment sessions, and then turn over the responsibility to the case manager to provide and coordinate subsequent treatment and monitoring. For example, a clinical health psychologist can provide initial relaxation and stress management skills and also help develop a behavior lifestyle change plan for diet and exercise. These brief interventions can then be turned over to the physician for further implementation, monitoring, and reinforcing. This type of model may be more appropriate for patients who do not have long-standing, chronic hypertension problems.

SUMMARY

Approximately 50 million adult Americans have hypertension, which is a major risk factor for stroke, MI, and CHF. Together, these diseases account for more than 50% of adult deaths in the United States. Proper blood pressure measurements are essential for the detection of hypertension. In terms of etiology, as much as 95% of all hypertension is of unknown cause.

The treatment of hypertension is one of the leading reasons for use of drugs in the United States. Once a good response to drug therapy has occurred and has been maintained for at least a year or longer, medications can often be reduced or discontinued in some patients. However, continuous monitoring of blood pressure must be maintained in the event of recurrence of hypertension. Research has also demonstrated the importance of lifestyle modifications for blood pressure control. Such modifications have multiple benefits besides lowering hypertension, such as decreasing the overall risk of CVD and other chronic diseases associated with maladaptive lifestyles. However, even though lifestyle modifications have been found to be effective, problems with adherence to them have arisen because of the lack of high motivation of patients to alter their diets and their activity levels. In this chapter, we provided suggestions for improving adherence to such modifications.

Finally, we discussed the most comprehensive approach to the management of hypertension: a multiple-model approach that uses a combination of nondrug and drug therapies. We presented an example of one such program that was developed to be used as either primary or adjunctive therapy for hypertension. It is based on the biopsychosocial model of hypertension, which emphasizes assessment/treatment directed at biological, psychological, and social factors.

RECOMMENDED READINGS

Joint National Committee on Detection, Evaluation, and Treatment of High Blood Pressure. (1997). The sixth report of the Joint National Committee on Detection, Evaluation, and Treatment of High Blood Pressure (JNC VI). *Archives of Internal Medicine, 157,* 2413–2446.

Kaplan, N. M. (1998). *Clinical hypertension* (7th ed.). Baltimore, MD: Williams & Wilkins.

Victor, R. (in press). Arterial hypertension. In L. Goldman & J. C. Bennett (Eds.), *Cecil textbook of medicine* (23rd ed.). St. Louis: W. B. Saunders.

GLOSSARY

adherence   The act or quality of doing what one is told or asked to do by a health care professional.

cardiovascular disease (CVD)   A disease of the cardiovascular system, composed of the heart and the blood vessels, that is responsible for the circulation of blood.

cholesterol   A fat-like substance in the form of leaflets or plates, found in animal fats and oils, and occurring in blood tissues and organs of the body. Recent guidelines suggest that an overall cholesterol blood level of less than 200 mg/dl is desirable; LDL ("bad cholesterol") of less than 100 mg/dl is optimal; and HDL ("good cholesterol") of 60 mg/dl is optimal.

diastole   Dilation of the heart ventricles occurring between the first and the second heart sound.

diuretic   A commonly prescribed antihypertensive medication that is effective for volume-dependent hypertension.

hypertension The medical condition in which blood pressure becomes chronically elevated (i.e., SBP of 140 mm Hg or greater, or DBP of 90 mm Hg or greater).

lipid levels Fatty acids, neutral fats, steroids, and phosphatides stored in the body that serve as a source of fuel.

pharmacogenetic profiling A profiling approach to determine what drugs are best for various patients with hypertension.

primary hypertension Hypertension of unknown cause or etiology. It is also sometimes called essential, benign, or idiopathic hypertension.

renin profiling A profiling approach based on the assumption that the measurement of plasma renin activity allows one to categorize all hypertension into two broad pathophysiological subsets associated with better response to certain medications; "V" drugs and "R" drugs.

systole The contraction of the ventricles of the heart.

triglyceride A neutral fat synthesized from carbohydrates for storage in animal adipose cells. Enzymatic hydrolyzes can then release free fatty acids in the blood. Recent guidelines suggest that a triglyceride blood level of less than 150 mg/dl is considered acceptable.

white-coat hypertension A condition noted in patients whose blood pressure is consistently elevated in the physician's office or clinic, but normal at other times.

REFERENCES

Baum, A., Gatchel, R. J., & Krantz, D. (Eds.). (1997). *An introduction to health psychology* (3rd ed.). New York: McGraw-Hill.

Finnerty, F. A. (1990). Stepped-down therapy versus intermittent therapy in systemic hypertension. *American Journal of Cardiology, 66,* 1373–1374.

Grande, A.M., Broggi, R., Colombo, S., Santillo, R., Imperiale, D, Bertolini, A., et al. (2001). Left ventricle changes in isolated office hypertension: A blood pressure-matched comparison with normotension and sustained hypertension. *Archives of Internal Medicine, 161,* 2677–2681.

Hyman, D. J., & Pavliak, V. N. (2001). Characteristics of patients with uncontrolled hypertension in the United States. *New England Journal of Medicine, 345,* 479–486.

Joint National Committee on Detection, Evaluation, and Treatment of High Blood Pressure. (1997). The sixth report of the Joint National Committee on Detection, Evaluation, and Treatment of High Blood Pressure (JNC VI). *Archives of Internal Medicine, 157,* 2413–2446.

Kaplan, N. M. (1998). *Clinical hypertension* (7th ed.). Baltimore, MD: Williams & Wilkins.

Moser, M. (2001). White-coat hypertension—To treat or not to treat: A clinical dilemma. *Archives of Internal Medicine, 161,* 2655–2666.

Pickering, T. (1995). Recommendations for the use of home (self) and ambulatory blood pressure monitoring. *American Journal of Hypertension*, 9, 1–11.

Rosen, R. C., Brondolo, E., & Kostis, J. B. (1993). Nonpharmacological treatment of essential hypertension: Research and clinical applications. In R. J. Gatchel & E. B. Blanchard (Eds.), *Psychophysiological disorders: Research and clinical applications*. (pp. 63–110). Washington, DC: American Psychological Association.

Schmeider, R. E., Rockstroh, J. K., & Messerli, F. H. (1991). Antihypertensive therapy: To stop or not stop? *Journal of the American Medical Association*, *265*, 1566–1571.

Verdecchia, P., Schillaci, G., Borgioni, C., Ciucci, A., & Porcellati, C. (1996). White coat hypertension. *Lancet*, *348*, 1443–1445.

Victor, R. (in press). Arterial hypertension. In L. Goldman & J. C. Bennett (Eds.), *Cecil textbook of medicine* (23rd ed.). St. Louis: W. B. Saunders.

Woodwell, D. (1997). *National Ambulatory Medical Care Survey: 1995 Summary advance data from vital and health statistics* (No. 286). Hyattsville, MD. National Center for Health Statistics.

5

CARDIOVASCULAR DISEASE

Cardiovascular disease (CVD) is the leading cause of death in the United States, accounting for 1 in every 2.5 deaths. According to the American Heart Association (AHA, 2001), approximately 60.8 million Americans were experiencing some form of CVD in 1998, and it accounted for about 950,000 deaths the same year. There were also 62.6 million physician office visits, and 5.3 million outpatient department visits, with a primary diagnosis of CVD in 1998. These high prevalence and medical care utilization rates suggest that a significant percentage of patients in a primary care setting will have some form of CVD, and psychologists working in primary care should have a solid understanding of the CVD condition.

WHAT IS CVD?

The term *cardiovascular disease* refers to a broad range of disorders of the heart. This section presents an overview of these disorders so that a psychologist can become familiar with conditions with which patients present in primary care. Interested readers are referred to an excellent book chapter by Scheidt (1996), which provides a comprehensive discussion of cardiology for nonphysicians.

CVD can be grouped into three major types: coronary heart disease (CHD; also known as coronary artery disease or CAD), valvular heart disease, and cardiomyopathy. CHD is disease of the coronary arteries, which is due in the vast majority of cases to atherosclerosis (plaques forming inside the arteries that cause narrowing or blocking). The reason artherosclerotic plaques grow is still not well understood; however, a number of risk factors for CHD have been identified. These factors, along with possible risk factors for which the evidence is less definitive, are listed in Table 5.1.

Patients with CHD can present with a number of serious syndromes. Each is related to atherosclerosis and, in some cases, the combined effect of a blood clot (thrombosis) encountering the plaque build-up further blocks the artery. The most common clinical syndromes are as follows:

- *Angina pectoris:* Angina pectoris refers to temporary discomfort in the chest that tends to be precipitated by physical exertion or mental stress. It generally lasts for less than 10 minutes and will improve with discontinuation of the precipitating activity.
- *Acute myocardial infarction:* Acute myocardial infarction (MI), or heart attack, occurs when the heart muscle is deprived of oxygen, usually due to arterial blockage, and it dies.
- *Ventricular arrhythmia:* Ventricular arrhythmia occurs when myocardial ischemia (insufficient oxygen to the heart) results in disruption of the rhythm of the heart. The disruption can be in the atria, which is usually not life threatening, or in the ventricles, which is often life threatening. Ventricular fibrillation is a frequent cause of sudden cardiac death.

Valvular heart disease involves narrowing or leakage in one or more of the four valves of the heart: the mitral value, aortic valve, tricuspid valve, and pulmonic valve. At least 50% of the time, the valve disease is related to rheumatic fever had as a child or adolescent. It can also be degenerative. The syndromes of aortic stenosis or mitral stenosis occur when narrowing

TABLE 5.1
Risk Factors for Coronary Heart Disease

Known Risk Factors	Possible Risk Factors
Age	Psychological stress
Male sex	Type A behavior pattern (anger and hostility)
Cigarette smoking	High blood triglycerides
Hypertension	
High-fat/high-cholesterol diet	
High total blood cholesterol	
High low-density lipoproteins	
Low high-density lipoprotein	
Sedentary lifestyle	
Major obesity	
Diabetes mellitus	

occurs in either the aortic or mitral valve. Symptoms of aortic stenosis are usually not present until late in the course of the disease, and they include chest pain with physical exertion, heart failure, and loss of consciousness. Symptoms of mitral stenosis tend to develop over long periods of time and include shortness of breath, fatigue, and atrial fibrillation. Aortic insufficiency or aortic regurgitation is a syndrome in which leakage occurs in the valve. As with aortic stenosis, the problem can be well developed before the individual becomes aware of symptoms, which include shortness of breath and congestive heart failure (CHF). Mitral insufficiency or regurgitation involves leakage of the mitral valve; however, symptoms are rare and the condition is not serious. Mitral valve prolapse is a congenital disorder in which the structures of the mitral valve are easily stretched and become thinner and weaker. Often this poses no clinical problem for the individual.

The third category of heart disease is cardiomyopathy. Cardiomyopathy is a weakening of the heart muscle itself. When the heart is no longer able to pump sufficient amounts of blood to the body, CHF results. The majority of cases in the United States are due to atherosclerotic disease, hypertension, alcohol, hypertrophic cardiomyopathy, or unknown causes.

COMMON MEDICAL TREATMENTS AND RECOMMENDATIONS

Reduction of risk for patients with known heart disease often includes lifestyle modification, medication, and sometimes surgery. The goal of therapy is to reduce the risk of MI or other trauma to the heart, prevent complications such as stroke, reduce discomfort, and maintain function and quality of life. Medical interventions can target risk factors such as hypertension and high blood cholesterol. Medications can reduce risk of thrombosis (blood clotting), dilate the blood vessels, reduce ischemia by decreasing the heart's need for oxygen, and prevent arrhythmias. The major classes of medications used for CVD and common examples are presented in Table 5.2. Psychologists working with patients with cardiac problems will benefit from familiarizing themselves with these medications and their actions to better understand the medical status and treatment of their patients.

When stenosis (arterial blockage) is diagnosed, a number of procedures can be used to clear the artery and allow blood flow to resume. Percutaneous transluminal coronary angioplasty involves directing a balloon-tipped catheter into the coronary artery. When the balloon reaches the blockage, it is inflated at high pressure to eliminate the obstruction of blood flow. Stents, which are small metal tubes, can be inserted into the coronary artery to support the arterial walls and prevent reoccurrence of stenosis. When coronary artery blockages cannot be treated with medications or angioplasty, surgery may be necessary. Blockages in the carotid artery can be cleaned out surgically

TABLE 5.2
Medications for Cardiovascular Disease

Class	Generic Name	Trade Name
ACE inhibitors		
Used as an antihypertensive. Also used to reduce acute MI in CHF patients.	Benazepril	Lotensin
	Captopril	Capoten
	Enalapril	Vasotec
	Fosinopril	Monopril
	Lisinopril	Prinivil, Zestril
	Quinapril	Accupril
	Ramipril	Altace
Antiarrhythmic drugs		
Used for preventing or suppressing atrial and ventricular arrhythmia.	Amiodarone	Cordarone
	Disopyramide	Norpace
	Flecainide	Tambocor
	Mexiletine	Mexitil
	Moricizine	Ethmozine
	Procainamide	Procan, Pronestyl
	Propafenone	Rythmol
	Quinidine	
	Sotalol	Betapace
Anticoagulants		
Interferes with clotting.	Heparin	
	Warfarin	Coumadin
Antilipids		
Used to reduce atherosclerosis by reducing LDL and total cholesterol or increasing HDL.	Cholestyramine	Questran
	Colestipol	Colestid
	Fluvastatin	Lescol
	Gemfibrozil	Lopid
	Lovastatin	Mevacor
	Pravastatin	Pravachol
	Probucol	Lorelco
	Simvastatin	Zocor
Antiplatelet agents	Aspirin	Multiple
Protects against clotting in the blood.	Dipyridamole	Persantine
	Ticlopidine	Ticlid
Beta blockers		
Used to reduce ischemia by decreasing the heart's need for oxygen. Reduces heart rate, blood pressure, and strength contraction.	Acebutolol	Sectral
	Atenolol	Tenormin
	Metoprolol	Lopressor, Toprol
	Nadolol	Corgard
	Pindolol	Visken
	Propranolol	Inderal
	Timolol	Blocadren
Calcium blockers		
Vasodilators used for preventing recurrent MI in some patients.	Amlodipine	Norvasc
	Diltiazem	Cardizem, Dilacor
	Felodipine	Plendil
	Isradipine	DynaCirc
	Nicardipine	Cardene
	Nifedipine	Procardia, Adalat

TABLE 5.2
Medications for Cardiovascular Disease *(continued)*

Class	Generic Name	Trade Name
	Nimodipine	Nimotop
	Verapamil	Calan, Isoptin, Verelan
Digoxin *Used for CHF and atrial fibrillation.*	Lanoxin	—
Diuretics *Used for reducing blood pressure by decreasing body fluid and dilating blood vessels.*	Bumetanide	Bumex
	Chlorthalidone	Hygroton
	Ethacrynic acid	Edecrin
	Furosemide	Lasix
	Hydrochlorothiazide	Esidrix, HydroDIURIL
	Metolazone	Zaroxolyn
	Spironolactone	Aldactone
	Triamterene	Dyrenium
Nitrates *Used for treatment of angina attacks.*	Isosorbide dinitrate	Sorbitrate, Isordil
	Isosorbide	Ismo, Imdur
	Nitroglycerin patches	Transderm-Nitro, Nitro-Dur
	Sublingual nitroglycerin	

through the procedure carotid endarterectomy. Coronary artery bypass graft surgery is a highly successful procedure that involves removing one or more healthy arteries or veins, often from the legs or near the sternum, and grafting them to the coronary arteries to bypass the obstructed area.

Surgery can also be indicated for patients with other forms of heart disease. Patients with valve disease will often need to have the valve surgically replaced. Vasodilating medications can sometimes be used to reduce pressure within the heart and delay the need for valve replacement. Patients with arrhythmias can be treated with an automatic implantable cardiodefibrillator (AICD; for inducible ventricular arrhythmia) or a pacemaker (for brachyarrhythmia). An AICD is a small electrical device implanted in the chest that delivers an electrical shock to the heart when it detects life-threatening ventricular fibrillation. A pacemaker is also implanted in the chest to prevent slow rhythms of the heart that fail to pump enough blood to the brain. With severe CHF and cardiomyopathy, heart transplantation can increase chances of survival. Given the high cost and limited availability of donor hearts, transplants are available only to a limited number of patients.

Although the procedures just discussed require the specialized skills of a cardiologist or cardiovascular surgeon, patients who have undergone these treatments, once stabilized, will often return to their primary care provider for ongoing care. Clinical health psychologists working in primary care should have a general understanding of the nature of these treatments and, specifically, the psychological demands and sequelae that often accompany them.

BARRIERS TO EFFECTIVE MANAGEMENT OF CVD

The effort required to manage CVD effectively can be difficult. In addition to complex medication regimens and medical procedures, patients often must attempt to change lifelong habits and well-ingrained patterns of interacting with the world. Common barriers to effective management of CVD include behavioral, physiological, environmental, and emotional factors. Risk factors in each of these areas can contribute to the onset of CVD, exacerbate the disease or loss of function, or diminish the prognosis for treatment and recovery. Fortunately, each has the potential to be modified.

Behavioral Barriers

Behavioral risk factors that can compromise cardiac health include tobacco use, a high-fat diet, a high-cholesterol diet, and inactivity. Smoking is a leading cause of CAD, because it increases the heart rate, raises blood pressure, constricts peripheral arteries, and increases the circulation of cholesterol in the bloodstream (Liese, Vail, & Seaton, 1996). The largest percentage of deaths from smoking-related illnesses are from CVD, and about one in five deaths from CVD is attributable to smoking (AHA, 2001). Approximately 27% of American men and 22% of American women are smokers, putting them at increased risk of heart attack and stroke. These numbers do not include the 4.1 million adolescents who also smoke. The nicotine in cigarettes makes smoking cessation a difficult endeavor for many people, and some will continue to smoke even after a diagnosis of CVD, heart attack, or stroke.

High blood cholesterol is categorized as another behavioral barrier because it is clearly related to dietary practices. The typical American diet is high in fat and cholesterol and contributes significantly to high total blood cholesterol, high LDL, and low HDL (all of which are risk factors). Only in recent years has sufficient evidence been gathered to conclude that cholesterol definitely plays a major role in the development of atherosclerotic plaques (Roberts, 1996). Total cholesterol level above 200 mg/dl significantly increases the risk of atherosclerotic events. Fortunately, however, cholesterol levels can be modified with health-enhancing results. Three large-scale randomized clinical trials have provided evidence that lowering total and LDL cholesterol levels reduces the frequency of fatal and nonfatal CAD (Roberts, 1996).

Medications can help to lower blood cholesterol, but dietary changes are also necessary. Food choices—including types of food, amounts of food, and frequency of eating—can be influenced by a variety of factors including culture, interpersonal influences, learned habits, advertising, availability of food choices, emotions, beliefs, and attitudes. Each of these factors often should be addressed to help patients overcome the barrier of unhealthy eating patterns. Heart-healthy eating is not simply a matter of *knowing* which foods are the right ones to eat. Indeed, a review of studies evaluating adherence rates to recommended diets for managing CVD concluded that patients generally do poorly, with rates ranging from only 13% to 76% (Dunbar-Jacob & Schlenk, 1996).

The third major behavioral barrier is lack of physical activity. Despite the rising popularity of running, health clubs, and other physical activity during the past 30 years, Americans still tend to be highly sedentary. Between 33% and 57% (depending on race and gender) of adults have no leisure physical activity (AHA, 2001). This puts a large proportion of the population at increased risk for CVD. The large amounts of time that many people spend on television watching and computer activities have likely contributed. Once cardiac problems arise, beginning regular exercise can be an even greater challenge due to physical symptoms, disability, and fear that exercise will trigger a cardiac event.

Physiological Barriers

The three primary physiological risk factors that are modifiable are obesity, hypertension, and diabetes mellitus. Individuals who are obese generally have higher total cholesterol and LDL levels than do people who are not obese (Garrison & Castelli, 1985). This is likely due to dietary differences between populations who are obese and those who are not, and, in fact, obesity may be best viewed as a cholesterol-dependent risk factor (Roberts, 1996). Hypertension may also be considered a secondary risk factor. People with hypertension have greater frequency of atherosclerotic events than normotensive individuals, but this is true only among those whose total blood cholesterol is higher than 150 mg/dl. Likewise, individuals with both Type I and Type II diabetes tend to have higher levels of cholesterol than those who are not diabetic (Roberts, 1996). Two thirds of people with diabetes die from CVD (AHA, 2001).

Environmental Barriers

Low socioeconomic status (SES), psychosocial stress, and social isolation have all been shown to interfere with the management of cardiovascular disorders. An extensive review by Kaplan and Keil (1993) highlighted the abundance of literature linking SES with established cardiovascular risk factors, including hypertension, smoking, total cholesterol level, body mass index, excess alcohol use, and diabetes. These authors also present evidence that SES may be an independent risk factor for CVD.

The ongoing stress of modern life can also pose a challenge for patients and their providers who are trying to manage CVD. High-stress role demands, both occupational and familial, certainly do not diminish when a person begins having cardiovascular difficulties. Many people believe they "thrive" under high-stress conditions and have difficulty removing themselves from potentially rewarding, albeit stressful, environments in which they have a history of occupational or personal success. Environmental factors, such as traffic, crime, and noise, are difficult to avoid. Family conflict can also be a persistent source of stress. A recent review of the effect of mental stress in patients with CAD concluded that both chronic and acute stress can be detrimental (Krantz, Sheps, Carney, & Natelson, 2000). Additionally, patients receiving medication for coronary disease and who had high baseline levels of daily stress were found to have smaller medication treatment effects than patients without high-stress scores (Rutledge, Linden, & Davies, 1999). Failure to recognize stress and understand its role in CVD can contribute to insufficient attention to stress management.

Occupational stress appears to be an independent risk factor for CVD (Baum, Gatchel, & Krantz, 1997). Several broad types of working conditions have been associated with CHD, including the psychological demands of the job, autonomy on the job, and job satisfaction. A combination of low levels of control over one's job and an excessive workload can be particularly important in heightening job-related stress and can increase risk of coronary disease. An interesting analysis of data from the Framingham Heart Study examined the risk of CVD in working women in particular. The researchers found that, although working women *in general* were not at greater risk for CVD than were housewives or men, women who were clerical workers, who had children, and whose bosses were nonsupportive were more likely to develop CHD (Haynes & Feinleib, 1980). This may be due to these women having low job control (e.g., clerical workers) and high demands (from family and work-related pressures). Fortunately, CVD risk has the potential to be reduced by modifying characteristics of the workplace to increase personal control and reduce unrealistic demands.

Inadequate social support can also compromise cardiovascular health. A review of 15 studies examining the impact of social factors on the future incidence of CAD found that a relatively small social network was, on average, associated with a two- to threefold increase in the incidence of CAD over time. Low levels of perceived emotional support increased the risk even more (Rozanski, Blumenthal, & Kaplan, 1999).

Emotional Barriers

Emotional risk factors include hostility reactions, depression, anxiety, and fear. Research on the role of emotions in the onset of coronary disease has yielded mixed results, and there are several gaps in the current knowledge (Kubzansky & Kawachi, 2000). The most evidence exists for anxiety, depression, and hostility reactions. Several studies have suggested an increased risk of CHD among patients with phobic anxiety (Coryell, Noyes, & Hause, 1986; Haines, Imeson, & Meade, 1987; Kawachi et al., 1994) or panic disorder (Coryell, Noyes, & Clancy, 1982; Weissman, Markowitz, Ouellette, Greenwald, & Kahn, 1990). Panic disorder affects 10% to 14% of coronary patients, compared to 2% to 5% in the general population (Shehan, 1982).

Depression is highly common in patients with cardiac problems and presents both direct and indirect barriers. Two depression symptoms, depressive affect and hopelessness, have been found to be independent predictors of survival among middle-age patients with cardiac disease (Barefoot et al., 2000). Additionally, women with CHD who also have high depression scores have been found to have nearly a threefold risk of smoking, one of the top behavioral risk factors (Rutledge et al., 2001).

The Type A behavior pattern (Friedman & Rosenman, 1959), a syndrome characterized by competition, hostility, time pressure, and exaggerated emphasis on achievement, was originally cast as a predictor of CAD. Studies of Type A personalities revealed mixed results leading to evaluation of individual components. Hostility, as an independent factor, has received a great deal of attention. Studies have found hostility to be associated with coronary stenosis (Low et al., 1998), restenosis after angioplasty (Goodman, Quigley, Moran, Meilman, & Sherman, 1996), and high blood pressure (Brownley, Light, & Anderson, 1996). Additionally, Helmers and colleagues (1995) found that patients with defensiveness combined with hostility had more functionally severe CAD than patients with high hostility but low defensiveness, suggesting that the combination of these traits may predispose CAD patients to a more adverse prognosis.

ROLE OF THE CLINICAL HEALTH PSYCHOLOGIST

The impact of psychosocial interventions in the treatment of CVD is well documented. Linden, Stossel, and Maurice (1996) performed a meta-analysis of 23 randomized controlled trials that evaluated the additional impact of psychosocial treatment for documented CAD. Patients who received psychosocial treatments showed greater reductions in psychological distress, systolic blood pressure, heart rate, and cholesterol level than did control patients. Furthermore, patients who did not receive psychosocial treatments had higher cardiac recurrence and mortality rates during the first 2 years of follow-up.

These studies evaluated the impact of psychosocial interventions that were part of a comprehensive cardiac rehabilitation program (generally including drug treatments combined with exercise rehabilitation and nutritional recommendations). Less is known about the impact of brief psychosocial interventions, provided in the primary care setting, on the course and prognosis of CVD, because researchers have just started to work in this area. Nevertheless, the studies that do exist, and logical application of what we know from studies conducted in non–primary care settings, suggest that health psychologists can certainly affect psychological distress and can potentially reduce risk of recurrent cardiac events and mortality through focused primary care interventions.

Assessment and intervention can be accomplished in three time frames. First, behavioral and lifestyle risk factors can be addressed with patients before signs of CVD are identified (primary prevention). Second, patients with early signs of heart disease can be worked with to prevent complications, slow progression of the disease, and maximize prognosis (secondary prevention). This can involve attention to behavioral risk factors, as well as psychological factors related to having a chronic and potentially life-threatening disease. Finally, a broad range of work (tertiary care) can be done with individuals who had a cardiac event (e.g., MI, stroke, surgery). Preferably, primary care psychologists will work with these patients as a follow-up to participation in a cardiac rehabilitation program that involves psychosocial interventions. In some settings and for some patients, however, formal cardiac rehabilitation programs are not available, and contact with a primary care psychologist may be the first intervention received from a behavioral medicine provider.

Primary Prevention

The primary modifiable risk factors for CVD are tobacco use, obesity, high blood cholesterol, and physical inactivity (AHA, 2001). According to the World Health Organization, 1 year after quitting tobacco, the risk of CHD decreases by 50%, and within 15 years, the relative risk of dying from CHD for an ex-smoker approaches that of a long-time nonsmoker (cited in AHA, 2001). Between 41% and 49% of Americans ages 20 years and older are at higher risk for CHD due to their elevated low-density lipoprotein levels. A 10% decrease in cholesterol levels may result in an estimated 30% reduction in the incidence of CHD (AHA, 2001). The risk of inactivity is equivalent to that observed for high blood pressure, high cholesterol levels, and cigarette smoking (Pate & Pratt, 1995). A recent study of more than 72,000 female nurses indicated that physical activity, including walking, is associated with substantial risk reduction of total and ischemic stroke compared with casual pace walking (Hu et al., 2000). Finally, overweight and obesity are the risk factors with the highest prevalence, with 35% to 62% of adult men (depending on race) and 25% to 64% of adult women having a body mass index (BMI) greater than 25 kg/m^2.

Given the push in many health care systems for primary care providers to spend decreasing time with patients during each visit, many find it difficult to inquire about these issues during an appointment that may be for a completely unrelated problem. Furthermore, once a risk factor is identified, providers must use additional time to either provide an intervention or direct the patient to another resource that can offer help. Primary care health psychologists can serve as physician extenders and thereby improve the feasibility of incorporating primary prevention into a primary care clinic.

Ensuring that screening is available for these risk factors among patients without cardiac disease will be an initial first step. Tobacco use, exercise habits, and BMI can be incorporated into the vital sign assessment completed by nurses or medical technicians prior to the patients' physician visit. Patients who report using tobacco or exercising inadequately, or who have a BMI greater than 25 can be informed that these factors represent risk for CVD and can be asked if they are interested in making changes to their lifestyle. If patients give an affirmative response, they are then asked if they would like a follow-up visit with the clinical health psychologist in the clinic to discuss strategies that are likely to be successful and to tailor a program to their individual needs. Many patients who are interested in reducing their risk through lifestyle change will prefer to try it alone, and this is all right. Those who are pessimistic, who have low self-efficacy, or who are information seekers will likely benefit from the offer of assistance. Interventions psychologists might use with these patients are discussed more specifically in chapters 9 and 11.

Interventions for Patients Diagnosed With Cardiac Disease

Patients with CVD should be educated about the potential risk of psychosocial stress on their condition. Including stress management skills training as part of a clinical pathway for *all* patients with CVD may help them identify areas for change that may not have come to light had only select "highly stressed" patients received the intervention.

In our experience, many patients hold a narrow view of stress that defines it as involving only major external demands. In other words, they do not consider stress to be relevant for them unless they are going through a divorce, losing their job, or experiencing other dramatic life-changing events. Patients should be educated to the fact that, although exposure to high-intensity stressors such as war (Meisel et al., 1991; Sibal, Armenian, & Alam, 1989) and natural disasters (Dobson, Alexander, Malcolm, Steele, & Miles, 1991) have been shown to increase incidence of fatal MI, it is a person's physiological and emotional responses to situations that primarily determine risk to the heart. Acute episodes of frustration, irritation, anger, and impatience in response to common daily events can trigger increased heart rate and premature ventricular contractions and lead to tachycardia and ventricular fibrillation (Powell, 1996).

Stressors that precipitate lethal arrhythmias are most commonly small, unexpected hassles occurring within 1 hour of the cardiac event (Kamarck & Jennings, 1991). Furthermore, these small stressors are common for most of us, and many of these events are likely not even remembered beyond their occurrence. This suggests that patients' self-report of not having stress in their lives may reflect inadequate perception and definition of stress rather than actual low risk. Therefore, it is wise to target all patients with cardiac problems with stress management intervention rather than only those who acknowledge stress in their lives.

A broad range of commonly used brief stress management approaches can be applied to patients with cardiac problems in the primary care setting. These can be provided individually in 15- to 30-minute sessions or through psychoeducational groups conducted in the primary care clinic.

Relaxation Training

Relaxation training has been shown to decrease blood pressure in patients who are not on medication (Kaufmann et al., 1988), reduce anxiety symptoms in patients with CVD (Dath, Mishra, Kumaraiah, & Yavagal, 1997), and decrease sympathetic arousal (Cottier, Shapiro, & Julius, 1984). A wide range of techniques can be taught, including diaphragmatic breathing, progressive muscle relaxation, autogenic relaxation, and mental imagery. Patients should be provided with a brief rationale for the use of relaxation that applies to their specific physical condition. For example, patients with hypertension can be told that relaxation exercises have the potential to decrease blood pressure. Relaxation can be framed as a means for controlling anger or frustration in patients with recognized emotional reactivity. Post-MI patients can be given relaxation exercises as a tool for decreasing risk of MI reoccurrence.

Because some people have never learned to relax effectively, psychologists should have them practice relaxation techniques during the office visit and assess whether the patient noticed any change in tension or other physiological responses. Patients who do not notice any effect from initial efforts to relax should be informed that relaxation is a skill and, like any other skill, it needs to be practiced to become proficient at it. These individuals should be encouraged to look for small signs of change as indicators of progress. Biofeedback equipment can be useful for helping individuals see progress when they do not feel any change. Individuals who have initial difficulty with relaxation are at risk for dismissing the techniques as ineffective if proper attention is not paid to developing skills, setting appropriate expectations, and reinforcing behavior change.

Monitoring forms for home practice can help increase adherence to relaxation recommendations. Additionally, it is often helpful to provide patients with a relaxation audiotape to assist home practice.

Cognitive–Behavioral Group Interventions

Cognitive–behavioral group interventions have been used effectively to reduce hostility and blood pressure in patients with CHD (Gidron, Davidson, & Bata, 1999). The eight-session treatment that was evaluated included skills training to reduce antagonism (e.g., listening), cynicism (e.g., cognitive restructuring), and anger (e.g., problem solving). Relapse prevention was also covered. This type of group can easily be adapted to the primary care setting.

Powell (1996) presented another simple, cognitive intervention that is useful in primary care for addressing emotional hyper-reactivity in patients with cardiac problems. She suggested targeting two key beliefs that underlie chronic emotional hyper-reactivity to minor stressors: (a) the belief that human behavior is a function of environmental stimuli (pure environmental determinism) and (b) the belief that environmental forces are subject to one's personal control and can be changed through personal efforts. Powell's intervention teaches that, when faced with anger or irritation, people have a choice of whether to try to change the environmental stressor or their own response to the stressor. She used the metaphor of a fish confronting a fisherman's hook to illustrate that there is an opportunity for decision as to whether one will "bite" or not. By immediately labeling stressors as "hooks," patients are taught to neutralize the arousal effect.

Problem-Solving and Assertiveness Training

Problem-solving and assertiveness training can also be applied to help patients address potentially modifiable situations that may be contributing to stress. Traditional methods for teaching these skills, through classes or individual therapy, can be applied to the primary care setting. Additionally, many patients are likely to benefit from handouts, pamphlets, and bibliotherapy recommendations addressing these issues. These materials, combined with counseling or role plays to assist patients in applying the concepts to their specific situations, may be most appropriate within the consultation model for primary care psychology.

Other Roles for Clinical Health Psychologists

Psychologists can also serve essential roles in assessing and treating comorbid anxiety with patients with CVD. Brief, self-help treatments, based on well-established cognitive behavioral principles and with minimal therapist contact, have been shown to be effective for many people with anxiety problems (Barlow, Lerner, & Esler, 1996). Craske and colleagues have published anxiety treatment manuals that can be easily adapted to the primary care setting (Craske, 2001; Craske, Barlow, & O'Leary, 1992). White (1995) developed a "stresspac" consisting of brief information about the nature of stress and anxiety, as well as mechanisms for coping, and provided it to patients with anxiety disorders presenting in the primary care setting. Patients receiving the "stresspac" improved significantly more than wait-list control and advice-only groups after 3 months, and those who required further individual therapy benefited from fewer sessions than did the other groups. Of course, patients should be evaluated as to the appropriateness and likely prognosis of a minimal-contact approach. Those with more severe symptoms, greater adverse impacts on their life from the anxiety, or risk for harm to self or others should be referred to specialty mental health care.

Standard cognitive–behavioral treatments for anxiety are appropriate for patients with CVD, although certain issues may need to be addressed. For many patients with chronic disease, psychological distress is related to increasing disability, changes in role functioning, end of life, and the impact of the disease on family and other significant people. Additionally, anxiety symptoms (e.g., palpitations, fatigue, shortness of breath) can mimic symptoms of cardiac disease, leading to confusion and fear of disease progression, which then, in a cyclical manner, increase symptoms. Patients with CVD and anxiety should be taught to discriminate and manage anxiety symptoms but not to dismiss potentially life-threatening cardiac symptoms that may need medical care. Indeed, timeliness of medical attention following a heart attack can significantly improve recovery, and it would be a grave error for patients to dismiss symptoms as "simply anxiety."

Likewise, the prevalence of depression among patients with cardiac problems, and its potential for complications in the management of cardiovascular illness, highlights another important role of the primary care psychologist. Routine screening for depression should be accomplished for all patients with cardiac problems, either by the primary care physician or as part of a behavioral risk assessment by the psychologist. The depression sections of the PRIME–MD (Spitzer et al., 1994) and the CES–D (Myers & Weissman, 1980) are self-report scales that are useful for this purpose. The Agency for Health Care Policy and Research guidelines (1993) suggested that the primary care provider should be the first line of treatment for depression, with referral to a mental health provider as a secondary option. This is important because many patients will not follow through on a referral to a mental health clinic. The psychologist, as a member of the primary care team, can play a key role in facilitating appropriate treatment. As with anxiety, discussed earlier, many patients with mild or subclinical depression can be treated successfully with brief, minimal-contact approaches. Bibliotherapy using Burns's (1980) *Feeling Good* handbook has been shown to reduce depressive symptoms (Jamison & Scogin, 1995). Recommendations for behavioral activation and increasing pleasurable activity can be a powerful tool for helping many people move toward decreased depressive symptoms and improved quality of life.

Structured psychoeducational groups for the treatment of depression can be incorporated into the primary care setting. Peterson and Halstead (1998) presented empirical support for a group treatment format that would be readily adaptable to the medical setting. Individuals with significant neurovegetative signs and psychosocial impairment may benefit from antidepressant medications, combined with psychological interventions, and the psychologist can make this recommendation to the physician when appropriate. Those with more severe symptoms, psychosis, or risk of harm to self or others should be referred to more intensive mental health care. Brief psychological treatment can effectively reduce depression and physiological risk factors for CVD (Black, Allison, Williams, Rummans, & Gau, 1998; Carney et al., 2000). However, we still do not know whether treatment for depression actually improves medical prognosis for CHD.

SUMMARY

As the leading cause of death in the United States, CVD is a major public health concern. The clear role of behavioral and psychosocial factors in the development and course of CVD makes psychologist involvement essential. Psychologists have become invaluable in cardiac rehabilitation and other specialty-level services. However, we are only beginning to learn about the impact of primary care psychology for patients with cardiac problems. The potential for involvement in primary prevention, secondary prevention, and tertiary care is high, and continuing research in these areas will further solidify psychologists' role in primary care treatment for CVD.

RECOMMENDED READINGS

Allan, R., & Scheidt, S. (Eds.). (1996). *Heart and mind: The practice of cardiac psychology*. Washington, DC: American Psychological Association.

Rozanski, A., Blumenthal, J. A., & Kaplan, J. (1999). Impact of psychological factors on the pathogenesis of cardiovascular disease and implications for therapy. *Circulation, 99*, 2192–2217.

GLOSSARY

angina pectoris   Temporary discomfort in the chest that tends to be precipitated by physical exertion or mental stress.

aortic insufficiency   A syndrome in which leakage occurs in the aortic valve (also called aortic regurgitation).

arrhythmia   When myocardial ischemia (insufficient oxygen to the heart) results in disruption of the rhythm of the heart.

atherosclerosis   Plaques forming inside the arteries causing narrowing or blocking.

automatic implantable cardiodefibrillator (AICD)   A small electrical device implanted in the chest that delivers an electrical shock to the heart when it detects life-threatening ventricular fibrillation.

blood triglycerides   The level of triglycerides, one of the circulating blood fats, in the blood.

brachyarrhythmia   Slow beating of the heart, sometimes at a rate that is insufficient to pump blood to the brain.

cardiomyopathy   Dysfunction of the heart muscle itself.

carotid endarterectomy   A procedure for clearing out narrowing in the carotid artery.

coronary artery bypass graft (CABG) surgery   Surgical procedure that involves removing one or more healthy arteries or veins, often from the legs or near the sternum, and grafting them to the coronary arteries to bypass the obstructed area.

coronary heart disease (CHD)   Disease of the artery that supplies blood to the heart. Also known as coronary artery disease (CAD).

high-density lipoproteins (HDL)   Commonly referred to as "good cholesterol," HDL carries cholesterol from the arteries to the liver. It is known to protect against arteriosclerotic plaque buildup; therefore, high HDL levels reduce risk for coronary artery disease.

hypertrophic cardiomyopathy   A genetic condition in which there is inconsistent thickening of the heart wall.

ischemia   A condition in which insufficient oxygen is present, particularly in the heart.

low-density lipoproteins (LDL)   Commonly referred to as "bad cholesterol," LDL carries cholesterol to the coronary artery. It is known to contribute to arteriosclerotic plaque buildup; therefore, high LDL levels are considered a risk for CAD.

mitral insufficiency   Leakage of the mitral valve; also called mitral regurgitation.

mitral valve prolapse   A congenital disorder in which the structures of the mitral valve are easily stretched and become thinner and weaker.

myocardial infarction (MI)   Occurs when the heart muscle is deprived of oxygen, usually due to arterial blockage, and dies. This event is commonly referred to as a heart attack.

pacemaker   An electrical device implanted in the chest to prevent slow rhythms of the heart that fail to pump enough blood to the brain.

percutaneous transluminal coronary angioplasty (PTCA)   A procedure for clearing arterial blockages that involves directing a balloon-tipped catheter into the coronary artery. When the balloon reaches the blockage, it is inflated at high pressure to eliminate the obstruction of blood flow.

stents   Small metal tubes that are inserted into the coronary artery to support the arterial walls and prevent reoccurrence of stenosis.

thrombosis   Blood clotting.

total serum cholesterol   A measure of the amount of cholesterol in the bloodstream. Normal level is below 200 mg/dl. High levels are a major risk factor for CHD.

Type A behavior pattern   A complex set of behaviors that are thought to increase risk for cardiovascular disease. It is characterized by pervasive free-floating hostility and a strong sense of time urgency, as well as an intense drive to achieve and to gain recognition, high competitiveness, extreme mental and physical alertness, and a tendency to increase the rate of physical and mental activities.

valvular heart disease   Narrowing or leakage in one or more of the four valves of the heart: the mitral value, aortic valve, tricuspid value, and pulmonic valve.

ventricular fibrillation   Electrical impulses moving through the heart in a chaotic way that causes the heart to stop pumping blood effectively. Cardiac arrest occurs within seconds of onset.

ventricular tachycardia   Rapid heart rate originating in the ventricle.

REFERENCES

Agency for Health Care Policy and Research. (1993). The severity of major depression and choice of treatment in primary care practice. In *Clinical practice guideline number 5. Depression in primary care: 2. Treatment of major depression* (AHCPR Publication No. 93-0551). Rockville, MD: U.S. Department of Health and Human Services.

American Heart Association. (2001). *2001 heart and stroke statistical update*. Dallas: Author.

Barefoot, J. C., Brummett, B. H., Helms, M. J., Mark, D. B., Siegler, I. C., & Williams, R. B. (2000). Depressive symptoms and survival of patients with coronary artery disease. *Psychosomatic Medicine, 62,* 790–795.

Barlow, D. H., Lerner, J. A., & Esler, J. L. (1996). Behavioral health care in primary care settings: Recognition and treatment of anxiety disorders. In R. J. Resnick & R. H. Rozensky (Eds.), *Health psychology through the lifespan: Practice and research opportunities* (pp. 133–148). Washington, DC: American Psychological Association.

Baum, A., Gatchel, R. L., & Krantz, D. (1997). *Introduction to health psychology* (3rd ed.). New York: McGraw-Hill.

Black, J. L., Allison, T. G., Williams, D. E., Rummans, T. A., & Gau, G. T. (1998). Effect of intervention for psychological distress on rehospitalization rates in cardiac rehabilitation patients. *Psychosomatics, 39,* 134–143.

Brownley, K. A., Light, K. C., & Anderson, N. B. (1996). Social support and hostility interact to influence clinic, work, and home blood pressure in Black and White men and women. *Psychophysiology, 33,* 434–445.

Burns, D. (1980). *Feeling good: The new mood therapy.* New York: Avon Books.

Carney, R. M., Freedland, K. E., Stein, P. K., Skala, J. A., Hoffman, P., & Jaffe, A. S. (2000). Change in heart rate and heart rate variability during treatment for depression in patients with coronary heart disease. *Psychosomatic Medicine, 62,* 639–647.

Coryell, W., Noyes, R., & Clancy, J. (1982). Excess mortality in panic disorder: A comparison with primary unipolar depression. *Archives of General Psychiatry, 39,* 701–703.

Coryell, W., Noyes, R., & Hause, J. D. (1986). Mortality among outpatients with anxiety disorders. *American Journal of Psychiatry, 143,* 508–510.

Cottier, C., Shapiro, K., & Julius, S. (1984). Treatment of mild hypertension with progressive muscle relaxation: Predictive value of indexes of sympathetic tone. *Archives of Internal Medicine, 144,* 1954–1958.

Craske, M. G. (2001). *Mastery of your anxiety and panic: Client workbook for agoraphobia (MAP-3).* San Antonio, TX: Harcourt.

Craske, M. G., Barlow, D. H., & O'Leary, T. (1992). *Mastery of your anxiety and worry.* Albany, NY: Graywind.

Dath, N. N. S., Mishra, H., Kumaraiah, V., & Yavagal, S. T. (1997). Behavioural approach to coronary heart disease. *Journal of Personality and Clinical Studies, 13,* 29–33.

Dobson, A. J., Alexander, H. M., Malcolm, J. A., Steele, P. L., & Miles, T. A. (1991). Heart attacks and the Newcastle earthquake. *Medical Journal of Australia, 155,* 757–761.

Dunbar-Jacob, J., & Schlenk, E. A. (1996). Treatment adherence and clinical outcome: Can we make a difference? In R. J. Resnick & R. H. Rozensky (Eds.), *Health psychology through the lifespan: Practice and research opportunities* (pp. 323–343). Washington, DC: American Psychological Association.

Friedman, M., & Rosenman, R. H. (1959). Association of specific behavior pattern with blood and cardiovascular findings. *Journal of the American Medical Association, 169,* 1286–1296.

Garrison, R. J., & Castelli, W. P. (1985). Weight and 30 year mortality of men in the Framingham study. *Annals of Internal Medicine, 106,* 1006–1009.

Gidron, Y., Davidson, K., & Bata, I. (1999). The short-term effects of a hostility-reduction intervention on male coronary heart disease patients. *Health Psychology, 18,* 416–420.

Goodman, M., Quigley, J., Moran, G., Meilman, H., & Sherman, M. (1996). Hostility predicts restenosis after percutaneous transluminal coronary angioplasty. *Mayo Clinic Proceedings, 71,* 729–734.

Haines, A. P., Imeson, J. D., & Meade, T. W. (1987). Phobic anxiety and heart disease. *British Medical Journal, 295,* 297–299.

Haynes, S. G., & Feinleib, M. (1980). Women, work, and coronary heart disease: Prospective findings from the Framingham heart study. *American Journal of Public Health, 70,* 133–141.

Helmers, K. F., Krantz, D. S., Merz, C. N. B, Klein, J., Kop, W. J., Gottdiener, J. S., et al. (1995). Defensive hostility: Relationship to multiple markers of cardiac ischemia in patients with coronary disease. *Health Psychology, 14,* 202–209.

Hu, F. B., Stampfer, M. J., Colditz, G. A., Ascherio, A., Rexrode, K. M., Willett, W. C., et al. (2000). Physical activity and risk of stroke in women. *Journal of the American Medical Association, 283,* 2961–2968.

Jamison, C., & Scogin, F. (1995). The outcome of cognitive bibliotherapy with depressed adults. *Journal of Consulting and Clinical Psychology, 63,* 644–650.

Kamarck, T., & Jennings, J. R. (1991). Biobehavioral factors in sudden cardiac death. *Psychological Bulletin, 109,* 42–75.

Kaplan, G. A., & Keil, J. E. (1993). Socioeconomic factors and cardiovascular disease: A review of the literature. *Circulation, 88,* 1973–1998.

Kaufmann, P. G., Jacob, R. G., Ewart, C. K., Chesney, M. A., Muenz, L. R., Doub, N., et al. (1988). Hypertension intervention pooling project. *Health Psychology, 7*(Suppl), 209–224.

Kawachi, I., Colditz, G. A., Ascherio, A., Rimm, E. B., Giovannucci, E., Stampfer, M. J., et al. (1994). Coronary heart disease/myocardial infarction: Prospective study of phobic anxiety and risk of coronary heart disease in men. *Circulation, 89,* 1992–1997.

Krantz, D. S., Sheps, D. S., Carney, R. M., & Natelson, B. H. (2000). Effects of mental stress in patients with coronary artery disease: Evidence and clinical implications. *Journal of the American Medical Association, 283,* 1800–1802.

Kubzansky, L. D., & Kawachi, I. (2000). Going to the heart of the matter: Do negative emotions cause coronary heart disease? *Journal of Psychosomatic Research, 48,* 323–337.

Liese, B. S., Vail, B. A., & Seaton, K. A. (1996). Substance use problems in primary care medical settings: Is there a psychologist in the house? In R. J. Resnick & R. H. Rozensky (Eds.), *Health psychology through the lifespan: Practice and research opportunities* (pp. 177–194). Washington, DC: American Psychological Association.

Linden, W., Stossel, C., & Maurice, J. (1996). Psychosocial interventions for patients with coronary artery disease: A meta-analysis. *Archives of Internal Medicine, 156,* 745–752.

Low, K. G., Gleisher, C., Colman, R., Dionne, A., Casey, G., & Legendre, S. (1998). Psychosocial variables, age, and angiographically-determined coronary artery disease in women. *Annals of Behavioral Medicine, 20,* 221–226.

Meisel, S. R., Kutz, I., Dayan, K. I., Pauzner, H., Chetboun, I., Arbel, Y., et al. (1991). Effect of the Iraqi missile war on incidence of acute myocardial infarction and sudden death in Israeli civilians. *Lancet, 338,* 660–661.

Myers, J. K., & Weissman, M. M. (1980). Use of a self-report symptom scale to detect depression in a community sample. *American Journal of Psychiatry, 137,* 1081–1084.

Pate, R. R., & Pratt, M. (1995). Physical activity and public health. *Journal of the American Medical Association, 273,* 402–408.

Peterson, A. L., & Halstead, T. S. (1998). Group cognitive behavior therapy for depression in a community setting: A clinical replication series. *Behavior Therapy, 29*, 3–18.

Powell, L. H. (1996). The hook: A metaphor for gaining control of emotional reactivity. In R. Allan & S. Scheidt (Eds.), *Heart and mind: The practice of cardiac psychology* (pp. 313–327). Washington, DC: American Psychological Association.

Roberts, W. C. (1996). Coronary atherosclerosis: Descriptions, manifestations, and prevention. In R. Allan & S. Scheidt (Eds.), *Heart and mind: The practice of cardiac psychology* (pp. 147–178). Washington, DC: American Psychological Association.

Rozanski, A., Blumenthal, J. A., & Kaplan, J. (1999). Impact of psychological factors on the pathogenesis of cardiovascular disease and implications for therapy. *Circulation, 99*, 2192–2217.

Rutledge, T., Linden, W., & Davies, R. F. (1999). Psychological risk factors may moderate pharmacological treatment effects among ischemic heart disease patients. *Psychosomatic Medicine, 61*, 834–841.

Rutledge, T., Reis, S. E., Olson, M., Owens, J., Kelsey, S. F., Pepine, C. J., et al. (2001). Psychological variables are associated with atherosclerosis risk factors among women with chest pain: The WISE study. *Psychosomatic Medicine, 63*, 282–288.

Scheidt, S. (1996). A whirlwind tour of cardiology for the mental health professional. In R. Allan & S. Scheidt (Eds.), *Heart and mind: The practice of cardiac psychology* (pp. 15–62). Washington, DC: American Psychological Association.

Shehan, D. V. (1982). Current concepts in psychiatry: Panic attacks and phobias. *New England Journal of Medicine, 307*, 156–158.

Sibal, A. M., Armenian, H. K., & Alam, S. (1989). Wartime determinants of arteriographically confirmed coronary artery disease in Beirut. *American Journal of Epidemiology, 130*, 623–631.

Spitzer, R. L., Williams, J. B. W., Kroenke, K., Linzer, M., de Gruy, F. V., III, Hahn, S. R., et al. (1994). Utility of a new procedure for diagnosing mental disorders in primary care: The PRIME-MD 1000 study. *Journal of the American Medical Association, 272*, 1749–1756.

Stroebel, C. F. (1982). *Q. R.: The quieting reflex*. New York: Putnam.

Weissman, M. M., Markowitz, J. S., Ouellette, R., Greenwald, S., & Kahn, J. P. (1990). Panic disorder and cardiovascular/cerebrovascular problems: Results for a community survey. *American Journal of Psychiatry, 147*, 1504–1508.

White, J. (1995). Stresspac: A controlled trial of a self-help package for anxiety disorders. *Behavioural and Cognitive Psychotherapy, 23*, 89–107.

6

ASTHMA

As Baum, Gatchel, and Krantz (1997) have summarized, the prevalence, morbidity, and mortality of asthma in the United States and other Western countries have increased drastically during the past two decades. As many as 10 to 15 million individuals in the United States have asthma, with an incidence of 4% to 5% in adults. The rate of asthma has also increased in minorities living in the United States, and these minorities are placed most often in the "severe or poorly controlled" category of asthma treatment. In 1990, the total cost of asthma care in the United States was $6.21 billion, $3.64 billion of which reflected the direct costs of asthma care (e.g., ambulatory care visits, hospital emergency room visits, outpatient services). Even more alarming is the fact that more than 5,000 people die from asthma each year. In spite of a wide range of efforts, the morbidity and mortality rates for asthma have steadily increased in the United States since 1979 (Centers for Disease Control and Prevention, 1995). Even though acute episodes of asthma can be fatal, the vast majority of deaths from asthma are definitely preventable (National Heart, Lung, and Blood Institute [NHLBI], 1997).

At the outset, we should note that considerable debate remains over the exact definition of what asthma is, as well as specific distinctions among terms such as *asthma attack*, *asthma flare*, and *asthma episode*. In this chapter, we use the term *asthma attack* to refer to an episode of acute airway obstruction.

Nevertheless, a broad, comprehensive definition of *asthma* views it as a lung disease that affects one's ability to breathe due to obstruction of airways, narrowing airways, inflammation, or hyper-responsiveness of air passages to a variety of stimuli (such as dust, pollen, and other allergens). When the lungs become inflamed, the airways become constricted and may fill with fluid, thus causing symptoms such as shortness of breath, wheezing, and coughing. It is extremely important to minimize lung inflammation due to asthma because chronic inflammation weakens the lungs and makes them more prone to chronic lung disease. Asthma can be precipitated by allergies, cold temperatures, exercise, infections, or stress.

Asthma is agreed to be most dangerous during an asthma *attack*. The frequency and regularity of asthma attacks can be quite variable. For some individuals, attacks may be rare, whereas for others, they are much more common. In addition, for some people, such attacks are usually precipitated by specific conditions, such as an allergic reaction; for others, they are quite unpredictable. Asthma attacks can also vary in severity. Differences in the pattern of episodes and the severity of each attack are one reason that problems arise when attempting to systematically study, treat, and classify asthma.

Again, as just noted, the alarming statistic about asthma is that more than 5,000 people die from it every year. Indeed, the tragic paradox of asthma care is that, in spite of significant improvements in preventive medications for asthma (such as bronchodilators and steroids to decrease inflammation), recent refinements in asthma care plans, and numerous educational efforts, we continue to see evidence of less than optimal treatment outcomes. Of the many factors contributing to this paradox, poor adherence to medication regimens continues to be a major issue among patients with asthma. Indeed, one study evaluated patients' questionnaires, medical records, and health insurance claims to determine patients' use of asthma medications (Voelker, 1997). In this study, more than 600 patient records from three managed care sites were reviewed over a 1-year time period. Results indicated that almost one fifth of 340 patients who received prescriptions did not fill them. Of those who did have their prescriptions filled, more than 70% did not take them as clearly prescribed, and many preferred to rely only on short-acting bronchodilators. Moreover, research reviewed by Haire-Joshu, Fisher, Munron, and Wedner (1993) concluded that, among adult patients with asthma who were receiving treatments in acute health care settings, treatment was undertaken primarily in response to acute episodes, and that acute self-treatment rather than preventive self-management is usually the norm. In addition, they found a reliance on over-the-counter medication, and patient delays in receiving treatment were quite commonplace. Findings such as these highlight the need for continuing enhancement of interventions focusing on increasing self-management behaviors among patients with asthma. We review such programs later in this chapter.

Finally, Creer and Bender (1993) have reviewed research that evaluated the various potential causes of asthma. This research has produced as many questions as answers, and more recent efforts have been made to evaluate the important factors involved in asthma management. For example, although a majority of patients display complete reversibility of airway obstruction with appropriate treatment, others do not—even with intensive treatment. Nevertheless, by improving asthma management, the number and severity of asthma attacks should decrease and the quality of life of individuals with asthma should increase. Moreover, adherence to medical recommendations, regarding both lifestyle changes and use of medications, is also an important determinant of asthma severity, as well as its effective management. Again, as discussed later, attention to these management and adherence issues appears to be the major focus of treating asthma and its negative impacts on one's life.

PEDIATRIC ASTHMA

Asthma is the most common chronic pediatric disease, and it is one of the leading causes of admission to pediatric hospitals. Rees (1964) originally isolated three causal factors when examining the case histories of children with asthma. The first factor he labeled as the *allergy factor*, which reflected situations in which some particular substance (e.g., an allergen, such as dust or pollen) caused a biochemical reaction that constricted the bronchi in the lungs. The second factor he termed the *infection factor*, which included bacterial or viral etiology, with the most common type of respiratory infection being acute bronchitis. Indeed, Rees noted that in about 35% of the children with asthma that he evaluated, their first asthma attacks occurred during a respiratory infection. Finally, the third factor was labeled the *psychological factor*, which included variables such as anxiety, depression, and other emotional reactions that potentially precipitated an asthma attack.

This disease has a significant effect not only on the children who have it, but also on their primary caregivers. Indeed, a significant correlation is usually seen between measures of asthma severity and quality of life, for both children and their caregivers. Williams et al. (2000) have highlighted the impact of asthma on the entire family and have emphasized the importance of having a management plan in place to deal with this disease. Moreover, the data clearly indicate that the management plan should be based on long-term comprehensive care, rather than on simply dealing with acute exacerbations, and it should include the children as well as the caregivers.

In addition to the effect that pediatric asthma has on quality of life, it may also have a significant impact on children's school attendance and performance, as well as their caregivers' work attendance. This may further impact the overall level of family functioning. For example, Diette et al. (2000) have noted that nocturnal awakening due to asthma often occurs in children with asthma whose illness is poorly controlled or managed. These children tend not to do well at school, and their caregivers experience a high frequency of absenteeism at the workplace. Thus, better management plans may not only increase quality of life but also aid in the prevention of poor daytime performance.

Children living in the inner city also seem to be affected disproportionately by asthma morbidity and mortality (see, e.g., Weil et al., 1999). This appears to be due to the fact that both children and adults in inner-city living environments tend to be exposed more often to dust mites and cockroaches, both of which are known allergens that can serve as triggers for asthma attacks. Moreover, they are thought to cause asthma in some patients. This is due to the fact that tiny particles of fibers that break off from both dust mites and cockroaches are easily inhaled and, when they invade the respiratory tract, they serve as irritants that may suppress immune functioning.

The federal government is now extremely concerned about the higher prevalence of asthma effects on inner-city residents. The National Cooperative Inner-City Asthma Study evaluated the factors that contributed to asthma morbidity among inner-city children (Evans et al., 1999). In this study, 1,528 children ages 4 to 9 years with asthma, and their primary caretakers, were evaluated. They were recruited from eight research centers and seven metropolitan inner-city areas in the United States. The measures assessing morbidity and mortality included the number of hospitalizations and unscheduled visits for asthma in the previous 3 months and the number of days of wheezing and functional status in the previous 2-week period. Psychological variables were also evaluated. One of the major findings of this study was that psychosocial factors, mainly the mental health of both the children and their caretakers, were significant predictors of asthma morbidity in children (Weil et al., 1999). We discuss such psychosocial factors later in this chapter. Finally, in another investigation emanating from the National Cooperative Inner-City Asthma Study, researchers found that individually tailored, multifaceted intervention, administered by social workers, could significantly reduce asthma symptoms in inner-city children (Evans et al., 1999).

COMMON MEDICAL TREATMENT AND PHYSICIAN RECOMMENDATIONS

Many primary care physicians are now, fortunately, beginning to view asthma from a biopsychosocial perspective and to develop treatment plans accordingly. For example, a study reported by Welsh, Magnusson, and

Napoli (1999) revealed how a multidisciplinary team approach at the Children's Hospital of Philadelphia was developed and implemented to treat pediatric asthma. This multidisciplinary team consisted of the medical staff, registered nurses, respiratory therapists, and case managers. This team allowed for more standardized and efficient treatment, because their approach followed the guidelines of an algorithm developed to provide the most appropriate and tailored program for each patient. They also took into account the psychological component of asthma, including case managers and focusing on patient education. Outcome measures produced by this program revealed a decreased length of hospital stays, with no increase in the readmission rate, as well as better cost efficiency.

Health care professionals now accept that such a multidisciplinary, biopsychosocial approach needs to be utilized to develop the best educational and self-management program for patients with asthma. Besides paying careful attention to the medical needs of patients with asthma, the psychological factors experienced by patients, such as anxiety, panic, and depression, need to be addressed. Likewise, social factors, such as living in an inner-city environment, need to be considered. Treatment plans will have to take these factors into account, and must focus on patient education and individually tailored treatment plans. These treatment plans should also address the important factor of nonadherence, and concerted efforts need to be made to ensure adherence to self-management programs. In other chapters in this text, we discuss ways to increase adherence (e.g., see chapter 3, "Diabetes Mellitus," and chapter 4, "Hypertension."). These efforts need to be made with patients who have asthma, especially in light of the potentially life-threatening nature of this disease.

What steps can be taken to increase adherence? Baum et al. (1997) have offered a number of basic methods, as summarized here:

1. First and foremost, physicians need to actively develop a good doctor–patient relationship; they need to try to be better communicators and to be warm and sensitive to patients. Indeed, Di Blasi, Harkness, Ernst, Georgiou, and Kleijnen (2001) have recently reviewed the literature and found that physicians who adopt a warm, friendly, and reassuring manner with patients are more effective in significantly influencing health outcomes than those physicians who keep consultations formal and do not offer reassurance.

2. Make certain that the information being communicated to patients is comprehensible. Allow them to ask questions. Also, provide them with an easy-to-read pamphlet or leaflet describing how they need to manage their asthma, on a step-by-step basis.

3. Enhance family and social support by having a family member/significant other accompany the patient to office visits and make them a part of the "treatment team."

4. Regular supervision of patients is important, either via telephone calls or actual home visits. Indeed, in recent inner-city asthma treatment programs, home visits are deemed important to ensure that home-based allergens are being controlled.

5. Self-monitoring or self-supervision is also important. Having patients keep a written record (on a form you provide them) of their self-management behaviors is quite beneficial. These records can then be reviewed during an office visit, any adherence problems can be discussed, and strategies developed to decrease the problems.

We should also note that, even though optimal treatment techniques for asthma are available, little has been done to educate primary care physicians about the National Asthma Education and Prevention Program guidelines (NHLBI, 1997; Stempel & Szefler, 1995) designed to improve the quality of asthma management. These guidelines delineate the proper medications and dosage levels to be used, the appropriate measurement of pulmonary function, the educational information to be provided to patients, and so on. Thus, physician adherence is also a potential problem that needs to be addressed.

Table 6.1 lists the important components of self-management that a health psychologist can provide in a primary care setting. The major goal of self-management programs should be to teach patients to perform self-initiated skills so they can become *proactive* partners in the management of their asthma. In the past, a major shortcoming of self-management programs has been a failure to motivate patients to enroll in—and continue to participate in—the prescribed education curriculum. Moreover, programs that initially may have had an impact on outcomes often failed to produce long-term improvement (Blaiss, 1997). Furthermore, previous measures developed to assess psychological factors relating to asthma self-management usually concentrated on the patient's level of asthma-related knowledge (Creer & Bender, 1993).

Questionnaires regarding patient knowledge of asthma routinely target two main objectives: (a) the evaluation of changes in asthma management knowledge that occur as a result of educational interventions and (b) an attempt to reveal misconceptions regarding asthma that might result in the underutilization of medical care and nonadherence to medication regimens. Creer and Bender (1993), however, pointed out that such instruments used to assess patient knowledge seldom accomplished their objectives because they frequently yielded a complex array of scores, whose clinical meaning was difficult to evaluate, especially in the absence of data regarding their reliability and validity. Obviously, we need to develop a better way of being certain that patients process, understand, and remember this information. Regular reinforcement and reminders during *each* clinical encounter will go a long way toward accomplishing this goal! Patients should be constantly reminded of the following five key facts:

TABLE 6.1
Important Components of Asthma Self-Management

Self-Management Regimen	Role of Health Psychologist
Use of a peak expiratory flow meter to keep track of asthma.[a]	Set up environmental cues as a reminder to use it.
Call doctor or change medicines when peak flow meter number drops too low.	—
Use asthma medicines and inhaler when appropriate.	Explore cognitions about medication use and other potential barriers.
Be aware of the early warning signs of an asthma attack (e.g., wheezing, shortness of breath, chest tightness, coughing, fatigue, feeling irritable/afraid/nervous, nocturnal awakening because of asthma).	Develop a symptom log to help increase early recognition.
Rest when asthma symptoms occur; stay calm; try to relax and do breathing exercises.	Teach a coach to help in diaphragmatic breathing.
Call doctor or nurse when having problems or questions.	—
Recognize things that make one's asthma worse (e.g., pollen, certain pets, pollution/ozone, stress, cigarette smoke, house dust, molds, colds/virus infections, changes in weather).	Develop a symptom log to help identify potential triggers.
Follow the care plan given by the doctor or nurse.	Advise physician or nurse to be very *specific* in recommendations; with struggling patients, make one change at a time, reinforcing incremental steps, and so on. Psychologists can also treat anxiety, depression, family stress, and so on, to enhance adherence.

[a]Peak expiratory flow zones: *Green zone* (80% to 100% of personal best) signals good control. Keep taking usual daily long-term-control medications (if taking any). Keep taking such medications even when in the yellow or red zones. *Yellow zone* (50% to 79% of personal best) signals caution because asthma appears to be getting worse. Quick-relief medications need to be added, and other asthma medicines may need to be increased (as directed by one's doctor). *Red zone* (below 50% of personal best) signals a medical alert. Add or increase quick-relief medicines and *immediately* call one's doctor.

1. Asthma can be managed so that patients can live a normal life.
2. Asthma is a disease that makes the airways in the lungs inflamed.
3. Many things in the home, school, work, and other places can cause asthma attacks.
4. Asthma needs to be watched and cared for over a long period of time.
5. Asthma can be controlled when patients manage their asthma and work with their doctor.

PSYCHOSOCIAL FACTORS AND ASTHMA

There can be no doubt that various psychosocial factors play an important role in the overall course of asthma. For example, the often sudden, unexpected nature of asthma attacks, as well as the prospect of such attacks occurring at any time, can generate a great deal of anxiety and fear in patients. In addition, patients with asthma continue to struggle with the uncertainty involved in their illness. As an example, Sexton, Stephanie, Calcasola, Bottomley, and Funk (1999) reported that people who had had asthma for a longer duration of time reported lower levels of uncertainty, whereas those who were hospitalized because of asthma, and those whose asthma was triggered by pollen, both reported higher levels of uncertainty. Individuals' perception of having an unpredictable and uncontrollable illness can significantly affect their overall emotional status.

Centanni et al. (2000) compared groups of patients with asthma, patients with chronic hepatitis, and healthy participants on psychological functioning. They found that anxiety and depression levels were significantly higher in patients with asthma than in both patients with hepatitis and healthy volunteers. Moreover, children and adolescents who have asthma also display a high prevalence of anxiety disorders (Vila, Nollet-Clemencon, deBlic, Mouren-Simeoni, & Scheinmann, 2000). Further studies support relationships among variables such as anxiety, affective distress, overall quality of life, and asthma. For example, Chaney et al. (1999) reported findings suggesting that individuals with long-standing asthma appear to be at increased risk for depression and for symptoms consistent with *learned helplessness*. In turn, Mancuso, Peterson, and Charlson (2000) reported that nearly one half of the patients with asthma evaluated in their study had a positive screen for symptoms consistent with depression. Moreover, those patients with asthma who had more depressive symptomatology were associated with poor health-related quality of life, relative to patients with asthma who had similar disease activity but fewer depressive symptoms. In addition, Mancuso et al. found that scores on quality-of-life measures were negatively correlated with perceived vulnerability and "panic–fear personality," as well as symptoms of irritability, fatigue, airway obstruction, hyperventilation, and panic–fear during attacks.

Finally, it also appears that emotional reactions such as anxiety play a major role in the overutilization of services in asthma treatment. Nouwen, Freestone, Labbe, and Boulet (1999) reported that, when comparing patients who had unscheduled visits to the emergency room to patients with asthma who had not visited the emergency room over the same period of time, those with the unscheduled emergency room visits reported more panic–fear symptoms, lower self-efficacy, and more perceived interference than the other group. Such overutilization is a major cost burden to the health care system. The estimated cost of asthma in the United States was $6.21 billion in 1990 (Creer & Bender, 1993).

Adherence Issues

As discussed previously, adherence to therapy is a significant psychosocial issue in the management of asthma. On average, only 40% of people with asthma adhere to a recommended therapeutic regimen (e.g., Bender, Milgrom, & Rand, 1997). Throughout this text, we have highlighted the fact that low rates of adherence to medication regimens pose a major challenge to the effective management of most acute and chronic diseases. Nonadherence can be divided into two basic categories: *unintentional* (i.e., accidental) and *intentional* (i.e., deliberate). Unintentional nonadherence may be a result of poor doctor–patient communication or a lack of ability to follow advice due to poor intellectual status and inadequate literacy, among other factors. Intentional nonadherence, on the other hand, occurs when a patient knows what is required, but decides not to totally follow this advice. For example, nonadherence to asthma medication regimens is a significant problem associated with unnecessary functional limitations and possible hospitalizations (Schmaling, Afari, & Blume, 2000). The exact reasons for such nonadherence are quite complex and can vary greatly among individuals. They may include some of the following factors:

- complexity of the treatment regimen that a patient is asked to follow
- communication problems between doctors and patients
- patient education, comprehension, and literacy
- how the administration of treatment is coordinated
- inaccurate patient beliefs about therapy, and their expectations concerning it
- psychosocial factors that may present formidable barriers to the management of the disease
- possible steroid medication side effects.

However, determining the various factors that directly influence or predict adherence in populations with asthma is still difficult to ascertain, despite a great deal of research in this area. What is known is that patients who characterize themselves as nonadherent may also be at greater risk for hospitalization (Put, Van den Bergh, Demedts, & Verleden, 2000). We should also point out that adherence in adolescents with any physical illness is an important medical and psychosocial issue. The fact that the prevalence of asthma in children and adolescents continues to increase, and morbidity is higher in the adolescent age group, suggests that adolescents with asthma may not be getting appropriate treatment for their condition. Nonadherence is most likely a factor in this higher morbidity rate in adolescents, and it does not appear to exist only in patients with a poor understanding of their illness. Various psychosocial factors play a role in adolescent nonadherence, including isolation and low self-esteem, which appear to be important traits in adolescents with asthma.

Kyngas (1999) evaluated the degree to which adolescents with asthma adhered to treatment regimens and the factors that were associated with this adherence. Results of this study indicated that 42% of the adolescents reported full adherence to treatment regimens, 40% reported satisfactory compliance, and the remaining 18% reported poor adherence. The poorest adherence was associated with not avoiding foods, animals, and pollens that typically triggered asthma attacks. The various factors that Kyngas found to be correlated with good adherence are summarized in Exhibit 6.1. Finally, research has also revealed that physicians' report of treatment alliance with the patient was associated with family functioning and asthmatic medication adherence (Gavin, Wamboldt, Sorokin, Levy, & Wamboldt, 1999).

SUMMARY

The prevalence, morbidity, and mortality of asthma in the United States and other Western countries have dramatically increased during the past two decades. As many as 10 to 15 million individuals in the United States have asthma. Even more alarming is the fact that more than 5,000 people die from asthma each year, even though the vast majority of deaths are preventable. Moreover, asthma is the most common chronic pediatric disease, and it is one of the leading causes of admission to pediatric hospitals. Children living in the inner city appear to be affected disproportionally by asthma morbidity and mortality.

Many primary care physicians are beginning to view asthma from a biopsychosocial perspective and to develop treatment plans accordingly. Multidisciplinary approaches are now being used to develop the best educational and self-management program for people with asthma. Besides paying careful attention to the medical needs of patients with asthma, the psychosocial factors of patients (such as anxiety, depression) and social factors (such as living in an inner-city environment) are considered. A major goal of such programs is to teach patients to perform self-initiated skills so that

EXHIBIT 6.1
Factors Associated With High Adherence in Adolescents With Asthma

- Good motivation
- A strong sense of perceived normality
- Lack of perceived threat to social well-being
- High energy and willpower
- Lack of fear of complications of treatment
- Support from parents, physicians, and nurses
- A positive attitude toward the disease and its treatment

Note. Source is Kyngas (1999).

they can be *proactive* partners in the management of their asthma. These programs also need to address the important factor of nonadherence and consider efforts to ensure adherence to self-management programs.

RECOMMENDED READING

National Heart, Lung, and Blood Institute. (1997). *Guidelines for the diagnoses and management of asthma* (No. 97-4053). Bethesda, MD: National Institutes of Health.

GLOSSARY

allergen   A substance capable of inducing allergy or some specific hypersensitivity, such as in the airway passages. These substances may be protein or nonprotein.

asthma   A lung disease that affects one's ability to breathe due to obstruction of airways, narrowing airways, having inflammation, or inducing hyper-responsiveness of air passages to a variety of stimuli (such as dust, pollen, and other allergens).

asthma attack   An episode of acute airway obstruction.

bronchi   Any of the larger airway passages of the lungs.

bronchodilator   A substance that dilates or expands the airway passages of the lungs.

metered-dose inhaler   An apparatus used for the administration of a specified amount of vapor or volatilized remedies by inhalation.

peak expiratory flow meter   An instrument that measures the maximum level of oxygen that can be exhaled. This measure helps to check how well one's asthma is controlled.

pediatric asthma   The most common chronic pediatric disease and one of the leading causes of admission to pediatric hospitals.

spacer   An attachment to an inhaler that allows the inhalation of only the amount of substance needed, thus eliminating the loss of any of the inhalant.

steroid   A group name for compounds that have an inflammation-decreasing characteristic.

REFERENCES

Baum, A., Gatchel, R. J., & Krantz, D. S. (1997). *An introduction to health psychology* (3rd ed.). New York: McGraw-Hill.

Bender, B., Milgrom, H., & Rand, C. (1997). Nonadherence in asthmatic patients: Is there a solution to the problem? *Annuals of Allergy Asthma Immunology, 79*, 117–186.

Blaiss, M. S. (1997). Outcomes analysis in asthma. *Journal of the American Medical Association, 278,* 1874–1880.

Centanni, S., DiMarco, F., Castagna, F., Boveri, B., Casanova, F., & Piazzini, A. (2000). Psychological issues in the treatment of asthmatic patients. *Respiratory Medicine, 94,* 742–749.

Centers for Disease Control and Prevention. (1995). Asthma United States 1989–1992. *Morbidity and Mortality Weekly Report, 43,* 952–955.

Chaney, J. M., Mullins, L. L., Uretsky, D. L., Pace, T. M., Werden, D., & Hartman, V. L. (1999). An experimental examination of learned helplessness in older adolescents and young adults with long-standing asthma. *Journal of Pediatric Psychology, 24,* 259–270.

Creer, T. L., & Bender, B. C. (1993). Asthma. In R. J. Gatchel & E. B. Blanchard (Eds.), *Psychophysiological disorders: Research and clinical applications* (pp. 151–204). Washington, DC: American Psychological Association.

DiBlasi, Z., Harkness, E., Ernst, E., Georgiou, A., & Kleijnen, J. (2001). Influence of context effects on health outcomes: A systematic review. *The Lancet, 357,* 757–762.

Diette, G. B., Markson, L., Skinner, E. A., Nguyen, T. T., Algatt-Bergstrom P., & Wu, A.W. (2000). Nocturnal asthma in children affects school attendance, school performance, and parents' work attendance. *Archives of Pediatrics and Adolescent Medicine, 154,* 923–928.

Evans, R., III, Gergen, P. J., Mitchell, H., Kattan, M., Kercsmar, C., Crain, E., et al. (1999). A randomized clinical trial to reduce asthma morbidity among inner-city children: Results of the National Cooperative Inner-City Asthma Study. *Journal of Pediatrics, 135,* 332–338.

Gavin, L. A., Wamboldt, M. Z., Sorokin, N., Levy, S. Y., & Wamboldt, F. S. (1999). Treatment alliance and its association with family functioning, adherence, and medical outcome in adolescents with severe, chronic asthma. *Journal of Pediatric Psychology, 24,* 355–365.

Haire-Joshu, D., Fisher, E. B., Munro, J., & Wedner, H. J. (1993). A comparison of patient attitudes toward asthma self-management airway acute and preventive care settings. *Journal of Asthma, 30,* 359–371.

Kyngas, H. A. (1999). Compliance of adolescents with asthma. *Nursing and Health Sciences, 1,* 195–202.

Mancuso, C. A., Peterson, M. G., & Charlson, M. E. (2000). Effects of depressive symptoms on health-related quality of life in asthma patients. *Journal of General Internal Medicine, 15,* 344–345.

National Heart, Lung, and Blood Institute. (1997). *Guidelines for the diagnosis and management of asthma* (No. 97-4053). Bethesda, MD: National Institutes of Health.

Nouwen, A., Freestone, M. H., Labbe, R., & Boulet, L. P. (1999). Psychological factors associated with emergency room visits among asthmatic patients. *Behavior Modification, 23,* 217–233.

Put, C., Van den Bergh, O., Demedts, M., & Verleden, G. (2000). A study of the relationship among self-reported noncompliance, symptomatology, and psychological variables in patients with asthma. *Journal of Asthma, 37,* 503–510.

Rees, L. (1964). The importance of psychological allergic and infective factors in childhood asthma. *Schizophrenia Bulletin, 8,* 1–11.

Schmaling, K. B., Afari, N., & Blume, A. W. (2000). Assessment of psychological factors associated with adherence to medication regimens among adult patients with asthma. *Journal of Asthma, 37,* 335–343.

Sexton, D. L., Stephanie, R. N., Calcasola, S. L., Bottomley, S. R., & Funk, M. (1999). Adults' experience with asthma and their reported uncertainty and coping strategies. *Clinical Nurse Specialist, 13,* 8–14.

Stempel, D. A., & Szefler, S. J. (1995). Going beyond the National Asthma Education Program Guidelines for the diagnoses and management of asthma. *Immunology, 75,* 457–460.

Vila, G., Nollet-Clemencon, C., deBlic, J., Mouren-Simeoni, M. C., & Scheinmann, P. (2000). Prevalence of DSM–IV anxiety and affective disorders in a pediatric population of asthmatic children and adolescents. *Journal of Affective Disorders, 58,* 223–231.

Voelker, R. (1997). Taking asthma seriously. *Journal of the American Medical Association, 278,* 11.

Weil, C. M., Wade, S. L., Bauman, L. J., Lynn, H., Mitchell, H., & Lavigne, J. (1999). The relationship between psychosocial factors and asthma morbidity in inner-city children with asthma. *Pediatrics, 104,* 1274–1280.

Welsh, K. M., Magnusson, M., & Napoli, L. N. (1999). Asthma clinical pathway: An interdisciplinary approach to implementation in the impatient setting. *Pediatric Nursing, 25,* 83–87.

Williams, S., Sehgal, M., Falter, K., Dennis, R., Jones, D., Boudreaux, J., et al. (2000). Effect of asthma on the quality of life among children and their caregivers in the Atlanta empowerment zone. *Journal of Urban Health, 77,* 268–279.

7

ACUTE AND CHRONIC
PAIN CONDITIONS

As Gatchel and Turk (1996) have indicated, pain accounts for more than 80% of all physician visits, affecting more than 50 million Americans and costing more than $70 billion annually in health care costs and lost productivity. Traditionally, the main focus in medicine was simply on the cause of the pain reported, with the assumption that the pain had a physical basis and that, once that basis was identified, the source of it could be either eliminated or blocked by medical interventions. As a result, assessment was focused almost entirely on identifying the physical basis for the pain. In the absence of such a physical basis, psychological causation was often suggested and, hence, the term *psychogenic pain* was coined. This is now an outdated, traditional viewpoint of pain, in which complaints were categorized by a simple dichotomy: The pain reported either had a physical basis or a psychological basis.

Fortunately, this view of pain is no longer accepted. Rather, a biopsychosocial perspective of pain is beginning to be more widely embraced (Gatchel & Turk, 1996), although some administrators of health care plans and physicians in primary care settings still need to be "converted." Psychosocial factors, along with biological factors, need to be considered when determining how to treat medical problems. Indeed, as discussed throughout this book, such a biopsychosocial approach is the most heuristic approach to treating medical problems. This again underscores the important role of mental health specialists in the assessment and treatment of medical patients, especially those with pain. This acknowledgment of the importance of psychosocial factors in pain has resulted in a large number of mental health specialists evaluating and treating patients with pain in free-standing pain clinics, in a variety of medical settings, and in private practices. Currently, the biopsychosocial perspective of pain has been found to be the most useful approach to understanding and managing it.

Recently, several important organizations in the United States have developed new standards for the evaluation of pain. For example, the Joint Commission on Accreditation of Healthcare Organizations (JCAHO, 2000) now requires that physicians consider pain to be a *fifth vital sign* (added to pulse, blood pressure, core temperature, and respiration) when evaluating patients. The JCAHO guidelines require that pain severity be documented, using a pain scale. In addition, the following assessments also need to be made of

- the patient's own words describing his or her pain
- pain location, duration, and aggravating and alleviating factors
- present pain management regimen and its effectiveness
- effects of pain
- the patient's pain goal
- physical examination.

All of these factors need to be documented on initial assessment. Except for the physical examination, these factors can be assessed by a clinical health psychologist. These new standards are now also being scored for compliance in accredited health care organizations. In addition, a nonprofit organization, the American Pain Foundation, has issued a "Pain Care Bill of Rights" (www.ampainsoc.org) informing patients of this requirement. Such initiatives as these have created a new mandate to successfully assess and manage all types of pain, malignant or nonmalignant, in all medical settings, including primary care.

Note that the Agency for Health Care Policy and Research, which is now the Agency for Healthcare Research and Quality (AHRQ), developed specific guidelines for the treatment of acute and chronic pain conditions. In partnership with the American Medical Association and the American Association of Health Plans Foundation, a National Guide Clearinghouse now exists that is a public database of evidence-based clinical practice guidelines. Internet users can gain free online access to these guidelines at http://www.guideline.gov, as well as at the AHRQ Web site at http://www.ahrq.gov.

Basic guidelines have also been developed for pain treatment program evaluations. Morley and Williams (2002) have recently provided an excellent overview of how to conduct and evaluate such treatment outcome studies.

Most patients seeking medical care for common pain complaints are regularly seen in primary care settings. For example, abdominal pain, back pain, chest pain, headache, and neck pain are among the 20 most common reasons for visits to primary care physicians in the United States (American Academy of Family Physicians [AAFP], 1987). Overall, affordable health care services in this country depend on well-organized and effective primary care services. Indeed, primary care physicians act as referral sources and are the "gatekeepers" for specialty care when patients require such treatment. As gatekeepers, primary care physicians can serve the important purpose of controlling access to unwanted, costly, and potentially detrimental treatment services. Thus, the major goal of primary care is to provide essential services to large numbers of people at an affordable cost to both the patient and to society at large (Von Korff, 1999).

THE CONCEPT, PREVALENCE, AND CLASSIFICATIONS OF PAIN

We need to distinguish pain as a neurological event from pain perception. The neurological event is called *nociception*, which originates in pain receptors/regions and then passes through nerve fibers and pathways to the central nervous system. Pain perception is the actual interpretation of pain sensation by the patient. This often can be a two-way path. That is, the perception of the nociceptive event can significantly influence one's emotional and behavioral response. The stress associated with the meaning of pain, in turn, can then have a significant effect on the original nociception by decreasing pain threshold. Indeed, various pain syndromes can often lead to pressures and changes of lifestyle that most people find unpleasant, at the very least.

Unplanned and unwanted lifestyle changes can lead to stress, so patients may begin to feel worse than they anticipated, and the stress actually can interfere with physical recovery. This can be explained in terms of a cycle in which pain and the changes that it brings lead to stress, which leads to increased pain, which leads to increased stress, and so on. Indeed, many studies have demonstrated that stress and anxiety significantly influence pain perception, with higher levels of stress or anxiety associated with higher levels of pain intensity (e.g., Cornwal & Doncleri, 1988). Moreover, stress may activate biological responses in the autonomic and musculoskeletal systems. Thus, for example, muscle spasms may occur along with anxiety accompanying tension headaches which, in turn, produces more pain and muscle tension, and so on. This *pain–stress cycle* can often be important to point out to patients (see Figure 7.1).

As noted earlier, approximately 80% of primary care visits are prompted by pain symptoms. The most common types of pain seen at

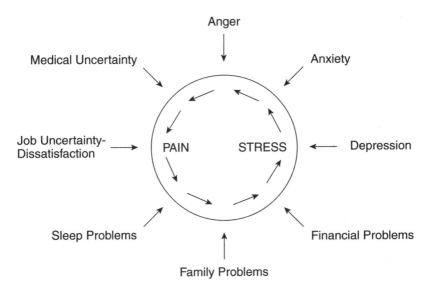

Figure 7.1. The pain–stress cycle, emphasizing the interaction of stress-related issues and the actual pain problem. It is helpful to draw patients' attention to this cycle. From *Personality Characteristics of Patients With Pain,* (p.17) by R. J. Gatchel and J. N. Weisberg, 2000, Washington, DC: American Psychological Association. Copyright 2000 by American Psychological Association. Reprinted with permission from the author.

primary care settings, which have also been the focus of epidemiological studies, are the following (Gatchel, 1996):

- *Abdominal pain:* This is more prevalent in women, and it decreases with age. Although the rates are the lowest among the elderly population, elderly people make up the greatest percentage of individuals seeking care for abdominal pain.
- *Back pain:* Although there do not appear to be gender differences, back pain prevalence tends to rise in men up to age 50.
- *Headache:* The prevalence for women with migraine is higher at all ages, and the female–to–male ratio tends to increase with age from menarche to about 42 years and then declines thereafter. Headache pain from migraine appears to have its highest prevalence among both men and women, ages 35 to 45.
- *Joint pain:* This type of pain is usually age specific, reflecting the degenerative changes that occur with aging. A higher rate of age-related joint pain appears to occur in women, who experience a greater degree of degenerative changes than do men.
- *Chest pain:* This is a very common symptom associated with many disorders and diseases, including heart, lung, esophageal, and panic disorders, to name just a few. Men and

women appear to share rates for chest pain that change little with age (about one third for both genders).

- *Facial pain:* The prevalence of this type of pain is about twice as high for women as it is for men. It rises with age among women through their mid-40s, dropping after age 65.
- *Fibromyalgia:* This diagnosis is often made in patients with unexplained widespread pain. The crucial physical finding in making this diagnosis is the presence of "tender points" (i.e., tenderness at the bony insertions of certain tendons and muscles). Most patients also complain of associated fatigue and sleep disturbances. This widespread pain appears to peak between ages 50 and 60 and appears to be more prevalent in women than in men.

Pain is usually broadly defined as *acute, chronic,* or *recurrent,* depending on its time course. This broad classification of pain duration is often used to better understand the biopsychosocial aspects that may be important when conducting the assessment and treatment. For example, many times, chronic pain is a result of unresolved acute pain episodes, resulting in accumulative biopsychosocial effects such as prolonged physical deconditioning, anxiety, and stress. This type of information, obviously, can be extremely helpful in directing specific treatment approaches to the type of pain that is being evaluated.

Acute Pain

Acute pain is usually indicative of tissue damage, and it is characterized by momentary intense noxious sensations (i.e., nociception). It serves as an important biological signal of potential tissue/physical harm. Some anxiety may initially be precipitated, but prolonged physical and emotional distress usually is not. Indeed, anxiety, if mild, can be quite adaptive in that it stimulates behaviors needed for recovery, such as the seeking of medical attention, rest, and removal from the potentially harmful situation. As the nociception decreases, acute pain usually subsides.

Chronic Pain

Chronic pain is defined as pain that lasts 6 months or longer, well past the normal healing period one would expect for its protective biological function. Arthritis, back injuries, and cancer can produce chronic pain syndromes and, as the pain persists, it is often accompanied by emotional distress such as depression, anger, and frustration. Such pain can also often significantly interfere with activities of daily living. Patients with chronic pain utilize health facilities often in an attempt to find some relief from the pain symptoms, and the pain has a tendency to become a preoccupation of an individual's everyday living.

Recurrent Pain

Intense, *episodic* pain, reoccurring for more than 3 months, is often referred to as *recurrent pain*. Recurrent pain episodes are usually brief (as are acute pain episodes); however, the recurring nature of this type of pain makes it similar to chronic pain in that it is very distressing to patients. Such episodes may develop without a well-defined cause, and they may begin to generate an array of emotional reactions, such as anxiety, stress, and depression/helplessness. Pain medication is often used to control the intensity of recurrent pain, but it is not usually helpful in reducing the frequency of the episodes that a patient experiences. Note also that patients often find it difficult to distinguish between chronic and recurrent pain. Patients will often present with "chronic-like" symptoms from prolonged episodes of, say, headache or back pain. These do not always fit the description of chronic pain but are usually persistent and can be just as disabling.

Keep in mind that all pain, whether acute, chronic, or recurrent, may often be accompanied by emotional distress. A health care professional needs to make a comprehensive biopsychosocial evaluation of a patient with pain to understand the different factors (such as physiological, sociocultural, environmental, and pathophysiological), associated with all three types of pain. This allows the health care professional to treat and predict response to treatment of these patients. Of course, to reiterate, the primary care setting is the "front line" for treatment of all types of pain.

MAJOR PSYCHOSOCIAL VARIABLES ASSOCIATED WITH PAIN

As noted by Turk and Monarch (2002), there are many individual differences in how people respond in the face of nociception and differences in the methods used to understand and interpret the painful stimuli. This makes the experience of pain dependent on cognitive–evaluative processes and on affective–motivational processes. In terms of the cognitive–evaluative process, individuals evaluate pain in terms of the perception of the consequences of the pain, the importance of the pain, and their perceived ability to cope with the pain. These various factors are delineated in Exhibit 7.1.

In terms of affective–motivational processes, cognitive appraisal of pain can lead to a variety of affective responses. Patients who perceive their pain as "out of control" or as a threat are more prone to emotional distress. This affect associated with pain spans the spectrum, from vague unpleasantness to more discrete emotions such as fear, anger, and depression. This rela-

EXHIBIT 7.1
The Cognitive–Evaluative Processes Associated With Pain

Beliefs About Pain

Certain beliefs about pain (e.g., the pain signifies ongoing tissue damage; the pain is likely to persist; the pain is indicative of some underlying disease; the pain will increase if one engages in exercise behaviors or simple activities) will result in maladaptive coping, feelings of helplessness, and exacerbation of pain, increased suffering, and greater disability.

Beliefs About Controllability

Beliefs that one's pain cannot be controlled can lead to negative effects: subsequent nociceptive input perceived as more intense than it actually is (i.e., overreaction); decreased activity level in the hope of minimizing the pain; inappropriate medication use; psychological sequelae such as demoralization, learned helplessness/depression and poor psychosocial functioning.

Self-Efficacy

Self-efficacy refers to one's belief or conviction that he or she can successfully perform certain required behaviors in a particular situation, to provide a desired outcome. This construct has been shown to be an important mediator of therapeutic change. It has been demonstrated that a patient's report of low self-efficacy regarding pain control is associated with low pain tolerance, poor psychosocial functioning, greater impairment and disability, and poor behavioral treatment outcome.

Cognitive Errors

Cognitive errors, such as *catastrophizing* (thoughts or images anticipating negative outcomes or aversive aspects of an experience), *overgeneralization* (assuming that the outcome of one event will apply to the outcome of all future or similar events), and *selective abstraction* (paying attention only to the negative aspects of an experience, while ignoring positive aspects), can greatly influence the experience of pain and disability, as well as the concomitant depression.

Coping

A number of overt and covert coping strategies can help individuals deal with pain, adjust to pain, or minimize the distress caused by pain. Overt behavioral coping strategies include simple rest, the use of relaxation methods, or the use of medication. Covert coping strategies include methods such as distracting oneself from pain, seeking information from various sources, and problem solving.

Note. Source is Turk and Monarch (2002).

tionship between affect and pain is both dynamic and complex. For example, Fernandez (1998) described this as a six-factor relationship:

1. When there is a personality trait or prior trauma, affect can be a predisposing factor.
2. The affect of anxiety, for example, can trigger pain.
3. Pain and affect can be correlational in nature.
4. Pain may be exacerbated by affect, such as in the case of anger creating tension that can aggravate the already existing pain (such as in the case of muscle tension headache).

5. Affect is often a consequence of pain, which is then referred to as *distress*.
6. Affect can perpetuate pain. If patients receive a great deal of secondary gain, such as increased nurturance and attention received from others, then they may use pain to get these needs continually met.

Thus, there is a dynamic relationship between affect and pain. Affect can be both a consequence and an exacerbating factor in pain. It can be explained as pain causing stress, which causes more pain, which causes more stress, and so on. This is similar to the cycle delineated earlier in Figure 7.1.

The motivational aspects of the affective–motivational part of pain perception refer to an individual's willingness to perform certain behaviors. Because pain is a subjective, private, and unpleasant experience, a number of negative emotions are usually associated with it and that can maintain it. Affect often leads to action, such as approach and avoidance (which are the simplest forms of action). Again, Turk and Monarch (2002) have delineated the common affective factors associated with pain:

- depression/learned helplessness
- anxiety/pain-related fear
- anger/frustration.

A CONCEPTUAL MODEL OF HOW ACUTE PAIN DEVELOPS INTO CHRONIC PAIN

Gatchel (1991, 1996) has characterized the progression from acute to chronic pain by means of a three-stage model (Figure 7.2). In Stage 1, referred to as the *acute phase*, normal emotional reactions, such as fear, anxiety, and worry, develop subsequent to the patient's perception of pain. This is a natural emotional reaction that often serves a protective function by prompting the individual to heed the pain signal and, if necessary, seek medical attention for it. However, if the perception of pain exists beyond a 2- to 4-month period (which is usually considered a normal healing time for most pain syndromes), the pain begins to develop into a more chronic condition, leading into Stage 2 of the model.

During this second stage, physiological and behavioral problems are often exacerbated. Learned helplessness, anger, distress, and somatization are typical symptoms of patients in this stage. Often, the extent of these symptoms depends on the individual's preexisting personality/psychosocial structure, in addition to socioeconomic and environmental conditions. The model proposes a *diathesis–stress* perspective, in which the stress of coping with pain can lead to exacerbation of the individual's underlying psychological characteristics.

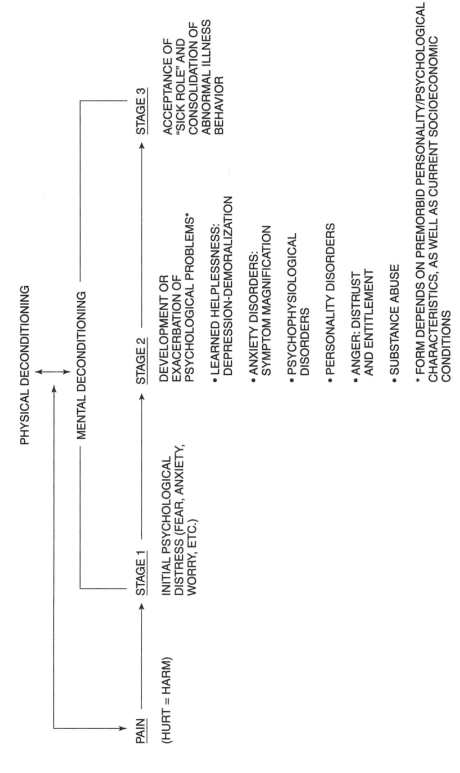

Figure 7.2. Gatchel's three-stage model. From *Contemporary Conservative Care for Painful Spinal Disorders* (p. 282), by T. G. Mayer, V. Mooney, and R. J. Gatchel, (Eds.) 1991, Philadelphia: Lea & Febiger. Copyright 1991 by Lea & Febiger. Reprinted with permission.

Finally, Stage 3, which represents the chronic phase of the model, is characterized by the progression to complex interactions of physical, psychological, and social processes. As the result of the chronic nature of the pain experience, and the stress that it creates, the patient's life begins to revolve around the pain and the behaviors that maintain it. The patient begins to adopt a "sick role," in which any excuse from social and occupational responsibilities becomes routine. As a consequence, the patient now becomes accustomed to the avoidance of responsibility, and other reinforcers serve to maintain such maladaptive behavior.

Of course, the key in treating pain is to not let it progress to the chronic stage, in which more complex biopsychosocial problems develop. Good patient care, which usually involves merely taking steps to reassure the patient that the pain is only temporary, thus allaying a great deal of the patient's anxiety and fears, goes a long way to help prevent the patient from becoming overly preoccupied with the pain and also helps to prevent premature catastrophizing about the symptoms.

COMMON MEDICAL TREATMENT
AND PHYSICIAN RECOMMENDATIONS

As noted earlier, patients who pursue medical care for the high prevalence of common pain problems usually go to their primary care physicians for advice (AAFP, 1987). However, very often these pain problems are not associated with objective anatomical findings and, therefore, a primary care provider is challenged with the significant task of trying to evaluate and plan treatment for only a symptom. Moreover, the symptoms presented are often episodic and variable in terms of severity and the time since onset. An easy solution, such as splinting a broken arm or suturing an open cut, is usually not available. Because of lack of training in understanding how to deal with pain, especially when it becomes chronic (where the important role of patients' attitudes, beliefs, coping abilities, and other psychosocial factors reviewed earlier are important in the management and outcome), primary care providers are significantly challenged with complex biopsychosocial problems that they are ill prepared to handle.

A number of examples are seen in the way in which primary care providers display a less than optimal approach in dealing with one type of pain: back pain. Such inadequacies have been observed in audiotaped analyses of the content and organization of primary care visits for back pain (Turner, LeResche, Von Korff, & Ehrlich, 1998; Von Korff, 1999). In these analyses, the visits were found to be quite similar and included a brief social greeting, followed by a brief history of the problem, and then a physical exam. Treatment recommendations were then made, usually consisting of a prescription of medicine for acute pain and some advice about self-care. Thus, in general, these visits for back pain revolved around simple discussions about pain history, diagnosis, and possible medications. The advice concerning patient self-management was found to be very unfocused. Moreover, results of these studies revealed the following:

- Patient worries about the pain symptoms were really not asked about or addressed.
- Relatedly, patients often feared serious disease or disability concerning the pain symptoms, without being told what the "red flags" or risks for these were.
- The physicians rarely took the opportunity to explain what was being looked for or "ruled out" during their evaluation.
- Staying active was often recommended to some patients, without addressing how to do so safely.
- Physicians rarely spent time identifying any functional difficulties associated with the pain syndromes or goals and plans for overcoming such difficulties.
- Relatedly, physicians did not attempt to identify and address such difficulties associated with performing work activities.
- Although many patients were already performing self-care activities, physicians missed opportunities to focus the visit on reinforcing such self-care and instead focused on simply the medical management of pain.
- Diagnostic information provided to patients was often quite ambiguous, leaving patients uncertain about what "improvement" meant or when it could be expected.
- Current information about the natural progression of back pain was usually not provided, and many patients were simply given overly optimistic prognoses.
- Palliative care was usually prescribed, typically the prescription of nonsteroid anti-inflammatory medicines, elementary advice about exercise, and a possible referral to physical therapy. On a less frequent basis, opioids or muscle relaxants were prescribed.
- Rarely were the recommendations written down, nor were patients given any documentation of the recommendations.

The preceding findings prompted the investigators of these studies to suggest that there is an urgent need for improvements in physicians' behavior during these important aspects of the initial primary care visit. This need for improvement is evidenced by the fact that approximately 30% of patients seeing a primary care physician for back pain subsequently have persistent problems 12 months later, and approximately 20% of these patients continue to experience moderate or severe activity limitations due to back problems (Von Korff & Saunders, 1996). As Pruitt and Von Korff

(2002) have highlighted, the insufficient preparation in medical school for dealing with pain problems, combined with time-pressured office visits in which complex biopsychosocial factors are present, as well as unrealistic patient expectations for immediate improvement, results in back problems being the most disliked conditions seen by primary care physicians. Obviously, the need is great to rectify these multiple hindrances to quality back care and to pain in general. A restructuring of the primary care team and services provided needs to be accomplished. Methods of accomplishing this are addressed next.

AN ASSESSMENT AND TREATMENT MODEL FOR PRIMARY CARE SETTINGS

The first step in the assessment process is the need to identify any pathophysiology or disease process that may be causing the pain symptoms. This can be accomplished by means of a thorough medical examination, as well as by diagnostic tests if needed. Unfortunately, a great many pain symptoms presented at the primary care clinic do not have any clear-cut pathophysiology that can be easily identified. Rather, more complex biopsychosocial issues are usually involved, and it is here that physicians struggle with attempting to identify behavioral problems in their patients and, if they do, often experience frustration in trying to change the patient's maladaptive behaviors. As we discussed earlier in this chapter, patients' beliefs, attitudes, daily behaviors, coping styles, and so on all need to be taken into account when comprehensively assessing the cause of pain symptoms. Unfortunately, the cognitive–behavioral skills necessary to assess the impact of these psychosocial variables are not part of traditional medical education. In addition, interventions that would be helpful in altering these psychosocial variables are not available in most primary care settings. To expect physicians to provide such interventions at the level that is necessary is quite unrealistic and is not time efficient. It is here that the clinical health psychologist can provide an invaluable service. Moreover, it is very important to carefully monitor patients at the acute phase to prevent the progression into chronicity (we reviewed this model of progression earlier in this chapter). Von Korff (1999) has outlined a *stepped-care framework* for managing back pain in the primary care setting. This same framework can be used in dealing with pain symptoms in general. There are three basic steps in this framework:

1. *Step 1.* This is the lowest intensity of intervention, which consists of addressing a patient's fear/avoidance beliefs about the pain through education, information, and advice about the importance of returning to activities of daily living as soon as possible. This level of intervention can usually be

brief during the initial office visit. It may be all that is necessary for a great number of patients with nonpathological pain.

2. *Step 2.* This refers to the need for increased intensity of intervention, and is reserved for patients who continue to report pain 6 to 8 weeks following the onset of an episode and who demonstrate persistent limitations in activities of daily living. The intervention at this level might include a structured exercise program or additional cognitive–behavioral strategies to deal with patient fears and to help them resume their usual work and recreational activities. At this step, an extended visit or multiple visits may be needed to improve outcomes for patients who need this level of intensity. Also, such interventions could be efficiently provided in a group format, with the assistance of health care providers from other disciplines, such as psychologists, physical therapists, health educators, or nurses.

3. *Step 3.* For those patients who failed to improve with either Step 1 or Step 2 interventions, Step 3 may be required for those who continue to experience significant disability and are at risk for becoming permanently disabled. Intervention at this stage may be more costly and complex than Step 1 and Step 2 interventions. Possible psychiatric comorbidity (e.g., major depression, anxiety disorders, substance abuse disorders), as well as secondary gain issues (e.g., relinquishing responsibilities at work, home, and social areas), need to be addressed. If these services cannot be provided in the primary care setting, such patients may need to be referred to specialty services, preferably an interdisciplinary pain management clinic (e.g., Deschner & Polatin, 2000; Mayer & Polatin, 2000).

As Von Korff (1999) has noted, this stepped-care framework can be applied in other than a progressive fashion. Many times, patients may come to the attention of the primary care provider who are already in need of Step 3 intervention for an ongoing pain problem that has failed to resolve and that has resulted in significant physical limitations. In such cases, a stratified approach is recommended, in which steps are "skipped," and patients can be immediately matched to the level of care appropriate for their needs.

The preceding three steps are similar to the primary, secondary, and tertiary care distinctions made earlier in the clinical research literature (e.g., Mayer et al., 1995), and subsequently reviewed by Gatchel (1996). These distinctions are helpful because they indicate that the type of biopsychosocial treatment required for each form of care is substantially different. In discussing back pain rehabilitation, for example, *primary* care is applied usually to acute cases of pain of limited severity. Basic symptom control methods are utilized in relieving pain during the normal early healing period. Frequently, some basic psychological reassurance that the acute pain episode is temporary, and will soon be resolved, is quite effective.

Secondary care represents "reactivation" treatment administered to those patients who do not improve simply through the normal healing process. It is administered during the transition from acute (primary) care to the eventual return to work. Such treatment has been designed to promote return to productivity before advanced deconditioning and significant psychosocial barriers to returning to work occur. At this phase, more active psychosocial intervention may need to be administered to those patients who do not appear to be progressing.

Finally, *tertiary* care requires an interdisciplinary and intensive treatment approach. It is intended for those patients experiencing the effects of physical deconditioning and chronic disability. In general, it differs from secondary treatment with regard to the intensity of rehabilitation services required, including psychosocial and disability management. The critical elements of interdisciplinary care, such as functional restoration, involve the following:

- formal, repeated quantification of physical deficits to guide, individualize, and monitor physical training progress
- psychosocial and socioeconomic assessment to guide, individualize, and monitor disability behavior-oriented interventions and outcomes
- multimodal disability management program using cognitive–behavioral approaches
- psychopharmacological interventions for detoxification and psychological management
- interdisciplinary, medically directed team approach with formal staffings, frequent team conferences, and low staff–to–patient ratios
- ongoing outcome assessment utilizing standardized objective criteria. Such interdisciplinary treatment programs have been shown to be extremely efficacious, as well as cost effective, in successfully treating patients with chronic pain, relative to less intensive, single-modality treatment programs (e.g., Deschner & Polatin, 2000; Mayer & Polatin, 2000).

In terms of primary and secondary care, the clinician must be aware of many psychosocial factors that can contribute to an acute pain episode becoming subacute and then chronic. Patients may progress through a number of stages (reviewed previously) as their pain and disability becomes more chronic (i.e., Stages 2 and 3). These may create significant *barriers to recovery* if they are not dealt with effectively. These barriers to recovery include the psychosocial variables discussed earlier, as well as functional, legal, and work-related issues that can greatly interfere with the patient's return to full functioning and a productive lifestyle.

Treatment personnel must also be alert to potential secondary gains of continued disability. Members of the health care team must be knowledgeable about all psychosocial issues while the patient is in treatment. This knowledge allows staff members not only to understand and serve the patient better but also to be more effective in problem solving if the patient's physical progress is slow or nonexistent. At other times, real interfering circumstances may be used as "smoke screens" or excuses for suboptimal performance and failure to adhere to the treatment regimen. Indeed, failure to make physical progress generally indicates psychosocial barriers to recovery. These barriers to recovery issues must be effectively assessed and brought to the attention of the entire treatment team. Steps can then be taken to understand their origins and avoid their interference with treatment goals.

If Step 1 care is regularly provided to every patient seen at a primary care clinic, significant potential definitely exists to reduce the chances of chronicity, to minimize disability, and to limit excessive use of health care services (Malmivaara et al., 1995). Exhibit 7.2 presents the major approaches that should be diligently adhered to in the primary care setting when treating patients reporting pain.

EXHIBIT 7.2
Major Approaches to Adhere to in Treating Patients
Reporting Pain in the Primary Care Setting

- Discuss the rationale for the physical exam, as well as any diagnostic tests that are needed.
- Assess the patient's pain (using the JCAHO guidelines), especially the pain's interference with daily activity.
- Reassure common patient worries regarding the "source and meaning" of pain, possible future disability or activity limitations, and so forth.
- Relate realistic and reassuring prognostic statements.
- Encourage self-care activities, such as exercise, continuation of routine activities, and medication management when appropriate. Offer praise or support for such efforts.
- Address patients' coping abilities, attitudes, beliefs, and daily behaviors related to the pain.
- Collaborate with patients to determine whether treatment recommendations can be adhered to reliably.
- Provide information and education about pain, preferably in a written booklet format.
- Write down the treatment recommendation for each patient.
- Follow up with patients after the initial visit to evaluate treatment gains.

SUMMARY

As we have discussed in this chapter, pain accounts for more than 80% of all physician visits, affecting more than 50 million Americans and costing more than $70 billion annually in health care costs and low productivity. Most patients seeking medical care for pain complaints are regularly seen in primary care settings. Because of the prevalence of pain, the JCAHO now requires that physicians consider pain to be a *fifth vital sign* when evaluating patients. The JCAHO guidelines also require that pain severity be documented, using a pain scale.

The common interaction between the physical basis of pain and psychosocial concomitants has led to the use of a biopsychosocial perspective of pain in which psychosocial factors, along with biological factors, need to be considered in its assessment and treatment. This again underscores the important role of clinical health psychologists in the assessment and treatment of medical patients, especially those with pain. Examples of assessment and treatment models for dealing with pain in the primary care setting were reviewed.

RECOMMENDED READINGS

Joint Commission on Accreditation of Healthcare Organizations. (2000). *Pain assessment and management: An organizational approach.* Oakbrook Terrace, IL: Author.

Turk, D. C., & Gatchel, R. J. (2002). *Psychological approaches to pain management* (2nd ed.). New York: Guilford Press.

Von Korff, M. (1999). Pain management in primary care: An individualized stepped-care approach. *Psychological Factors in Pain, 22,* 360–373.

GLOSSARY

acute pain Pain that is usually indicative of tissue damage and that is characterized by momentary intense noxious sensations (i.e., nociception).

barriers to recovery Psychosocial, functional, legal, and work-related factors that can significantly interfere with a patient's return to full functioning and a productive lifestyle.

catastrophizing Thoughts or images anticipating negative outcomes or aversive aspects of an experience.

chronic pain Pain that lasts 6 months or longer, well past the normal healing period one would expect for its protective biological function.

fifth vital sign Pain is now viewed as the fifth vital sign (added to pulse, blood pressure, core temperature, and respiration) and must be evaluated in all patients.

interdisciplinary pain management   An intensive tertiary treatment approach to dealing with the complex biopsychosocial features of chronic pain. It involves a team approach, with close collaboration among physicians, nurses, psychologists, physical therapists, case managers, and other required health care professionals needed for care of patients with pain.

nociception   A neurological event, originating in pain receptors/regions, that is originally responsible for pain.

overgeneralization   The assumption that the outcome of one event will apply to the outcome of all future or similar events.

pain–stress cycle   A cycle in which pain and the changes it brings lead to stress, which leads to increased pain, which leads to increased stress, and so on.

primary care   Term usually applied to acute cases of pain of limited severity.

psychogenic pain   An older term used to suggest that pain was caused solely by psychological factors.

recurrent pain   Intense, episodic pain reoccurring for more than 3 months.

secondary care   This represents "reactivation" treatment administered to those patients with pain who do not improve simply through the normal healing process.

selective abstraction   Paying attention only to the negative aspects of an experience, while ignoring positive aspects.

self-efficacy   One's belief or conviction that he or she can successfully perform certain required behaviors, in a particular situation, to produce a desired outcome.

stepped-care framework   A framework proposed for dealing with pain symptoms. Step 1 is the lowest intensity of intervention; Step 2 refers to the need for increased intensity of intervention; and Step 3 refers to the potential need for more intensive treatment, such as referral to an interdisciplinary pain management clinic.

tertiary care   Refers to the most intensive treatment approach to pain, such as interdisciplinary pain management.

three-stage model of pain progression   A conceptual model of how acute pain develops into chronic pain, progressing through three distinct stages.

REFERENCES

American Academy of Family Physicians. (1987). *Facts about family practice.* Kansas City, KS: Author.

Cornwal, A., & Doncleri, D. C. (1988). The effect of experimentally induced anxiety on the experience of pressure pain. *Pain, 35,* 105–113.

Deschner, M., & Polatin, P. B. (2000). Interdisciplinary programs: Chronic pain management. In T. G. Mayer, R. J. Gatchel, & P. B. Polatin (Eds.), *Occupational musculoskeletal disorders: Function, outcomes and evidence* (pp. 629–638). Philadelphia: Lippincott, Williams & Williams.

Fernandez, E. (1998). The role of affect in somatoform and factitious disorders. *Current Review of Pain, 2,* 109–114.

Gatchel, R. J. (1991). Early development of physical and mental conditioning in painful spinal disorders. In J. G. Mayer, V. Mooney, & R. J. Gatchel (Eds.), *Contemporary conservative care for painful spinal disorders* (pp. 278–289). Philadelphia: Lea & Febiger.

Gatchel, R. J. (1996). Psychological disorders and chronic pain: Cause and effect relationships. In R. J. Gatchel & D. C. Turk (Eds.), *Psychological approaches to pain management: A practitioner's handbook* (pp. 33–54). New York: Guilford Press.

Gatchel, R. J., & Turk, D. C. (1996). *Psychological approaches to pain management: A practitioner's handbook.* New York: Guilford Press.

Joint Commission on Accreditation of Healthcare Organizations. (2000). *Pain assessment and management: An organization approach.* Oakbrook Terrace, IL: Author.

Malmivaara, A., Hakkinen, U., Aro, T., Heinrichs, M.L., Koskenniemi, L., Kuosma, E., et al. (1995). The treatment of acute low back pain—bed rest, exercises, or ordinary activity? *New England Journal of Medicine, 335,* 351–355.

Mayer, T. G., & Polatin, P. B. (2000). Tertiary nonoperative interdisciplinary programs. The functional restoration variant of the outpatient chronic pain management program. In T. G. Mayer, R. J. Gatchel, & P. B. Polatin (Eds.), *Occupational musculoskeletal disorders: Function, outcomes and evidence* (pp. 639–650). Philadelphia: Lippincott, Williams & Williams.

Mayer, T. G., Polatin P., Smith, B., Smith, C., Gatchel, R. J., Herring, S., et al. (1995). Spine rehabilitation: Secondary and tertiary nonoperative care. *Spine, 20,* 2060–2066.

Morley, S., & Williams, A. C. (2002). Conducting and evaluating treatment outcome studies. In D. C. Turk & R. J. Gatchel (Eds.), *Psychological approaches to pain management* (2nd ed., pp. 52–70). New York: Guilford Press.

Pruitt, S. D., & Von Korff, M. (2002). Improving the management of low back pain: A paradigm shift for primary care. In D. C. Turk & R. J. Gatchel (Eds.), *Psychological approaches to pain management* (2nd ed., pp. 301–316). New York: Guilford Press.

Turk, D., & Monarch, E. S. (2002). Biopsychosocial perspective on chronic pain. In D. C. Turk & R. J. Gatchel (Eds.), *Psychological approaches to pain management* (2nd ed., pp. 3–29). New York: Guilford Press.

Turner, J. A., LeResche, L., Von Korff, M., & Ehrlich, K. (1998). Primary care back pain patient characteristics, visit content, and short-term outcomes. *Spine, 23,* 463–469.

Von Korff, M. (1999). Pain management in primary care: An individualized stepped-care approach. *Psychological Factors in Pain, 22,* 360–373.

Von Korff, M., & Saunders, K. (1996). The course of back pain in primary care. *Spine, 21,* 2833–2837.

8

INSOMNIA

Insomnia is one of the most common problems among primary care patients. As reviewed by Morin (1993), approximately 20% to 40% of adults report experiencing sleep difficulties within any given year, and 10% to 15% indicate that insomnia is chronic. Only a small percent of primary care patients, however, visit their care providers specifically to discuss sleep difficulties. A recent study found that 69% of primary care patients acknowledged having insomnia when asked about it (Shochat, Umphress, Israel, & Ancoli-Israel, 1999). Fifty percent of these reported occasional insomnia, and 19% had chronic insomnia. Women and elderly people have the highest prevalence rate; however, people of all ages (including children) experience insomnia. Despite the high prevalence, most people with insomnia do not seek medical assistance. Greater attention to sleep concerns has the potential to significantly affect quality of life within a primary care clinic's population.

Insomnia can involve sleep onset problems, sleep maintenance problems, or early morning awakening. Sleep onset difficulties are more common in younger people, whereas middle-of-the-night awakening is more common with older adults. Early morning awakening is often related to depression or anxiety. Insomnia can also be categorized on the basis of its presumed cause. Primary insomnia, also called *psychophysiological insomnia,* results from the interaction of multiple factors, the most salient of which are the learned sleep habits and conditioned physiological arousal in response to bedtime cues that lead to wakefulness. Secondary insomnia, on the other hand, involves sleep difficulties related to another primary factor, such as medical illness, pain, medications, depression, or anxiety. It also may be secondary to environmental factors, such as noise or uncomfortable room temperature. Insomnia conditions can also be distinguished by their duration. Acute insomnia refers to short-term episodes of poor sleep, often triggered by emotional or physical triggers. Insomnia is considered chronic when it persists for more than 6 months.

Morin (1993) presented combined criteria for chronic insomnia that incorporates the two major nosological systems for sleep disorders: the *Diagnostic and Statistical Manual of Mental Disorders*, fourth edition (American Psychiatric Association, 1994), and the *International Classification of Sleep Disorders* (American Sleep Disorders Association, 1990). These components include the following:

- Subjective complaints are made about poor sleep.
- Difficulties are experienced initiating or maintaining sleep. Sleep-onset latency or middle-of-the-night awakenings must be greater than 30 minutes. Sleep efficiency (the percentage of time in bed that is spent actually sleeping) must be lower than 85 percent.
- Sleep difficulties are present three or more nights per week.
- Sleep difficulties persist for at least 6 months.
- Subjective reports are made about fatigue, performance impairment, or mood disturbance that are attributed to poor sleep.
- Sleep difficulties cause significant impairment in social or occupational functioning or cause marked distress.

Spielman and Glovinsky (1997) have suggested that three categories of factors contribute to insomnia. *Predisposing factors* are those that increase a person's vulnerability to poor sleep. Examples include a propensity toward physiological, cognitive, or emotional reactivity, a family history of insomnia, and gender (Morin, 1993). *Precipitating factors* are conditions that trigger an episode of insomnia. Often, this is some type of psychosocial stress that has led to physical or emotional arousal. *Perpetuating factors*, on the other hand, include the maladaptive sleep habits and cognitions that develop in response to the acute phase of insomnia, such as use of sleep medication or alcohol as a sleep aid, daytime napping, excessive caffeine use, and anxiety about not being able to sleep at night. Spielman and Glovinsky note that the influence of each of these factors changes over time. Acute insomnia is primarily related to a combination of predisposing factors and precipitating factors. As insomnia persists over time, the role of perpetuating factors increases, and the influence from the original precipitating factors decreases. By the time insomnia is chronic, the perpetuating factors have developed enough to maintain insomnia, even though the original triggers are much reduced.

COMMON MEDICAL TREATMENTS
AND RECOMMENDATIONS

Primary care physicians commonly use medications to help their patients who complain of poor sleep. Note, however, that prescriptions for sleep aids have decreased substantially during recent years (Walsh & Schweitzer, 1999). The National Sleep Foundation (1999) suggested situations in which sleep medications may be indicated, as listed in Exhibit 8.1. Sleep medications should ideally be used only for a brief period of time. Extended use of sleep aids can lead to rebound insomnia when the medications are discontinued, as well as habituation, which requires an ever higher dose to get the same effect. Patients are, however, commonly maintained on sleep aids long term. If used for extended periods, the medication should be used only intermittently.

Benzodiazepine receptor agonists have long been the medication of choice for sleep aids. They are effective for inducing and maintaining sleep (Nowell et al., 1997). Short-acting benzodiazepines, such as triazolam, are preferred because they help avoid daytime sedation, unless they are also being used to control daytime anxiety. Longer acting hypnotics, such as flurazepam, also increase the risk of injuries among older adults due to falls. Generally, physicians use the lowest dose that is effective because higher doses increase the probability of rebound insomnia on discontinuation. Benzodiazepines should not be used by pregnant women, by people who

EXHIBIT 8.1
Indications for Use of Medication for Aiding Sleep

- The insomnia has a known cause that is best treated with medication.
- The insomnia is interfering with the accomplishment of daily activities.
- Behavioral approaches have not been effective.
- Significant insomnia-related distress is present, and medications are being used in conjunction with the early phases of behavior therapy.
- Insomnia is short term.
- Insomnia is expected (i.e., concurrent with a medical/biological condition, stressful event, or traveling across time zones).

Note. Adapted from *Sleep Aids: Everything You Wanted to Know But Were Too Tired to Ask.* Retrieved October 15, 2001, from http://www.sleepfoundation.org/publications/sleepaids.html. Copyright 1999 by the National Sleep Foundation. Adapted with permission.

may need to get up and function during the middle of their normal sleep time, or by those with sleep apnea (because it can exacerbate breathing problems). Antidepressants are also commonly used for insomnia, although they are not recommended for patients who are not affected by depression. The sedative effect of antihistamines, such as Benedryl, makes them a frequently prescribed sleep aid, as well.

Newer, nonbenzodiazepine sleep aids have been shown to be effective without some of the negative side effects or complications of benzodiazepines. Zolpidem and zaleplon both have a short half-life, so they cause minimal residual daytime sleepiness, memory loss, or motor incoordination when used at recommended dosages. Additionally, neither medication shows evidence of tolerance or rebound, at least up to 4 weeks of nightly administration (Doghramji, 2001).

THE CLINICAL HEALTH PSYCHOLOGIST AND INSOMNIA MANAGEMENT

A number of nonpharmacological treatment approaches have been applied to insomnia with varying degrees of success. The most commonly used approaches are discussed here.

Sleep Hygiene Education

Many people with insomnia practice sleep habits that interfere with good sleep. Sometimes, these habits develop in response to an initial insomnia problem. For example, a person may increase consumption of caffeine in the early evening to counter drowsiness that stems from poor sleep the previous night. Other times, poor sleep practices are long-held habits of which the individual may not be aware. For example, a person may routinely bring work home to do late into the evening, thus maintaining cognitive arousal and tension right up until bedtime. Reviewing sleep practices with the patient and recommending improvements in sleep hygiene, where indicated, is a necessary, although often not sufficient, component to sleep treatment. Sleep hygiene recommendations are listed in Exhibit 8.2.

Stimulus Control Therapy

A primary factor in the development of psychophysiological insomnia is the learned association between bedroom stimuli and wakefulness. The goal of stimulus control therapy (Bootzin, Epstein, & Wood, 1991) is to reassociate bedroom stimuli and sleep to improve insomnia. Patients are instructed to avoid all activities in the bedroom except sleep and sex. They should remove from the bedroom all stimuli that may be associated with

EXHIBIT 8.2
Sleep Hygiene Recommendations

Avoid caffeine. The half-life of caffeine ranges between 3 and 7 hours, depending on the individual, so it is best for individuals to avoid any source of caffeine (coffee, tea, soda, chocolate, medications) after early afternoon.

Avoid tobacco. Nicotine is a stimulant that can interfere with sleep onset or return to sleep when individuals smoke close to bedtime or on middle-of-the-night awakening. Additionally, heavy tobacco users who smoke on awakening can become conditioned to wake when nicotine levels in their system drop.

Maintain a wind-down time prior to bedtime. Cognitive and physiological arousal can interfere with sleep onset. Establishing a prebedtime routine that includes an hour of relaxing activity can decrease arousal and help condition sleepiness at the designated bedtime.

Have a light snack prior to bedtime. A small, easy-to-digest snack can reduce hunger that may interfere with sleep. Foods with caffeine (e.g., chocolate) or that cause intestinal gas (e.g., raw vegetables) should be avoided.

Maintain a comfortable room temperature.

Keep the room dark. Heavy window covers or eye shades can be used to reduce light in the bedroom.

Reduce ambient noise. Uncontrollable noise (e.g., traffic noise) can be minimized by using earplugs.

Avoid alcohol. Alcohol can increase sleepiness and, therefore, may be used by some people to promote sleep onset. It will, however, fragment sleep and change sleep architecture. Therefore, it is not a good sleep aid.

Avoid clock-watching. Turn clocks so they cannot easily been seen from the bed.

Exercise. Sustained, moderate exercise may help with sleep onset and sleep fragmentation. Exercise too close to bedtime, however, is likely to interfere. Late afternoon may be the best time for exercise in reference to sleep.

---

wakefulness, such as televisions, computers, and desks, and avoid reading or talking on the phone while in bed. Additionally, individuals are instructed to get out of bed if, after 15 to 20 minutes of trying, they are unable to fall asleep. They should go into another room and engage in a mundane activity until they feel sleepy again. At that point in time, they should return to bed for another attempt at sleep. If, again, they are unable to fall asleep after 15 to 20 minutes, patients should repeat the cycle.

Because stimulus control guidelines may be contrary to the patients' beliefs about sleep, the psychologist should clearly outline the rationale for each recommendation. For instance, patients may believe that it is better to lie in bed awake than to get up if unable to sleep because they are, at least, getting rest if they remain in bed. Furthermore, patients may believe that getting up only serves to increase arousal and, therefore, may be reluctant to get up. Education should be given about the nature of learned associations and how they can be extinguished by avoiding the pairing of wakefulness and bedroom stimuli while, at the same time, increasing the occurrence of sleepiness in the bedroom. It may be helpful to discuss the fact that wakeful rest is not restorative like sleep. Therefore, continuing to lie awake in bed is unlikely to produce changes in daytime drowsiness. Finally, patients should be informed that sleep often gets worse before it gets better, and diligence in adhering to the guidelines will be required for several weeks before any change is observed. For this reason, frequent contacts with the patient, either through a clinic visit or via telephone, are generally helpful during the early phase of treatment.

Sleep Restriction

Individuals with insomnia often spend an excessive number of hours in bed attempting to get the sleep they feel is needed. For instance, a patient may go to bed in the early evening, knowing he or she will require several hours to fall asleep, and then will stay in bed late into the morning, in a state of repeated dozing, trying to make up for time spent awake during the night. In all, the patient may be in bed 12 or more hours to get 7 hours of sleep.

Sleep restriction treatment (Spielman, Saskin, & Thorpy, 1987) is designed to consolidate sleep by reducing the "sleep window" to the number of hours the patient is already getting. Using a sleep diary, the average number of hours of sleep the patient gets is determined. Patients then establish a set bedtime and wake-up time to allow them to be in bed for only the number of hours determined at baseline. For example, a patient who typically goes to sleep at 9:00 p.m. and stays in bed until 8:00 a.m., to get 6 hours of sleep, might set a bedtime of 1:00 a.m. and a wake-up time of 7:00 a.m. to get the same 6 hours of sleep. Through these steps, the demand on the patient changes from trying to fall asleep to trying to stay awake. To avoid excessive daytime drowsiness, the total sleep time prescribed should not be less than 5 hours. Patients continue to maintain a sleep diary and, when they are sleeping at least 85% of the designated sleep window for three consecutive nights, the window is increased by moving the bedtime back by 20 minutes. This continues until the patient is getting a desired number of hours of sleep. If sleep is repeatedly less than 85% of the sleep window, the sleep window should be shortened by 20 minutes again.

As with stimulus control therapy, sleep restriction can be difficult to maintain over the time necessary to show improvement. Frequent contacts may be necessary to offer support and to help guide the patient through the process.

Relaxation Training

Relaxation training (e.g., Bernstein & Borkovec, 1973) helps poor sleepers reduce physiological tension that may be interfering with sleep onset. Relaxation exercises can be used before bedtime during a wind-down period or after going to bed. A variety of techniques can be applied, including progressive muscle relaxation, mental imagery, diaphragmatic breathing, or autogenic relaxation, depending on patient preference. Some patients may also benefit from listening to relaxation instructions on audio-tape while trying to fall asleep.

Biofeedback

Physiological feedback can be useful for assessing tension before sleep onset and for helping some individuals decrease somatic tension (Bootzin & Rider, 1997; Hauri, 1991). Biofeedback is often combined with relaxation training to facilitate learning of techniques.

Paradoxical Intention

As insomnia persists over time, attempts to fall asleep can be accompanied by significant anxiety due to expectations of not being able to sleep. This anticipation of insomnia contributes to inability to fall asleep, as a sort of self-fulfilling prophecy. Paradoxical intention (Ascher & Efran, 1978) aims to avoid this anxiety by having the patient stay awake as long as possible. Similar to the idea of sleep restriction, this changes the demand on the patient from trying to fall asleep to trying to stay awake.

Cognitive Therapy

Maladaptive beliefs about sleep can contribute to increased arousal and tension. Cognitive therapy focuses on challenging sleep-related myths and other alarming cognitions to promote sleep. An extensive description of cognitive therapy for sleep has been provided by Morin (1993).

WHICH TREATMENTS WORK?

The American Academy of Sleep Medicine (AASM) has reviewed the evidence supporting the use of various nonpharmacological treatment modalities for insomnia (Chesson et al., 1999). From this review, the AASM has published practice parameters that grade the support for treatments as follows:

- *Evidence Level I:* randomized well-designed trials with low alpha and beta errors
- *Evidence Level II:* randomized trials with high beta error
- *Evidence Level III:* nonrandomized controlled or concurrent cohort studies
- *Evidence Level IV:* nonrandomized historical cohort studies
- *Evidence Level V:* case studies.

The AASM provided recommendations for treating insomnia based on this review. Recommendations with Level I or overwhelming Level II evidence were categorized as *standard*, those with Level II or a consensus of Level III evidence were categorized as *guidance*, and those with inconclusive or conflicting evidence were listed as *opinion*.

The AASM used 48 articles published between 1970 and 1997 that evaluated stand-alone, nonpharmacological treatment modalities. They found no Level I evidence studies. Stimulus control was found to be the one treatment approach with the strongest evidence to date, and it was classified as a standard recommendation supported by Level II evidence. Progressive muscle relaxation, paradoxical intention, and biofeedback were categorized as guideline recommendations, each being supported by Level II and Level III evidence. Sleep restriction and multicomponent (cognitive) behavioral therapy (which was graded as a single therapy due to its increasingly common use) were considered opinion recommendations, supported by Level III and Level V evidence, and some Level II evidence in the case of sleep restriction. Treatments with insufficient evidence to be recommended as a single therapy include sleep hygiene education, imagery training, and cognitive therapy. The AASM concluded that three treatments are empirically validated and well-established according to the criteria of the American Psychological Association (1995): stimulus control, progressive muscle relaxation, and paradoxical intention. Each of these treatments is brief and focused and can be readily applied to the primary care setting.

Although the AASM review assessed the support for each treatment component separately, multicomponent treatments are commonly practiced. Several studies have evaluated the effectiveness of multicomponent behavioral treatments for insomnia in clinical settings that can be applied to the primary care setting.

Hryshko-Mullen (2000) reported the results of 42 patients treated through the Wilford Hall Insomnia Program, a six-session, multicomponent insomnia treatment program. This program is based on self-management principles and can be conducted in a group or individual format. When conducted in a group setting, the sessions are typically 1.5 hours long. Additionally, two individual sessions and a phone contact are interspersed throughout the treatment period to reinforce and individualize the material. Sleep diaries are maintained for a least a 2-week baseline before treatment, as well as throughout treatment. During the program, patients are introduced to sleep hygiene guidelines, as well as to the principles of stimulus control and sleep restriction. Participants are taught relaxation exercises and instructed in cognitive techniques to reduce worry that may be contributing to insomnia. The final session is spent discussing relapse prevention.

Hryshko-Mullen (2000) reported that the 42 patients in the study had chronic insomnia, with an average of almost 10 years of sleep difficulties. Following treatment, patients with sleep-onset latency difficulties experienced a 53% decrease in the time required to fall asleep. Patients experiencing difficulties with middle-of-the-night awakening experienced a 40% decrease in time awake during the night.

Hryshko-Mullen (2000) noted that clinical health psychologists may be the health care providers with the most advanced training in the behavioral treatment of insomnia, and they advocate that primary care physicians and other providers involved with the evaluation of patients with insomnia seek out health psychologists to provide this care. The Wilford Hall Insomnia Program is based in a specialty clinical health psychology clinic; however, it is especially well suited for the primary care setting. The group format may facilitate easy access to treatment for a large number of patients who might be identified with sleep complaints if primary care physicians were to begin inquiring about sleep with all patients. Furthermore, the multicomponent treatment approach may be best for a population-based intervention, because it is likely to offer something helpful for everyone who is referred.

Espie and colleagues (2001) evaluated a similar cognitive–behavioral therapy (CBT) program; however, theirs was conducted by primary care nurses in a general medical clinic. One hundred and thirty-nine patients presenting to the clinic with chronic insomnia were randomized to either a six-session group-administered CBT or a self-monitoring control condition. Nurses administering treatment received extensive training from a clinical psychologist, a senior health promotions officer, and a pharmacist prior to providing treatments. The multicomponent intervention included sleep education, sleep hygiene, stimulus control, relaxation therapy, and cognitive therapy. Patients in the CBT group reduced mean sleep-onset latency from 61 to 28 minutes, and decreased time awake after sleep onset by 31 minutes, compared with only minimal change for the self-monitoring group. When the control group was subsequently treated, they also experienced similar improvements. Benefits had been maintained by both groups at the 1-year follow-up. This study lends support to the possibility that other primary care team members can effectively provide insomnia interventions, with psychologists serving in training and support roles.

Edinger and colleagues (2001) recently published a double-blind, randomized controlled trial of CBT for treatment of chronic primary insomnia in the *Journal of the American Medical Association*. Adults with sleep maintenance problems (average duration of 13.6 years) were randomly assigned to receive either 6 weeks of CBT, which included sleep education, stimulus control interventions, and time-in-bed restrictions; a progressive muscle relaxation treatment; or a placebo treatment involving quasi-desensitization. Patients were evaluated 6 months after treatment with polysomnographs and sleep diaries to measure sleep efficiency, time awake after initial sleep onset, and total sleep time. Questionnaires measured global insomnia symptoms, sleep-related self-efficacy, and mood. Patients treated with CBT showed a 54% reduction in their wake-after-sleep-onset, compared to 16% for the relaxation group and 12% for the placebo group. Sleep efficiency for the CBT group improved more than that for either of the other groups, with an increase from 78% at baseline to 85% at the end of treatment. Studies such as this, which are published in premier medical journals, are likely to have high credibility with physician colleagues. Clinical health psychologists might, therefore, benefit from having copies on hand to distribute to primary care team members to aid their efforts to increase referrals for insomnia treatment.

Even minimal contact interventions consisting of bibliotherapy alone have shown some promise for treating insomnia. Mimeault and Morin (1999) randomly assigned 54 adults with insomnia to a bibliotherapy condition, in which they received six treatment booklets through the mail, or to a wait-list control group. Half of the bibliotherapy group also received a 15-minute telephone contact offering professional guidance. Participants in both treatment conditions improved their sleep efficiency and reduced their total wake time. The wait-list control group showed no change. Minimal contact approaches such as this may be another option for psychologists who need highly efficient, yet effective, treatments for the primary care setting. Further evaluation of the effectiveness of this type of approach within an actual clinical setting remains to be conducted.

SECONDARY INSOMNIA

Finally, note that secondary insomnia is likely to be seen in primary care settings as often—if not more often—as primary insomnia. Sleep difficulties that are caused by physical or psychiatric problems traditionally have been viewed as refractory to insomnia interventions and, thus, they have received little attention in the literature (Lichstein, Wilson, & Johnson, 2000). Lichstein and colleagues recently studied the effectiveness of treating older adults with secondary insomnia using relaxation and stimulus control. This was the first randomized trial to look at a broad range of secondary insomnia conditions that included both psychiatric and medical conditions as the primary factor. Forty-four participants, older than 58 years, were carefully screened for secondary insomnia and randomly assigned to either a treatment group consisting of relaxation and stimulus control interventions (four sessions) or to a no-treatment control group. Treatment group participants showed greater improvements in middle-of-the-night wake time, sleep efficiency, and ratings of sleep quality after completion of treatment and at a 3-month follow-up.

Lichstein and colleagues (2000) advocate for aggressive treatment of secondary insomnia using modalities similar to those used for primary sleep difficulties. They note, however, that, by definition, secondary insomnia is dependent on another primary condition and will not improve until the primary condition resolves. Therefore, they propose that the treatment effects are possible because, to some degree, the sleep problems being treated are actually primary insomnia. They propose that a high percentage of secondary insomnias may be misdiagnosed.

Lichstein et al. (2000) elaborated by discussing three types of secondary insomnia. *Absolute secondary insomnia* refers to sleep difficulties that are directly related to a primary condition. They noted that this is most likely to occur with newly presenting insomnia that occurs in the aftermath of acute illness. *Partial secondary insomnia* refers to sleep problems that are related to the primary condition; however, the primary condition does not account for 100% of the variance. The primary condition may have simply exacerbated preexisting sleep problems, or other perpetuating factors may have contributed to the maintenance of the problem. As discussed earlier, the precipitating factors (e.g., acute illness) often are not the same factors that maintain insomnia over time, so it is likely that at least part of the condition diagnosed as secondary insomnia is, in actuality, primary insomnia. The third type of secondary insomnia is *specious secondary insomnia*. This refers to sleep problems that appear to be related to another primary condition but, in fact, are not related at all.

Although the study by Lichstein and colleagues (2000) represents only an initial attempt to evaluate the treatment of secondary insomnia, it clearly suggests that medical or psychiatric patients with sleep difficulties may benefit from focused attention on their sleep. The conventional view that the primary condition must be resolved before sleep can improve may leave patients suffering more than is necessary.

SUMMARY

Given the high prevalence of both primary and secondary insomnia, primary care psychologists need to be adept at assessment and treatment. A great amount of suffering can be relieved with the straightforward behavioral approaches discussed in this chapter, all of which are amenable to the primary care setting. Varying levels of evidence exist for stimulus control therapy, sleep restriction, relaxation training, biofeedback, paradoxical intention, and multicomponent CBT. The benefits of these treatments can include improved daytime functioning, better health, reduced distress, and avoidance of difficulties caused by misuse of sleep medications. Clearly, treatment of insomnia is one of the areas in which psychologists are likely to be most valued when they are integrated into primary care.

RECOMMENDED READINGS

Chesson, A. L., Anderson, W. M., Littner, M., Davila, D., Hartse, K., Johnson, S., et al. (1999). Practice parameters for the non-pharmacologic treatment of chronic insomnia. *Sleep, 22,* 1128–1132.

Edinger, J. D., Wohlgemuth, W. K., Radtke, R. A., Marsh, G. R., & Quinlan, R. E. (2001). Cognitive behavioral therapy for treatment of chronic primary insomnia: A randomized controlled trial. *Journal of the American Medical Association, 285,* 1856-1864.

Morin, C. M. (1993). *Insomnia: Psychological assessment and management.* New York: Guilford Press.

GLOSSARY

absolute secondary insomnia   Sleep difficulties that are directly related to a primary condition.

acute insomnia   Short-term episodes of poor sleep.

chronic insomnia   Insomnia that persists for more than 6 months.

partial secondary insomnia   Sleep problems that are related to another primary condition; however, the primary condition accounts for only a portion of the insomnia; evidence exists for other predisposing, precipitating, or perpetuating factors.

perpetuating factors   Habits and cognitions that maintain insomnia over time.

precipitating factors   Conditions that trigger an episode of insomnia.

predisposing factors   Factors that increase a person's vulnerability to insomnia.

primary insomnia   Insomnia that is not related to another known condition (see *psychophysiological insomnia*).

psychophysiological insomnia   Insomnia that results from the interaction of multiple factors, the most salient of which are the learned sleep habits and conditioned physiological arousal in response to bedtime cues that lead to wakefulness.

secondary insomnia   Sleep difficulties related to another primary factor, such as medical illness, pain, medications, depression, or anxiety.

sleep architecture   The structure of the various stages of sleep over the course of a sleep period.

sleep efficiency   The percentage of time in bed that is spent actually sleeping.

sleep-onset latency   The time required to initially fall asleep.

sleep window   Total time between initially going to bed and attempting to fall asleep and finally getting out of bed to start the day.

specious secondary sleep   Sleep problems that appear to be related to another primary condition but, in fact, are not related at all.

REFERENCES

American Psychiatric Association. (1994). *Diagnostic and statistical manual of mental disorders* (4th ed.). Washington, DC: Author.

American Psychological Association. (1995). Training in and dissemination of empirically-validated psychological treatments: Report and recommendations. *The Clinical Psychologist, 48,* 3–23.

American Sleep Disorders Association. (1990). *International classification of sleep disorders. Diagnostic and coding manual.* Lawrence, KS: Allen Press.

Ascher, L. M., & Efran, J. S. (1978). Use of paradoxical intention in a behavioral program for sleep onset insomnia. *Journal of Consulting and Clinical Psychology, 46,* 547–550.

Bernstein, D. A., & Borkovec, T. D. (1973). *Progressive muscle relaxation: A manual for the helping professions.* Champaign, IL: Research Press.

Bootzin, R. R., Epstein, D., & Wood, J. M. (1991). Stimulus control instructions. In P. J. Hauri (Ed.), *Case studies in insomnia* (pp. 19–28). New York: Plenum Press.

Bootzin, R. R., & Rider, S. P. (1997). Behavioral techniques and biofeedback for insomnia. In M. R. Pressman & W. C. Orr (Eds.), *Understanding sleep: The evaluation and treatment of sleep disorders* (pp. 315–338). Washington, DC: American Psychological Association.

Chesson, A. L., Anderson, W. M., Littner, M., Davila, D., Hartse, K., Johnson, S., et al. (1999). Practice parameters for the non-pharmacologic treatment of chronic insomnia. *Sleep, 22,* 1128–1132.

Doghramji, K. (2001). *Sleepless in America: Diagnosing and treating insomnia.* Retrieved November 14, 2000, from http://psychiatry.medscape.com/Medscape/Clinical Mgmt/CM.v02/public/index-CM.v02.html

Edinger, J. D., Wohlgemuth, W. K., Radtke, R. A., Marsh, G. R., & Quinlan, R. E. (2001). Cognitive behavioral therapy for treatment of chronic primary insomnia: A randomized controlled trial. *Journal of the American Medical Association, 285,* 1856–1864.

Espie, C. A., Inglis, S. J., Tessier, S., & Harvey, L. (2001). The clinical effectiveness of cognitive behaviour therapy for chronic insomnia: Implementation and evaluation of a sleep clinic in general medical practice. *Behaviour Research and Therapy, 39,* 45–60.

Hauri, P. J. (1991). Sleep hygiene, relaxation therapy and cognitive interventions. In P. J. Hauri (Ed.), *Case studies in insomnia* (pp. 65–84). New York: Plenum Press.

Hryshko-Mullen, A. S. (2000). Behavioral treatment of insomnia: The Wilford Hall Insomnia Program. *Military Medicine, 165,* 200–207.

Lichstein, K. L., Wilson, N. M., & Johnson, C. T. (2000). Psychological treatment of secondary insomnia. *Psychology and Aging, 15,* 232–240.

Mimeault, V. & Morin, C. M. (1999). Self-help treatment for insomnia: Bibliotherapy with and without professional guidance. *Journal of Consulting and Clinical Psychology, 67,* 511–519.

Morin, C. M. (1993). *Insomnia: Psychological assessment and management*. New York: Guilford Press.

National Sleep Foundation. (1999). *Sleep aids: Everything you wanted to know but were too tired to ask*. Retrieved October 15, 2001, from http://www.sleepfoundation.org/ publications/sleepaids.html

Nowell, P. D., Mazumdar, S., Buysee, J. J., Dew, M. A., Reynolds, C. F., & Kupfer, D. J. (1997). Benzodiazepines and zolpidem for chronic insomnia: A meta-analysis of treatment efficacy. *Journal of the American Medical Association, 278*, 2170–2177.

Shochat, T., Umphress, J., Israel, A. G., & Ancoli-Israel, S. (1999). Insomnia in primary care patients. *Sleep, 22*, S359–393.

Spielman, A. J., & Glovinsky, P. B. (1997). The diagnostic interview and differential diagnosis for complaints of insomnia. In M. R. Pressman & W. C. Orr (Eds.), *Understanding sleep: The evaluation and treatment of sleep disorders* (pp. 125–160). Washington, DC: American Psychological Association.

Spielman, A. J., Saskin, P., & Thorpy, M. J. (1987). Treatment of chronic insomnia by restriction of time in bed. *Sleep, 10*, 45–56.

Walsh, J. K., & Schweitzer, P. K. (1999). Ten-year trends in the pharmacological treatment of insomnia. *Sleep, 22*, 371–375.

9

OBESITY

Obesity (overweight or extreme overweight status) is a common chronic condition in the United States. Its prevalence increased substantially during the 1990s, such that 1 of every 3 adults is now considered overweight. More importantly, obesity directly or indirectly contributes to the development of medical disorders such as cancers, diabetes, and hypertension (Stunkard & Wadden, 1993). Diabetes is associated with obesity when its onset is during adulthood. Individuals who are overweight have a high incidence of high blood pressure and high blood levels of cholesterol and triglycerides, all of which can lead to heart disease. Being overweight has even been linked to the development of certain types of cancer. For example, in women, cancer of the uterus, gallbladder, cervix, ovary, breast, and colon are all associated with being overweight. Men who are obese also have a higher mortality rate from colon, rectal, and prostrate cancer than do men of normal weight (Kaplan & Saddock, 1998).

Even more striking is the fact that obesity has been widely identified as a major cause of morbidity and mortality in the United States. An estimated 300,000 adults in the United States die each year of causes attributed to obesity (Kuczmarski, Flegal, Campbell, & Johnson, 2000). Recent studies have suggested that thinner men and women live longer and that relatively modest gains of weight after age 18 can result in small but measurable increases in health risk (Manson et al., 1995).

Obesity is also becoming a major problem in children and adolescents in this country, contributing to poor future health outcomes. Approximately 1 of 5 children between ages 6 and 17 is overweight, a statistic prompting the National Institute for Health Care Management and Education Foundation to sponsor a conference on "Coordinating Efforts on Childhood Obesity" ("A burgeoning epidemic," 2001). This is a great concern because obesity has been related to the development of cardiovascular risk factors such as elevated blood pressure and cholesterol (Jelalian & Saelens, 1999). In addition, childhood obesity is significantly related to obesity in adulthood. This is because, early in life, adipose tissue (i.e., fat) grows by increases in both cell number and cell size. In adulthood, this adipose tissue only grows in size. As a consequence, the weight gain during childhood may be much more difficult to lose later in life.

All mammals have fat cells (known as *adipocytes*). These specialized cells store enormous quantities of fat. They serve an important survival function: They have enabled the species to survive through the cycles of feast and famine that characterized life until quite recently. In times of abundance, we could preload our fat cells with a great deal of calories to permit us to survive during a period of famine.

An interesting theory in this regard is based on the notion of a set point. The term *set point* refers to the idea that the body regulates its weight to maintain a certain amount of body fat and energy balance for survival purposes (Keesey, 1993). Each person has a particular set point (or ideal weight) that is the target for that individual. Unfortunately, for some individuals, this set point may be too high. This may be a result of genetic factors, but research has also considered weight regulation based on the number and size of fat cells. Research would suggest that the number of fat cells one has is determined primarily by genetics or early nutrition (Faust, 1980). Once a person matures past childhood, the number of fat cells is already determined and is impossible to decrease. Thus, such findings suggest that, whenever possible, it is important to prevent childhood obesity and the increase in the overall number of fat cells that results. If childhood obesity persists, individuals may have to live with a weight problem for the rest of their lives.

Obesity is not only associated with morbidity and mortality problems but can also be psychosocially stigmatizing to individuals who are overweight. The emphasis on being thin and the prejudices associated with being overweight in our society have been well documented. Obesity is considered to be unattractive, and individuals who are extremely overweight may find themselves teased, shunned, or otherwise not treated very well. Many individuals desire to lose weight, and those who are overweight generally feel bad about themselves (Brownell & Rodin, 1994). Friedman and Brownell (1995) conducted a meta-analytic study that identified some consistent psychological risk factors of obesity, including the following:

- Obesity is related to poor body image and body dissatisfaction in White American adolescent girls, college-age women, and women in general.
- Children who are obese have lower levels of self-esteem regarding their bodies.
- Being overweight is related to poor self-concept in adolescent girls and college-age women.

Thus, adolescent girls and women, in particular, and sometimes children, appear to experience some negative psychological consequences from being overweight. Some individuals who are severely obese seek treatment because they are experiencing significant psychological distress (e.g., Stunkard & Wadden, 1993). However, in general, most individuals who are overweight or obese are well adjusted and do not appear to experience significant psychiatric disturbances relative to peers who are not obese (Baum, Gatchel, & Krantz, 1997).

THE CONTINUING EPIDEMIC OF OBESITY IN THE UNITED STATES

With the realization that obesity has become a major public health threat in this country, the National Heart, Lung, and Blood Institute (NHLBI) of the National Institutes of Health (NIH) launched an "Obesity Education Initiative" in 1991. The major goal of this initiative was to reduce the prevalence of individuals who are overweight or obese, along with the prevalence of physical inactivity, to reduce the risk of coronary heart disease and the overall morbidity and mortality caused by this disease. However, the prevalence of obesity continues to increase among U.S. adults even now (Mokdat et al., 2001). The Mokdat et al. study estimated the prevalence of obesity, diabetes, and use of weight control strategies among adults in the United States during 2000, using a random-digit telephone survey conducted in each of the 50 states. This resulted in responses from 184 to 450 adults in each state, ages 18 years or older. The major measures evaluated in this study were body mass index (BMI, calculated from self-reported weight and height), self-reported diabetes, prevalence of weight loss or maintenance attempts, and weight control strategies used. The results of this study are summarized in Exhibit 9.1. As can be seen, the prevalence of obesity and diabetes has continued to increase despite previous "calls for action," like those from the NHLBI. The authors concluded that rates are likely to continue to increase in the years ahead unless effective interventions are implemented. As discussed later in this chapter, some promising approaches have been developed and targeted for clinical and public health action.

EXHIBIT 9.1
Summary of Findings Regarding the Prevalence of Obesity
(Body Mass Index $\geq$ 30 kg/m^2) in the United States,
Using a Random-Digit Telephone Survey Conducted in All States

- Overall prevalence of 19.8% among U.S. adults.
- A total of 38.8 million U.S. adults are obese (19.6 million men and 19.2 million women).
- A 61% increase in obesity since 1991.
- In 1991, four of the participating states had obesity rates of 15% or greater; in 2000, all participating states (except Colorado) had obesity rates of 15% or greater.
- In 1991, none of the participating states had obesity rates of 20% or greater; in 2000, 22 of the states had obesity rates of 20% or greater.
- In 2000, Mississippi had the highest obesity rate (24.3%), and Colorado had the lowest rate (13.8%).
- Among races, Black Americans have the highest rate of obesity (29.3%).

Note. Source is Mokdad (2000).

With these continuing trends, the U.S. government has again increased its efforts to combat obesity. Indeed, overweight and obesity now are listed as one of 10 leading health indicators included in this nation's health objectives for the 21st century. In 2001, the Surgeon General again called for a concerted effort to reduce the prevalence of individuals who are overweight or obese in the United States (U.S. Department of Health and Human Services, 2001). In coordination with the NIH, the Centers for Disease Control and Prevention, and the Office of Public Health and Science, the Surgeon General has delineated several strategies for achieving this goal, including the following:

- Improve the accessibility to nutrition information for all segments of the population.
- Focus on preventive methods in children.
- Strengthen the link between nutrition and physical activity in health promotion efforts.
- Maintain a strong national program for nutrition research.
- Work closely with the public and private sectors on local, state, and national levels to sustain the aforementioned strategies.

The most widely used definition of overweight and obesity involves the use of the BMI, a measure of body weight relative to height, which is calculated by dividing the weight in kilograms by the height in meters squared (Figure 9.1). This BMI definition is commonly used in clinical research and has been embraced by the U.S. government and the World Health Organization. Overweight is defined as a BMI greater than or equal to 25 kg/m.^{2} Obesity, which is a subset of overweight, is defined as a BMI greater than or equal to 30 kg/m.^{2} Extreme or morbid obesity is classified as a BMI of 40 kg/m^2 or more.

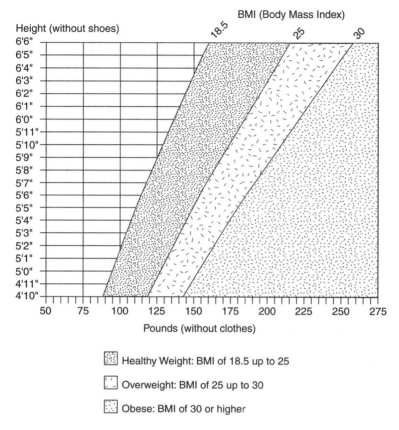

BMI (Body Mass Index)

Height (without shoes)

Pounds (without clothes)

Healthy Weight: BMI of 18.5 up to 25

Overweight: BMI of 25 up to 30

Obese: BMI of 30 or higher

Figure 9.1. Chart to determine BMI. Source is DHHS & USDA (2000).

A more precise measure of overweight is available, but the cost associated with using it is quite high. The most precise method involves determining fat composition by using hydrostatic weighing. With this method, percentage of body fat is computed from body density (i.e., the ratio of body mass to volume). This calculation is accomplished by submerging the individual in water, weighing him or her while under water, and then comparing that weight with the air-weight of the person. Although the most precise, this method is obviously too expensive to use with the general population. The BMI measurement correlates about 0.70 with more exact measures such as this one (Keys, Fidanza, Karvonen, Kimura, & Taylor, 1972).

A number of other methods can also be used to measure and define overweight or obesity. Obesity is frequently defined as weight that is 20% or greater than the standard weights listed in the height/weight tables published by life insurance companies. The table most frequently used today is the "Desirable Weight for Men and Women" table published by the Metropolitan Life Insurance Company. However, a major criticism of this table is the assumption that weight does not change significantly after age 25 and that people can be divided into "large," "medium," and "small" frames. Moreover, this table is based predominantly on White American men from the Eastern part of the United States who applied for life insurance in 1959 (Rothblum, 1989). Such tables are frequently used in physicians' offices. However, problems (such as outdated norms) are associated with using such tables to define overweight and obesity.

A popular method currently used by many health clubs is to define overweight in terms of subcutaneous fat folds. The major rationale for this approach is that one half of the body's total fat content is located in fat deposits directly beneath the skin. Using this method, the skin is pinched with a caliper in several different places, and then the measurements are averaged. This caliper procedure is both fast and easy to accomplish but also highly unreliable because the error in predicting body fat from fat folds could be ±200%!

Finally, another measurement that is sometimes used is simply looking at waist measures. The NIH has published data (NHLBI, 1998) indicating that one is more likely to develop many obesity-related illnesses if the following criterion is met: a woman with a waist that measures more than 35 inches; a man with a waist that measures more than 40 inches. Obviously, this is a very crude definition that lacks a great deal of precision.

Overall, the BMI method is usually the most appropriate one to use because it is precise enough without being overly costly.

TRADITIONAL MEDICAL TREATMENT APPROACHES

A disturbing recent finding has been that only 42.8% of individuals who are obese who have had a routine checkup in the past year had been specifically advised by their health care professionals to lose weight (Mokdad et. al, 2001). This is unfortunate, because people who do receive advice from a health care professional to lose weight are much more likely to attempt to lose weight than those who do not receive such advice (Galuska, Will, Serdula, & Ford, 1999). Health professionals who do advise individuals who are overweight or obese to lose weight usually suggest the combination of a low-calorie diet and increased physical activity. The U.S. Department of Health and Human Services and the U.S. Department of Agriculture has published a formal report, *Dietary Guidelines for Americans* (DHHS & USDA, 2000) in which physicians are encouraged to use the BMI measurement to determine a healthy weight. Physicians are also advised to encourage patients to remain physically active and to choose a diet that is low in saturated fat, cholesterol, sugar, and salt. Moreover, the "food pyramid" is recommended for proper nutrition; it suggests the following daily servings: six or more servings of grains; at least two servings of fruit; at least three servings of vegetables; two to three servings of dairy products; two to three servings of meat, beans, or eggs; and ingesting sweets, fats, and oils sparingly.

Note, however, that debate still remains concerning what the proper food pyramid is. Willett (2001) argued that there are some misleading suggestions in the original food pyramid recommendations. These include the following:

- The global suggestion to ingest fats and oils sparingly is too nonspecific. The problem is really related to saturated fats and trans fats (such as the partially hydrogenated vegetable oils found in many margarines and baked goods).
- Plant oils and whole grains should be the foundation of a healthy diet.
- Grains per se are not necessarily healthy. One should eat whole grains rather than refined grains. Even the much-touted "complex carbohydrates" (such as white rice or bread and pasta made with white flour) rather than whole wheat flour are quite starchy and have a high *glycemic index*, that is, they rapidly elevate blood glucose levels and trigger high secretion rates of insulin.
- A "Mediterranean diet," which includes a great deal of fresh fruits and vegetables, whole grains, monounsaturated fats like olive oil, and only small amounts of red meat and dairy products should be encouraged.

Different organizations, such as the American Heart Association, the NIH, and the American Cancer Association, suggest that the food pyramid be used as a general guide for making food choices, but they also suggest that one's total diet should not contain more than 30% fat (with no more than 7% being polyunsaturated, 10% saturated, and the balance monounsaturated), 15% protein, and 55% carbohydrates. The DHHS and USDA guidelines (2000) provide more specific details concerning such dietary issues.

Once dietary recommendations are made, patients need to follow through on these recommendations. Mokdad et al. (2001) reported that only 17.5% of U.S. adults are following guidelines for increasing physical activities and monitoring their diet. Thus, health care professionals do not appear to be monitoring their patients' weight loss efforts appropriately.

Note also that one potentially important factor related to the increasing prevalence of individuals who are overweight or obese in this country is the trend toward smoking cessation. Devlin, Yanovski, and Wilson (2000) have indicated that one quarter of the increased overweight in men during the past 10 years and one sixth of the increase for women may be attributable to smoking cessation. Public awareness of the dangers caused by smoking, including second-hand smoke, has been heightened, which has resulted in it becoming socially unacceptable. As a consequence, certain groups in the United States have experienced a reduction in rates of smoking. However, when people stop smoking, they often tend to gain weight (e.g., Grunberg, Brown, & Klein, 1996), thus discouraging some people from trying to quit. This happens because the effects of smoking, such as increases in the rate of metabolism and other biochemical factors leading to a decrease of adipose tissue enlargement (Devlin et al., 2000), are suddenly eliminated. Moreover, research suggests that weight gain accompanying withdrawal from nicotine often results from increased preferences for sweet-tasting foods (Grunberg, 1986). Thus, many individuals are faced with a significant dilemma: They are under significant pressure to decrease smoking for obvious health purposes but, simultaneously, such cessation may contribute to weight gain. Physicians have not been able to adequately address this paradox or dilemma faced by both their patients and themselves. Later in this chapter, we discuss smoking cessation methods.

BIOBEHAVIORAL TREATMENT OF OBESITY

Successful weight loss is usually defined as losing 10% of one's absolute body weight. This definition is based on the suggestion by the NHLBI (1998) that a 10% reduction in body weight results in a significant decrease in health risk factors. As discussed later, numerous clinical studies have demonstrated that individuals are able to lose weight and maintain this loss for several months. Some studies have even reported that long-term weight loss is a possibility. For example, Klem, Wing, McGuire, Seagle, and Hill (1997) gathered data on more than 2,500 people who were successful losing an average of 50 pounds and were able to maintain that loss for approximately 5 years. However, most clinical research studies suggest that long-term maintenance of weight loss is difficult. Before discussing this important issue of long-term maintenance of weight loss, a brief review of the initial biobehavioral programs developed for weight loss is provided.

Stuart (1967) was a classic study responsible for the subsequent widespread use of behavioral treatment of obesity. His program consisted of gradually restricting and eliminating stimuli that elicited maladaptive eating behavior. For example, the program involved guidelines such as the following: Restrict eating to specific times and places; do not eat while engaged in other enjoyable activities (like watching television or listening to the radio); remove high-fat foods from the home; avoid restaurants; and do not go grocery shopping when hungry. Using this approach, Stuart reported that, at the 1-year follow-up, participants in the program had lost from 26 to

46 pounds. Although weight loss of this magnitude has not been consistently found in studies conducted since then, biobehavioral treatment of obesity has been found to be effective (Baum et al., 1997). Many of these techniques are used in popular weight reduction programs such as Weight Watchers.

As Jeffery et al. (2000) have reviewed, the research on biobehavioral interventions for treating obesity has spanned more than 20 years. They point out that the major achievement during this time period has been the ability to enhance the magnitude of initial weight losses, which increased by approximately 75% between 1974 and 1994. For example, in 1974, the average weight loss was 5%, as compared to a 9% average weight loss in the period between 1990 and 1994. The most recognizable reason for this increased success may be related to the increase in treatment length. The almost doubling of average weight losses during the two decades mentioned has been accompanied by approximately doubling of the treatment duration. However, improvements in long-term weight loss have consistently lagged behind these improvements in short-term weight loss (with 6 months being the suggested time point for evaluating initial weight loss). Jeffery et al. have suggested a number of factors that need to be included in any long-term maintenance of weight loss. These are presented in Exhibit 9.2.

Now turning to the issue of initial weight loss approaches, note that population surveys have clearly indicated that weight control efforts are quite common (French & Jeffery, 1994). For example, one study reported that approximately 75% of women and 47% of men reported a history of dieting to lose weight at some time during their lives. Moreover, 31% of women and 6% of men reported having participated in some formal weight loss program, with 26% of women and 13% of men reporting that they were currently dieting to lose weight (Jeffery, Adlis, & Forster, 1991). In a review of the weight loss literature, Brownell and Wadden (1992) suggested that the assumption that a single treatment approach could be used effectively with all individuals was quite outdated. They proposed that, at the start of treatment, a three-part process for establishing a treatment plan should be developed with each individual, as delineated here:

1. Before establishing a plan for weight loss, patients need to be classified by their degree of obesity. People at increasing levels of obesity will naturally require a more aggressive and more intensive treatment.
2. A *stepped-care* approach should be utilized, based on patients' needs. The least intensive, expensive, and potentially dangerous approaches are used first with all individuals. Only nonresponders get the next intensive step, and so on. Thus, additional treatment components are added as needed, and they range from self-diet or self-help programs, to commercial

EXHIBIT 9.2
Factors to Consider to Improve Long-Term Maintenance of Weight Loss

- *Increase the intensity of initial treatment.* The very-low-calorie diet (VLCD), originally used for highly intensive obesity treatment, is now considered safe for outpatient populations. This VLCD approach requires individuals to restrict their food intake for periods of 2 to 3 months, and to achieve intake levels much lower than conventional low-calorie diets. Of course, this should be done under careful medical supervision. Prepared foods, such as liquid mixtures, are often substituted for some, or all, normal meals. Although this approach has produced large initial weight losses, it has not been that successful in producing long-term weight loss maintenance. Obviously, it needs to be included with other factors, as reviewed elsewhere in this exhibit, to achieve that goal.

- *Extend the length of treatment.* Some support has been extended to treating people for a longer period of time (20 vs. 40 weeks). A longer period of treatment is associated with greater weight loss, although the rate of weight regain was comparable for the two different time periods. However, a review of studies using extended contact schedules (e.g., at least biweekly for between 20 and 52 weeks after weight loss) suggests that this extended contact approach shows promise. Obviously, however, patient motivation will have to be maintained to achieve this.

- *Use of appropriate behavioral approaches to energy balance.* There appears to be no difference in the ease of maintaining a fat-restricted diet versus an energy-restricted diet. Thus, the type of diet selected should depend on patient preference and ease of adherence. More attention has now been given to including an exercise program along with dieting. Such a combined approach appears to be beneficial for weight control in the long run.

- *Enhance patient motivation.* Throughout this book, we have discussed the important issue of adherence and methods to increase it. Enhancing motivation for weight control and complying with methods prescribed are still major obstacles in the field of obesity and weight loss. Social support appears to be one promising approach to use. It may be quite useful for long-term maintenance, especially if carefully followed by physicians who provide a venue for such support groups.

- *Teaching Maintenance-Specific Skills.* In any biobehavioral treatment program, it is essential to build in a relapse prevention strategy, in which individuals identify situations in which adherence lapses may occur, learn coping skills to avoid such lapses, and get "back on track" if lapses do occur. Such skills can be quite useful in combination with social support groups. Again, clinical health psychologists can be quite useful in providing such services.

- *Medication.* Various medications, such as sibutramine (a serotonin reuptake inhibitor) and Xenical (which inhibits the digestion of dietary fat), are starting to be more widely evaluated for efficacy. With the enthusiasm surrounding such medications, we can expect even newer ones to be developed. It will be important to use such medications in combination with behavioral methods to reduce weight and increase exercise, as well as with the other aforementioned factors reviewed in this exhibit.

Note. Source is Jeffery (2000).

or behavioral programs, to hospital-based programs or very-low-calorie diet approaches, to private counseling or residential programs, all the way to possible bariatric surgery.

3. Selecting a particular weight loss treatment involves a matching decision in which all aspects of the individual are considered to find the most beneficial program for him or her. For example, some people might respond best to a group-oriented program, whereas others may respond to individual treatment. Some may need supervised exercise, whereas others may be capable of exercising on their own.

Note that most weight reduction programs should include a number of approaches, in addition to dieting, to produce weight loss and to aid in long-term maintenance of this weight loss. These include the following:

- Introduce exercise as a method of increasing resting metabolic rate and "burning" calories.
- Use social support for both the diet and exercise programs.
- Provide coping skills to help individuals overcome high-risk relapse situations (such as originally utilized by the earlier reviewed classic study by Stuart, 1967) and also overcome responses to violations of diet or episodes of binge eating.
- Emphasize low-fat diets that may help to overcome some of the adverse metabolic effects of weight loss.

Dieting Issues to Consider

The traditional method usually prescribed to lose weight is dieting. Surveys have indicated that, during any one year, up to 25% of men and 50% of women diet to lose weight (e.g., Serdula, in press). Indeed, dieting has become a very profitable, billion-dollar business in the United States. However, as discussed earlier, weight loss by this method is difficult, and the maintenance of that weight loss even more so. The forms of these diets vary greatly in terms of the degree of restrictions in calories, the relative amounts of macronutrients (i.e., fat, protein, carbohydrates) allowed, medical supervision, and cost. Initially, standard low-calorie diets (LCDs) were the most popular dietary weight loss methods. However, subsequently, more controversial very-low-calorie diets (VLCDs) were developed to produce larger and more rapid short-term weight loss. As reviewed by the National Task Force on the Prevention and Treatment of Obesity (NTFPTO, 1993), a VLCD is a hypocaloric diet containing 800 kcal or less per day, or less than 12 kcal/kg of ideal body weight per day. In contrast, a LCD provides 800 to 1,500 kcal per day, or 12 to 20 kcal/kg of ideal body weight per day. Even though some controversy still exists regarding the safety and long-term efficacy of VLCDs, they are now considered safe for outpatient populations

(Jeffery et al., 2000). However, they must be administered under careful medical supervision.

Finally, we need to discuss *weight cycling*, or the so-called "yo-yo" dieting effect, which is a common phenomenon that has possible adverse health effects (Brownell & Rodin, 1994). The effects of weight cycling have been investigated in an interesting series of experimental studies with rats by Brownell and colleagues. A number of significant results were revealed. Brownell, Greenwood, Stellar, and Shrager (1986) reported that rats actually gained weight more efficiently after dieting. In addition, the rats that had lost and regained weight subsequently had a greater preference for fat in their diets than did those rats that were never put on the diet (this would be expected on the basis of the set point theory, and the need for body fat for survival reasons, discussed earlier in this chapter). In another component of that study, a group of rats was placed on a high-fat diet until they became obese. They were then put on a diet to lose the weight and get back to their initial weight. Afterward, these rats were given unrestricted access to food. It was found that they quickly and easily regained all of the weight lost earlier. This diet–regain regimen was then repeated. Findings demonstrated that, during their first diet, the rats required about 21 days to lose the weight. However, with the second diet, the rats took approximately 46 days (i.e., about twice as long) to lose the same amount of weight. In addition, researchers found that it took 45 days for the rats to regain the weight after their first diet; after the second diet, it took only 14 days to regain the weight.

Brownell (1988) subsequently replicated parts of this study using human participants. He found that, regardless of whether participants had lost weight quickly or slowly during the dieting period, the rate of weight loss was slower during their second dieting period. Thus, the yo-yo weight loss and subsequent weight gain is a phenomenon about which clinicians need to be aware. Moreover, chronic dieting appears to be a significant factor in development of binge eating behaviors in some individuals (Patton et al., 1990). One obvious reason for this is that dietary restriction can lead to feelings of food deprivation that, in turn, can lead to overeating. Moreover, dietary restrictions may result in a "forbidden-apple" phenomenon, in which food becomes more desirable, thus leading to overeating. In addition, the set point theory reviewed earlier would suggest that dieting might actually increase weight in the long run. That is to say, periodic dieting is similar to periodic famines in that, subsequently, weight increases over the long run as the body attempts to control deprivation by lowering metabolism and storing fat for possible future times of food deprivation.

Pharmacotherapy and Weight Loss

A study by Weintraub (1992) initially demonstrated that, in patients who received the combination of dl-fenfluramine and phentermine, individuals experienced continued weight loss for as long as 3 years. Unfortunately, however, this so-called "fen-phen" medication, which suppresses appetite, was found to cause heart valve damage in a substantial number of patients and has been removed from the market. However, other appetite suppressant medications, such as dextroamphetamines and their derivatives, are still used. Sibutramine (Meridia) is currently very popular, along with other serotonin reuptake inhibitors. The drug, bupropion SR (sustained release), also marketed as Wellbutrin for depression and Zyban for nicotine addiction, has also been found to be beneficial for weight loss and the maintenance of such loss (Anderson et al., 2002). Even Prozac and Ritalin are sometimes used. Xenical, which inhibits the digestion of dietary fat, is also being evaluated. In assessing the efficacy of such pharmacotherapy for obesity, the NTFPTO (1996) concluded that such medication use, when combined with behavioral approaches to modify diet and increase physical activity, appears to help some patients who are obese to lose weight and to maintain weight loss for at least 1 year. However, few studies have documented its safety and efficacy for more than 1 year. This task force report concluded that it should be used only for carefully selected patients.

Practical Issues to Consider in Weight Loss Programs

Now that we have completed our discussion of the near epidemic and the associated negative health consequences of obesity, as well as important issues of dieting and the problem of long-term maintenance of weight loss, we are ready to review some basic issues that primary care practitioners should consider and incorporate into their standard patient health care practices:

- Evaluate and monitor the weight of patients. This can be easily done using the BMI to determine a potential weight problem. Figure 9.1 presents a convenient chart to use in this evaluation.
- If weight is a problem, recommend to the patient the need to lose weight for health maintenance purposes. Point out recent clinical research indicating that a combination of a healthy diet to lose weight and exercise can significantly reduce the risk of developing cancers, such as prostrate cancer, as shown in a study by Tymchuk, Barnard, Heber, and Aronson (2001).
- Be prepared to recommend methods, such as an appropriate diet that is nutritionally healthy (as discussed earlier in this chapter), and regular exercise. Make sure patients avoid the latest "fad" diets, many of which are based on faulty propositions and are nutritionally deficient.
- Follow up with your patients about their health status.

- If patients find it difficult to lose weight on their own, then referral to a weight management program should be made. Clinical health psychologists can be valuable in providing such services, making appropriate referrals, and gathering follow-up information concerning the weight losses made. A stepped-care approach should be considered, as discussed earlier in this chapter. Make patients aware of the importance of long-term maintenance and the importance of avoiding the negative effects of weight cycling.
- Make patients aware of the effects of smoking cessation on dieting and that those effects can make weight loss more difficult to obtain. However, the health benefits of smoking cessation far outweigh the additional efforts needed for weight management.

A Final Word About Smoking Cessation

As mentioned earlier in this chapter, both patients and physicians face a dilemma when the simultaneous needs exist to lose weight and to decrease smoking. However, this should not prevent attempts to do both, especially in light of the fact that smoking causes one sixth of all deaths in the United States each year. Indeed, some weight gain is a minor health risk compared to the risks of smoking. Nicotine is a very addictive drug contained in cigarettes, but one half of all individuals who have ever smoked have been able to quit according to the Agency for Health Care Policy and Research (AHCPR, 1996). The AHCPR has published a helpful guide to help individuals quit smoking. The specific topics covered include the following:

- the potentially beneficial effect of the use of a nicotine patch or nicotine gum for some individuals (Information is provided concerning who should use this method and how to determine what strength is right for a particular individual.)
- the importance of getting support and encouragement through counseling or support groups
- how to handle sudden urges to smoke
- how to prepare before attempting to quit
- facts about smoking, quitting, and gaining weight
- how to avoid relapse
- additional resources individuals can contact for help in their efforts to quit smoking.

SUMMARY

Obesity is a major public health threat in the United States, and its prevalence continues to increase among U.S. adults. Moreover, obesity is also becoming a major problem in children and adolescents in this country, with approximately 1 of 4 children between ages 6 and 17 being overweight. In addition, a child who is obese is more prone to be obese in adulthood. This is a great concern because obesity, overall, directly or indirectly, contributes to the development of medical disorders such as cancers, diabetes, and hypertension.

As discussed, only 42.8% of individuals who are obese who have had a routine checkup in the past year have been specifically advised by their health care professionals to lose weight. This is unfortunate, because individuals who do receive advice from health care professionals to lose weight are much more likely to attempt to lose weight than those who do not receive such advice. Physicians are advised to encourage patients who are obese to lose weight by remaining physically active and to choose a diet that is low in saturated fat, cholesterol, sugar, and salt. Biobehavioral treatment programs have been developed in which a stepped-care approach should be utilized, based on the patient's individual needs. Other approaches for producing weight loss include starting an exercise program, seeking social support for both the diet and exercise program, practicing coping skills to help individuals overcome high-risk relapse situations, and emphasizing low-fat diets that may help individuals overcome some of the adverse metabolic effects of weight loss.

RECOMMENDED READINGS

Devlin, M. J., Yanovski, S. Z., & Wilson, G. T. (2000). Obesity: What mental health professionals need to know. *American Journal of Psychiatry, 157,* 854–866.

Jeffery, R. W., Drewnowski, A., Epstein, L. H., Stunkard, A. J., Wilson, G. T., Wing, R. R., et al. (2000). Long-term maintenance of weight loss: Current status. *Health Psychology, 19,* 5–16.

National Heart, Lung, and Blood Institute, Obesity Education Initiative Expert Panel. (1998). Clinical guidelines on the identification, evaluation, and treatment of overweight and obesity in adults—The evidence report. *Obesity Research, 6,* 51S–210S.

U.S. Department of Agriculture. (2000). *Report of the Dietary Guidelines Advisory Committee on the dietary guidelines for Americans.* Washington, DC: Author. Copies can be purchased from the National Technical Information Service (703-605-6000).

GLOSSARY

adipocytes Specialized cells that can store enormous quantities of fat.

adipose tissue Fat tissue.

appetite suppressant medications Popular medications, often dextroamphet-amines or their derivatives, used for weight reduction.

body mass index (BMI) The most widely used definition of overweight and obe-sity. It is a measure of body weight relative to height, which is calculated by dividing the weight in kilograms by the height in meters squared.

bariatric surgery Surgery for the treatment of individuals who are obese, such as removing part of the intestines to decrease the amount of absorption of fat into the body.

"fen-phen" medication A combination of dl-fenfluramine and phentermine medi-cation, which suppresses appetite; originally found to prompt weight loss. How-ever, because of adverse health complications, it is no longer on the market.

food pyramid A dietary guideline recommended for proper nutrition. It recom-mends the following: six or more servings of whole grains per day; at least two servings of fruit; at least three servings of vegetables; two to three servings of dairy products; two to three servings of meat, beans, or eggs; ingesting sweets, fats, and oils sparingly.

glycemic index The rate at which certain foods elevate blood glucose levels and trigger insulin secretion.

hydrostatic weighing The most precise method of weight measurement, in which percent body fat is computed from body density (i.e., the ratio of body mass to volume).

low-calorie diet (LCD) Diet that provides 800 to 1,500 kcal per day, or 12 to 20 kcal/kg of ideal body weight per day.

macronutrients A class of nutrients, including fat, proteins, and carbohydrates.

obesity A subset of overweight, defined as a BMI greater than or equal to 30 kg/m.^{2} Similarly, overweight is defined as a BMI of 25 kg/m^2 or greater.

set point theory A theory that proposes that the body regulates its weight to maintain a certain amount of body fat and energy balance for survival purposes.

stepped-care approach to weight loss A weight loss approach based on the patient's needs, progressing from less intensive to more intensive methods.

very-low-calorie diet (VLCD) Diet that provides 800 kcal or less per day, or less than 12 kcal/kg of ideal body weight per day.

weight cycling Also known as "yo-yo" dieting, it refers to the cycle of losing weight by dieting, then regaining weight by not strictly adhering to the diet, and so on.

"yo-yo" dieting See *weight cycling*.

REFERENCES

A burgeoning epidemic—Obesity in children. (2001). HABIT, 4(13). Retrieved October 16, 2001, from http://www.habit@cfah.org

Agency for Health Care Policy and Research. (1996, April). *AHCPR consumer guide: You can quit smoking* (AHCPR Publication No. 96-0695). Rockville, MD: Author.

Anderson, J.W., Greenway, F. L., Fujioka, K., Gaddi, K. M., McKenney, J., & O'Neal, P. M. (2002). Bupropion SR enhances weight loss: A 48-week double-blind placebo-controlled trial. *Obesity Research, 10*, 633-641.

Baum, A., Gatchel, R. J., & Krantz, D. S. (1997). *Introduction to health psychology* (3rd ed.). New York: McGraw-Hill.

Brownell, K. D. (1988). Yo-yo dieting. *Psychology Today*, pp. 20–23.

Brownell, K. D., Greenwood, M. R. C., Stellar, E., & Shrager, E. E. (1986). The effects of repeated cycles of weight loss and regain in rats. *Physiology and Behavior, 38*, 459–464.

Brownell, K. D., & Rodin, J. (1994). The dieting maelstrom: Is it possible and advisable to lose weight? *American Psychologist, 49*, 781–791.

Brownell, K. D. & Wadden, T. A. (1992). Etiology and treatment of obesity: Understanding a serious, prevalent, and refractory disorder. *Journal of Consulting and Clinical Psychology, 60*, 505–517.

Devlin, M. J., Yanovski, S. Z., & Wilson, G. T. (2000). Obesity: What mental health professionals need to know. *American Journal of Psychiatry, 157*, 854–866.

Faust, I. M. (198). Nutrition and the fat cell. *International Journal of Obesity, 4*, 314–321.

French, S. A., & Jeffery, R. W. (1994). Consequences of dieting to lose weight: Effects on physical and mental health. *Health Psychology, 13*, 195–212.

Friedman, M. A., & Brownell, K. D. (1995). Psychological correlates of obesity: Moving to the next research generation. *Psychological Bulletin, 117*, 3–20.

Galuska, D. A., Will, J. C., Serdula, M. K., & Ford, E. S. (1999). Are health care professionals advising obese patients to lose weight? *Journal of the American Medical Association, 282*, 1576–1578.

Grunberg, N. E. (1986). Behavioral and biological factors in the relationship between tobacco use and body weight. In E. S. Katkin & S. B. Manuck (Eds.), *Advances in behavioral medicine* (Vol. 2, pp. 126–142). Greenwich, CT: JAI Press.

Grunberg, N. E., Brown, K. I., & Klein, L. C. (1996). Tobacco smoking. In A. Baum, C. McManus, S. Newman, R. West, C. McManus. (Eds.), *Cambridge handbook of psychology, health, and medicine* (pp. 126–142). Cambridge, England: Cambridge University Press.

Jeffery, R. W., Adlis, S. A., & Forster, J. L. (1991). Prevalence of dieting among working men and women. The healthy worker project. *Health Psychology, 10*, 274–281.

Jeffery, R. W., Epstein, L. H., Wilson, G. T., Drewnoski, A., Stunkard, A. J., & Wing, R. R. (2000). Long-term maintenance of weight loss: Current status. *Health Psychology, 19*, 5–16.

Jelalian, E., & Saelens, B. E. (1999). Empirically supported treatments in pediatric psychology: Pediatric obesity. *Journal of Pediatric Psychology, 24*, 223–248.

Kaplan, H. I., & Saddock, B. J. (1998). *Synopsis of Psychiatry* (rev. ed.). Baltimore, MD: Lippincott, Williams & Wilkins.

Keesey, R. E. (1993). Psychological regulation of body energy: Implications for obesity. In A. J. Stunkard & T. A. Wadden (Eds.), *Obesity: Theory and therapy* (pp. 79–96). New York: Raven Press.

Keys, A., Fidanza, F., Karvonen, M. J., Kimura, N., & Taylor, H. L. (1972). Indices of relative weight and obesity. *Journal of Chronic Disease, 25*, 329–343.

Klem, M. L., Wing, R. R., McGuire, M. T., Seagle, H. M., & Hill, J. O. (1997). A descriptive study of individuals successful at long-term maintenance of substantial weight loss. *American Journal of Clinical Nutrition, 66*, 239–246.

Kuczmarski, R. J., Flegal, K. M., Campbell, S. M., & Johnson, C. L. (1994). Increasing prevalence of overweight among US adults: The National Health and Nutrition Examination Surveys, 1960 to 1991. *Journal of the American Medical Association, 272*, 205–211.

Manson, J. E., Willett, W. C., Stampfer, M. J., Colditz, G. A., Hunter, D. J., Hankinson, S.E., et al. (1995). Body weight and mortality among women. *New England Journal of Medicine, 333*, 677–685.

Mokdad, A. H., Serdula, M. K., Dieta, W. H., Bowman, B. A., Marks, J. S., & Koplan, J. P. (2000). The continuing epidemic of obesity in the United States. *Journal of the American Medical Association, 284*, 1650–1661.

National Heart, Lung, and Blood Institute, Obesity Education Initiative Expert Panel. (1998). Clinical guidelines on the identification, evaluation, and treatment of overweight and obesity in adults—The evidence report. *Obesity Research, 6*, 51S –210S.

National Task Force on the Prevention and Treatment of Obesity. (1993). Very low-calorie diets. *Journal of the American Medical Association, 270*, 967–974.

National Task Force on the Prevention and Treatment of Obesity. (1996). Long-term pharmacotherapy in the management of obesity. *Journal of the American Medical Association, 276*, 1907–1915.

Patton, G. C., Johnson-Sabine, E., Wood, K., Mann, A. H., & Wakeling, A. (1990). Abnormal eating attitudes in London school girls—A prospective epidemiological study: Outcome of twelve month follow-up. *Psychosomatic Medicine, 20*, 383–394.

Rothblum, E. D. (1989). Women and weight: Fad and fiction. *Journal of Psychology, 124*, 5S–24S.

Serdula, M. (in press). Weight control practices of U.S. adolescents and adults. *Annals of Internal Medicine*.

Stuart, R. B. (1967). Behavioral control of overeating. *Behavior Research and Therapy, 5*, 357–365.

Stunkard, A. J., & Wadden, T. (Eds.). (1993). *Obesity: Theory and therapy* (2nd. ed.). New York: Raven Press.

Tymchuk, C. N., Barnard, R. J., Heber, D., & Aronson, W. J. (2001). Evidence of an inhibitory effect of diet and exercise on prostrate cancer cell growth. *Journal of Urology, 166,* 1185–1189.

U.S. Department of Health and Human Services. (2001). *Surgeon General launches effort to develop action plan to combat overweight, obesity* [Press Release]. Washington, DC: U.S. Surgeon General.

U.S. Department of Health and Human Services & U.S. Department of Agriculture. (2000). Nutrition and your health: Dietary guidelines for Americans. (5th ed.) Washington, DC: Author.

Weintraub, M. (1992). Long-term weight control: The National Heart, Lung, and Blood Institute's funded multimodal intervention study. *Clinical Pharmacology, 51,* 581–641.

Willett, W. C. (2001). *Eat, drink, and be healthy: The Harvard Medical School guide to healthy eating.* Cambridge, MA: Harvard University Press.

10

GASTROINTESTINAL DISORDERS

As succinctly summarized by Baum, Gatchel, and Krantz (1997), the gastrointestinal (GI) system (i.e., digestive system) is responsible for processing the food that we consume and converting it to usable nutrients. It extends from the mouth, salivary glands, and esophagus, through the stomach, to the small and large intestines and the anus. This system is quite long, complex, and still not totally understood. Basically, as food passes through this large and circuitous system, it is broken down into various nutrients by chemicals and fluids, such as saliva, that are secreted by organs along the way. These nutrients are then absorbed into the bloodstream and carried to other parts of the body. Waste is disposed of at the end of this long system.

The digestive process occurs in various stages, beginning with chewing and the action of the salivary enzymes in the mouth that initiate the breakdown of food that we eat. As food slips down the esophagus, it is pushed toward the stomach by a process called *peristalsis*. These contractions continue to occur as food reaches the stomach and is exposed to gastric acids and enzymes. In turn, these acids and enzymes break down the food further as it sits in the stomach and then is gradually emptied into the intestines. The passage through the small and large intestines occurs at various speeds as food goes through the final breakdown and then is absorbed through the intestinal lining into the bloodstream. This is further aided by secretions from the pancreas, liver, and gallbladder, including bile and pancreatic enzymes that help to reduce fat to tiny particles that can be absorbed. This absorption process, mostly of water, continues in the large intestine. The undigested material is converted into waste material that is stored in the rectum.

Psychosocial factors, such as stress, can increase the amount of acid in the stomach by increasing acid release and by causing the stomach to empty slower, leading to acid residing in the stomach for a longer time than normal; too much acid can give rise to ulcers. Relatedly, stress and anxiety can cause drying of the mouth, thus reducing the amount of saliva available to initially break up food. Certain behaviors, such as chewing less thoroughly, can also reduce the amount of saliva and slow the rate at which the stomach empties into the intestines or food is absorbed into the intestines. Defects in the stomach's mucosal lining, which protects it against acids secreted in the stomach, may further contribute to the development of ulcers.

STRUCTURAL GI DISORDERS: COMMON MEDICAL TREATMENT AND PHYSICIAN RECOMMENDATIONS

Structural GI disorders have identifiable structural or biochemical abnormalities. A few of the more common structural GI disorders are Crohn's disease, intestinal ulcers, and ulcerative colitis (Maunder, 1998; Whitehead, Crowell, Robinson, Heller, & Schuster, 1992). *Crohn's disease* affects the large and the small intestines or only one of the two. It is also one of two inflammatory bowel disorders (the other being ulcerative colitis). Much debate remains regarding the precise pathogenesis of this disease, although autoimmune and bacterial factors have been implicated (Anderson, 2001). Major symptoms of Crohn's disease include weight loss due to nutritional disturbances, abdominal pain, diarrhea, vomiting, and fever. More serious complications can also occur such as intestinal obstruction, bleeding, infection, and abscess formation. Moreover, the immunosuppressant medications and surgeries used to treat this disease can lead to various additional complications and problems for these patients.

An *ulcer* is a lesion or sore in the lining of the stomach or in the upper part of the small intestine or duodenum that is located immediately below the stomach. Approximately 2% of the population has ulcers, making it the most prevalent type of structural GI disorder. There are two major types of ulcers based on the location of the lesion. *Gastric ulcers* are located in the gastric mucosa, whereas *peptic ulcers* are located in the mucous membrane of the esophagus, stomach, or duodenum. (A *duodenal ulcer* is a type of peptic ulcer located in the duodenum.) Although these two types of ulcers have certain characteristics in common, significant differences do exist between them. For example, peptic ulcers are often associated with increased gastric secretion of hydrochloric acid and pepsin; in contrast, gastric ulcers can be characterized by normal, subnormal, or elevated gastric secretion levels. Moreover, emotional factors appear to play a more important role in peptic ulcers than gastric ulcers (Yager & Weiner, 1970). These two types of ulcers are also viewed by clinicians as separate disorders that may be associated with different causes. Therefore, the general term *ulcer* can be very misleading, because it refers to at least two diseases that differ in their location, history, and response to treatment.

Recently, some peptic ulcers have been found to be caused by a bacteria (*Helicobacter pylori*), which means the ulcers can be readily treated with antibiotics. However, other ulcers are not as easily explained. Of the two major types of ulcers, the greatest percentage appear to be peptic ulcers, which tend to occur at an earlier age than do ulcers in the stomach. These peptic ulcers are sometimes "quiet" in the sense that they cause no pain or discomfort; hence, they tend to go unnoticed and remain unreported for quite some time. As the lesion grows larger, the person feels some discomfort ranging from a "burning sensation" in the stomach, which is usually the first sign of an ulcer, to more severe pain. These symptoms can be accompanied by nausea and vomiting. Many ulcers heal by themselves, although treatment can markedly reduce the pain and speed recovery (Welgan, Meshkinpour, & Hoehler, 1985). However, if the ulcer perforates blood vessels in the walls of the stomach lining, some vomiting of blood will occur. Such continued hemorrhaging and internal bleeding can be life threatening.

With the isolation of *H. pylori* in the etiology of peptic ulcers, antibiotic medication is now a major treatment modality. It is also being prescribed to treat gastric ulcers. In addition, traditional recommendations are made, such as the use of antacids, antispastics, and acid-suppressing medications and the avoidance of hot, spicy foods, alcohol, and other potentially stomach-irritating foods.

Finally, we should also briefly address another type of prevalent structural GI disorder: elimination disorders, specifically urinary incontinence and fecal incontinence. (Keep in mind, though, that the urinary tract is not officially part of the GI system; it is part of the gastrourinary system.) Conservative estimates suggest that at least 11 million adults in the United States have urinary incontinence (Agency for Health Care Policy and Research, 1992). Moreover, more than 50% of all residents in nursing homes experience incontinence. In addition to the health care costs and loss of income (as a result of the inability to work) associated with incontinence, its psychosocial impact ranges from embarrassment to social isolation and depression (Tries & Eisman, 1995). It also has an additional negative impact on health because it often leads individuals to abandon various activities, such as exercise, that promote a healthy lifestyle.

Fortunately, behavioral treatment methods, including biofeedback, are effective in treating these disorders. Such patients can be referred by the primary care physician for a consultation with an appropriate clinical health psychologist for treatment. In terms of urinary incontinence, Tries and Eisman (1995) have delineated a comprehensive assessment–treatment program that includes relaxation training, biofeedback, and home exercises. The program has the following goals:

- Decrease the frequency of episodes of incontinence.
- Decrease urinary urgency.
- Decrease the abnormal frequency of voiding to four to eight times per day and one time per night.
- Decrease the number and size of protective garments worn.
- Decrease overall voiding dysfunction and the risk for bladder infection and instability.

In terms of fecal incontinence, Tries, Eisman, and Lowery (1995) have similarly developed an effective biobehavioral program. This program includes the following components:

- Use biofeedback procedures for modifying responses such as sphincteric contractions and elevated striated sphincter muscle activity when present.
- Help patients to improve their sensation of rectal distension, as well as the coordinated motor responses to the distension.
- Train in relaxation to help patients better cope with the anxiety and panic often associated with an urge to stool.
- Encourage alterations in diet and daily bowel habits to reduce symptoms of bowel dysfunction.
- Instruct in a home program to maximize overall treatment gains.

FUNCTIONAL GI DISORDERS: COMMON MEDICAL TREATMENT AND PHYSICIAN RECOMMENDATIONS

In contrast to structural GI disorders, functional GI disorders are defined as "variable combinations of chronic or recurrent GI symptoms not explained by structural or biochemical abnormalities" (Herschbach, Henrich, & Von Rad, 1999, p. 148). Maunder (1998) further described the functional GI disorders as persistent clusters of GI symptoms that do not have a specific basis in identifiable biological or structural problems. As he discussed, the Rome criteria were developed in 1988 by an international working team of gastroenterologists. Subsequently, the Rome II criteria (Drossman, Corazziari, Talley, Thompson, & Whitehead, 2000) were published, improving on the initial Rome criteria. Exhibit 10.1 lists the func-

EXHIBIT 10.1

Functional Gastrointestinal Disorders

Esophageal Disorders

Globus
Functional chest pain of presumed esophageal origin
Functional dysphagia
Functional heartburn
Rumination syndrome
Unspecified functional esophageal disorder

Gastroduodenal Disorders

Aerophagia
Functional vomiting
Functional dyspepsia (ulcer-like dyspepsia, dysmotility-like dyspepsia, unspecified [nonspecific] dyspepsia)

Bowel Disorders

Functional abdominal bloating
Functional constipation
Functional diarrhea
Irritable bowel syndrome
Unspecified functional bowel disorder

Functional Abdominal Pain

Functional abdominal pain syndrome
Unspecified functional abdominal pain

Functional Disorders of the Biliary Tract and Pancreas

Gallbladder dysfunction
Sphincter of Oddi dysfunction

Anorectal Disorders

Functional anorectal pain (levator ani syndrome, proctalgia fugax)
Functional fecal incontinence
Pelvic floor dyssynergia

Functional Pediatric Disorders

Abdominal pain (functional dyspepsia, ulcer-like dyspepsia, dysmotility-like dyspepsia, unspecified [nonspecific] dyspepsia, irritable bowel syndrome, functional abdominal pain, abdominal migraine, aerophagia)
Disorders of defecation (infant dyschezia, functional constipation, functional fecal retention, functional nonretentive fecal soiling)
Functional diarrhea
Vomiting (infant regurgitation, infant rumination syndrome, cyclic vomiting syndrome)

Note. Source is Drossman, Corazziari, et al. (2000).

tional GI disorders, broken down by categories, as delineated by the Rome II criteria. Note also that Leibbrand, Cuntz, and Hiller (2002) have developed the Gastro-Questionnaire, which is based on many of the Rome II criteria, as a reliable and economic means for the assessment of functional GI disorders.

Functional GI disorders are the most prevalent clinical condition seen in gastroenterology clinics, and they account for a major portion of primary care visits (Drossman, Creed, et al., 2000). Over 3 months in 1992, their prevalence was about 69% of the U.S. population (Drossman, Li, et al., 1993). Psychosocial factors are quite important in these disorders. Various clinical research studies have revealed that patients with functional GI disorders are more anxious, depressed, and hypochondriacal than people without functional GI problems. The majority of this research has focused on personality patterns, stressful life events, and abnormal illness behavior in individuals either with irritable bowel syndrome (IBS) or functional dyspepsia (Ford, Miller, Eastwood, & Eastwood, 1987; Herschbach et al., 1999; Porcelli, De Carne, & Fava, 2000). However, readers must keep in mind that it is still unclear as to whether the psychosocial problems that accompany GI disorders are the cause, result, or merely side effects of the disorders, or whether they are part of some other syndrome. Nevertheless, such psychosocial problems need to be addressed concurrently with the physical symptomatology. Indeed, as we discussed in chapter 1, the *biopsychosocial model* is increasingly being shown to be the most heuristic approach to medical illnesses in general (Gatchel, 1999; Turk, 1996), including GI disorders (Drossman, 1998).

Drossman's article (1998) was his presidential address to the Association of Gastroenterologists. This article, along with the Rome II criteria, can be used in primary care settings to support the acceptance of the biopsychosocial model in assessing and treating GI disorders. This model focuses on the complex interaction of variables—biological, psychosocial, and medicolegal—that patients encounter when dealing with a persisting, distressing medical condition. It accounts for the likelihood that patients' lives are seriously affected in a variety of ways by their medical conditions, thus requiring a comprehensive assessment and treatment approach designed to address all aspects of required care, both biological as well as psychosocial. This is in contrast to alternative, purely biological approaches designed to seek out the often-elusive "quick-and-easy" treatment plan that will result in a "medical cure."

We now discuss some of the more prevalent functional GI disorders and offer a synopsis of the type of treatment management techniques that have been found to be beneficial.

BIOPSYCHOSOCIAL TREATMENT

Irritable Bowel Syndrome

IBS is one of the most common functional GI disorders. Indeed, most studies examining a specific type of GI disorder focus more often on IBS than on the other functional GI disorders. It affects approximately 34 million adults in the United States and costs almost $10 billion annually in medical care (Foxhall, 2001). Initial research on this disorder was able to differentiate patients with IBS from control participants by demonstrating that people with IBS displayed increased motor reactivity to numerous stressors. Small bowel motility patterns (often referred to as *discrete clustered contractions*) were found to be specific to IBS. However, only about one fourth of these contractions were associated with abdominal pain, and the question remains concerning an explanation for the pain that often accompanies IBS (Drossman, 1998; Porcelli et al., 2000). Whitehead, Engel, and Schuster (1980) found that patients with IBS have visceral hypersensitivity, which is defined as an exaggerated experience of pain in response to mildly painful or even normal visceral stimuli. Patients with IBS reported more pain than patients without IBS, and the hypersensitivity and pain were more specific to the bowel.

The Rome II criteria for IBS are delineated as follows: at least 12 weeks or more, which need not be consecutive, in the preceding 12 months of abdominal discomfort or pain that has two out of three features: relieved with defecation, and/or onset associated with a change in frequency or stool, and/or onset associated with a change in form (appearance) of stool. These symptoms further support this diagnosis: abnormal stool frequency (i.e., more than three bowel movements a day or fewer than three bowel movements a week), altered stool form (lumpy and hard or loose and watery stool), abnormal stool passage (straining, urgency, or feeling of incomplete evacuation), passage of mucus, and a bloating feeling or feeling of abdominal distension.

Blanchard (1993, 2001) has been very influential in treating IBS with a biopsychosocial approach. Beginning with the Albany Multicomponent Behavioral Treatment Program for IBS, Neff and Blanchard (1987) developed an approach based on the idea that individuals with IBS are very anxious and overaroused and that they often cannot adaptively solve their problems. Moreover, they focus on their bowel symptoms but do not have correct information about normal bowel functioning. This leads them to label themselves as "sick" or "in need of help." This program had four components:

1. The individual gains information and education about normal bowel functioning. In this way, patients are assured that their symptoms are both real and distressing, and any misconceptions or myths about normal bowel functioning are addressed to alleviate such concerns.
2. Patients receive training in abbreviated progressive muscle relaxation. They are also required to participate in regular home practice of this relaxation.
3. Training in thermal biofeedback for hand warming is provided as a means of allowing patients to prove to themselves that they can gain voluntary control over some aspect of their bodies (in this case, hand temperature). The researchers

hoped this would lead patients to believe that they could gain control over their bowels also.

4. Training in cognitive stress coping techniques is provided to teach patients more effective ways of dealing with stressful events in their everyday lives. Moreover, they can learn to counteract negative cognitive attributions and distortions. Such negative thinking is thought to be a contributing factor to their distress, anxiety, and arousal.

More recently, Blanchard (2001) provided a detailed account of how to work effectively with patients with IBS. He also suggested methods that practitioners should use to get patients with IBS referred into their practices (such methods can also be used with other patients with functional GI disorders). The first is to consult with physicians who are likely to be seeing such patients. Providing a list of studies in prestigious medical journals on biopsychosocial treatments for IBS to the physician is an important first step in this process. In his many years of experience, Blanchard noted that a primary care physician who has a good relationship with a psychologist will not hesitate to refer a patient with chronic IBS to that practitioner (Foxhall, 2001). Gastroenterologists usually do not make mental health referrals and have to be convinced of the benefits of doing so. This is when marketing services to these physicians is important. Blanchard went on to note that gastroenterologists eventually are happy to refer their patients with chronic IBS to a psychologist simply because they realize they have little to offer in terms of consistently successful drug interventions. Such a situation often leaves the patient and physician frustrated. Having a psychologist to refer these patients to becomes a positive incentive for such referrals. Moreover, Blanchard indicated that, for reimbursement purposes, published research studies reveal that 50% to 90% of patients with IBS have some major Axis I psychiatric diagnosis through which reimbursement can be sought for treating these patients (Foxhall, 2001).

When the need arises for a consultation with a clinical health psychologist, it becomes very important to prepare the patients with functional GI disorders for such a referral. Drossman, Creed, et al. (2000) noted several reasons for such preparation: (a) Patients often feel stigmatized by such a referral, and they often lack knowledge of the benefits of psychosocial assessment and treatment. (b) Patients usually view their problems as "physical" and hence prefer to visit a medical physician because of their perception that mental health professionals deal only with psychological problems. (c) If such a referral is made after the initial medical evaluation, patients may interpret it as a rejection and assume the physician thinks the problem is "all in their heads." To avoid these potential problems, psychologists can educate referring physicians on ways to approach the referral. Drossman and colleagues have suggested the following approach:

- The physician should not totally "turn over" the care to the mental health professional. Patients may perceive such a referral as ignoring their somatic problems and might thus feel rejected or insulted, prompting them to seek another doctor for a second opinion.

- The physician should maintain some continued involvement, ranging from regular visits (if medical treatment is required) concurrent with the psychosocial treatment, to occasional visits for reevaluation, to no regularly scheduled visits but with the clear understanding of continued availability if the need arises.

- The physician should discuss with patients their symptoms in terms of a biopsychosocial disorder, rather than just a medical illness, to stimulate the patient's interest in, and motivation for, further exploring the psychosocial factors involved (such as stress, worry, and uncertainty). Indeed, we have reviewed the importance of taking a biopsychosocial approach to medical disorders throughout this book.

Is IBS caused by psychological distress, or is the psychological distress caused by the IBS? Both are reasonable possibilities. It may be that patients with IBS have a higher level of stress because of the recurrent bouts of the syndrome and their constant fear of such recurrences. Either way, however, the psychological treatment approach will be beneficial. As Blanchard (2001) noted, patients with IBS who respond successfully to such psychological treatment are helped in two ways: Their GI symptoms are reduced, and their psychological state is likely to improve to a significant degree.

Dyspepsia

Dyspepsia, which is also called *nonulcer dyspepsia (NUD)*, is associated with a variety of upper abdominal complaints such as heartburn, epigastric pain, postprandial bloating, nausea with occasional regurgitation, and vomiting. No structural abnormalities can be identified with these upper GI symptoms, and NUD is one of the most common clinical problems in medical outpatients. If predominant heartburn is not included as a symptom in dyspepsia, then approximately 25% of the population each year reports chronic or recurrent symptoms. Therefore, NUD is associated with a potentially significant economic and health burden to the medical system and, due to its diagnostic uncertainty, patients with this disorder often go through unnecessary test procedures (Lee et al., 2000).

Moreover, this disorder seems to have a significant comorbid psychosocial component. One study found that 53% of patients with NUD were diagnosed with generalized anxiety disorder (Maunder, 1998). Lee et al. (2000) also reported that patients with NUD, relative to normal patients, were associated with a significantly larger number of stressful life events, less social support, and less adaptive problem-focused coping. Thus, in treating these patients, it will be extremely important for health care providers to have help in dealing with the comorbid psychosocial problems displayed by them. Again, similar to IBS, a biopsychosocial treatment approach should be applied to better manage these patients. Consultation with a psychologist will greatly aid in the comprehensive treatment of such patients.

Rumination Syndrome

The major characteristic of this disorder is regurgitation of recently ingested food into the mouth. If reflux of acid-rich gastric contents into the esophagus occurs that is accompanied by symptoms of heartburn, then it is called *gastroesophageal reflux*. When it causes or contributes to tissue damage or inflammation (e.g., esophagitis), then it becomes a structural GI disorder called *gastroesophageal reflux disease*.

Little clinical research has been conducted to evaluate rumination disorders. In one study, though, Bradley et al. (1993) evaluated 17 patients to determine whether or not stressful stimuli can affect acid reflux symptoms. The Millon Behavioral Health Inventory was used to divide patients into one of two groups: those with psychological tendencies to report GI symptoms during stress (high GI susceptibility) and those without such tendencies (low GI susceptibility). The groups subsequently were administered three neutral tasks and then three stressful tasks. The effects of these tasks on anxiety, heartburn symptom rating, and the physiological degree of acid exposure were recorded. Results revealed that the group with low GI susceptibility had a lower level of anxiety relative to the group with high GI susceptibility, which had higher levels of anxiety for both the neutral and stress-related tasks. Patients with high GI susceptibility also reported higher levels of heartburn when under stress (Drossman, 1998). These results indicate that at least a subgroup of patients with gastroesophageal reflux reacts to stress in a maladaptive way in terms of anxiety and heartburn symptomatology. Again, this is another example of a GI disorder in which a stress management program, integrated into the primary care clinic, would be an appropriate and necessary adjunctive treatment modality to utilize.

Functional Chest Pain of Presumed Esophageal Origin

This chest pain syndrome is characterized by episodes of midline, angina-like pain that is thought to arise from the esophagus. In making these diagnoses, all structural abnormalities have been ruled out. The criteria for this type of functional chest pain have become broad enough to include patients who have chest pain with normal or near-normal noncardiac chest pain. In terms of the psychosocial characteristics of these patients, research has found that the prevalence of panic disorder varies from 60% to 76% in different studies, with the comorbidity of this disorder with major depression and agoraphobia being higher than the expected rates in the general population (Maunder, 1998). Thus, again, adjunctive psychosocial management needs to be employed with these patients.

GENERAL TREATMENT ISSUES TO CONSIDER WHEN MANAGING PATIENTS WITH GI DISORDERS

As Gatchel and Weisberg (2000) have noted in discussing the assessment and treatment of patients with pain, treatment professionals must be astutely aware that many medical patients are very sensitive to the term *psychological treatment* because they perceive it as suggesting that their physicians believe their medical condition is not real but merely imaginary. An effort, therefore, must be made to convince patients that the reason they are being asked to undergo any psychological or behavioral treatments is to deal comprehensively with their general psychophysiological functioning. Being seen as part of the primary care clinic team rather than as an outside provider can also decrease resistance to treatment. We discussed earlier the issue of patient preparation highlighted by Drossman, Creed, et al. (2000).

A pervasive misperception usually exists regarding psychological treatments—and psychology in general—that has developed because so many patients in the past have been told that their medical condition is not real. Patients must be educated about the role of psychological treatment as a component of an overall comprehensive program. Clinical health psychologists might want to use the term *behavioral health consultant* to describe their role and also note that they are health psychologists by training. Indeed, clinical health psychologists may find it useful to use the term *behavioral medicine evaluation and treatment* rather than *psychological evaluation and treatment* in their first encounters with patients in a medical setting. This helps to diffuse some of the misperceptions about the evaluation and treatment process, and it can reinforce to patients the medical nature of this assessment and treatment process.

In our practice, we emphasize with our patients that one reason for the behavioral medicine evaluation and treatment is that various medical conditions, especially if chronic in nature, can lead to pressures and changes of lifestyle that most people find unpleasant, at the very least. Unplanned and unwanted lifestyles changes can lead to stress, so patients often feel worse than they ever anticipated, and the stress can interfere acutely with physical recovery. We explain this in terms of a cycle in which the medical condition and the changes it brings lead to stress, which leads to increased medical symptoms, which leads to increased stress, and so on. This *medical symptom–stress cycle* is then pointed out to the patients as important to confront (see Figure 10.1). We also explain that the behavioral medicine evaluation and treatment will focus on stress-related issues that are intertwined with the actual medical condition. Of course, for ethical reasons, we must then reveal that the evaluation and treatment process involves psychological issues related to their medical conditions. By this time, though, the preparation of patients makes them less resistant to the idea of having psychological evaluation and treatment.

Note also that we try to avoid using terms such as *psychological problems* and *psychopathology* whenever possible. Instead, we use the terms *stress, biopsychosocial disorders, behavioral medicine,* and so on, which have a more neutral connotation. Most patients are not alarmed by these terms, and consequently they are more open to the evaluation and treatment process. Indeed, the lay public in general is quite familiar with the notion of stress and does not associate it with any negative psychiatric connotations. The evaluation and treatment process is discussed as a means to deal with stress factors that could be interacting with their medical conditions. Patients are frequently quite receptive and understanding of this purpose. Therefore, a great deal of education of the patient is needed before the psychological assessment and treatment process is initiated to reduce resistance to undergoing this process. We also reviewed this earlier when discussing IBS.

Figure 10.1. The medical symptom–stress cycle, emphasizing the interaction of stress-related issues and physical symptomatology. It is helpful to draw patients' attention to this cycle.

Finally, initiating any treatment focusing on the somatic aspect of the disorder, such as the use of biofeedback and stress management, as a way of dealing with the role of stress and its physiological counterpart, tension, usually helps patients to engage in the treatment process more easily and in a nonthreatening manner. Moreover, such treatment modalities begin to teach patients that they can indeed control their physiology which, in turn, increases their confidence that they can actively control their medical conditions. Indeed, biofeedback and stress management procedures have been found to be highly efficacious in reducing anxiety and tension in patients. These reductions, in themselves, are very rewarding to patients who immediately begin to feel a sense of relief that their overall functioning is being positively affected. Once patients are "hooked" on the treatment, they become less resistant or threatened by open talk about more personal types of stressors or cognitions that are contributing to their medical conditions.

A FINAL NOTE CONCERNING THE BIOPSYCHOSOCIAL MODEL

As previously noted, a realistic model that is increasingly being proposed for the treatment of GI disorders, as well as other medical conditions in which mental health professionals provide adjunctive treatment directly in the primary care setting, is the *biopsychosocial model*. The premise behind this model is that, by having mental health professionals work directly in the primary care setting, patients with GI disorders and other syndromes may feel less stigmatized and it may be more convenient for them than a mental health referral (Drossman, Creed, et al., 2000; Kroenke & Swindle, 2000). Studies have shown that this approach is quite helpful in improving outcomes for depression. Moreover, Van Dulmen, Fennis, and Bleijenberg (1996) have reported that psychological treatments, such as cognitive–behavioral therapy or other modalities that modify maladaptive cognitions and negative automatic thoughts, are very successful with patients with GI disorders.

SUMMARY

The GI system, which is responsible for processing the food that we consume and converting it to usable nutrients, is quite long, complex, and still not totally understood. Structural GI disorders, such as Crohn's disease, intestinal ulcers, and ulcerative colitis, have identifiable structural or biochemical abnormalities. In contrast to structural GI disorders, functional GI disorders are not easily explained by structural or biochemical abnormalities.

Functional GI disorders are the most prevalent clinical conditions seen in gastroenterology clinics, and they account for a major portion of primary care visits. Psychosocial factors are quite important in these disorders, and the biopsychosocial model again is accepted as the most heuristic approach to understanding the complex interaction of biological and psychosocial factors in patients with GI disorders. In this chapter, we discussed a number of effective biopsychosocial treatments for various GI disorders. General treatment issues that need to be considered when managing GI patients were also reviewed.

RECOMMENDED READINGS

Blanchard, E. B. (2001). *Irritable bowel syndrome: Psychological assessment and treatment*. Washington, DC: American Psychological Association.

Drossman, D. (1998). Presidential address: Gastrointestinal illness and the biopsychosocial model. *Psychosomatic Medicine, 60,* 258–267.

Drossman, D., Corazziari, E., Talley, N. J., Thompson, W. G., & Whitehead, W. E. (2000). *Rome II, the functional gastrointestinal disorders: Diagnoses, pathophysiology and treatment. A multinational consensus* (2nd ed.). McLean, VA: Degnon Associates.

GLOSSARY

Crohn's disease   A structural GI disorder affecting the large and small intestines (or only one of the two). Major symptoms include weight loss due to nutritional disturbances, abnormal pain, diarrhea, vomiting, and fever.

duodenal ulcer   A peptic ulcer located in the duodenum.

duodenum   The first or proximal portion of the small intestine.

dyspepsia   Also referred to as *nonulcer dyspepsia,* this disorder is associated with a variety of upper abdominal complaints such as heartburn, epigastric pain, postprandial bloating, and vomiting.

fecal incontinence   An elimination disorder characterized by loss of anal sphincter control.

functional chest pain of presumed esophageal origin   Chest pain characterized by episodes of midline, angina-like pain thought to arise from the esophagus, with all structural and cardiac abnormalities ruled out.

functional GI disorder   A GI disorder characterized by combinations of chronic or recurrent GI symptoms that are not explained by structural or biochemical abnormalities.

gastric ulcer   An ulcer located in the gastric mucosa of the stomach.

gastroenterologist   A physician who specializes in disorders of the digestive tract.

gastroesophageal reflux   The regurgitation of recently ingested food, as well as reflux of acid-rich gastric contents.

gastroesophageal reflux disease   A disease caused when chronic gastroesophageal reflux causes or contributes to tissue damage in the esophagus.

Helicobacter pylori (H. pylori)   A bacteria that has been found to cause the development of peptic ulcers.

irritable bowel syndrome (IBS)   A widespread functional disorder of the lower GI tract. Symptoms include abdominal discomfort or pain, abnormal stool frequency, altered stool form, and bloating or a feeling of abdominal distension.

peptic ulcer   An ulcer located in the mucous membrane of the esophagus, stomach, or duodenum.

postprandial bloating   A bloating feeling occurring after a meal.

Rome II criteria   A listing of specific symptoms, with a specified minimum number present, required to yield a diagnosis of a functional GI disorder.

rumination syndrome   The regurgitation of recently ingested food into the mouth, with subsequent remastication and swallowing or spitting out of the food.

structural GI disorder   A GI disorder that has identifiable structural or biochemical abnormalities as its etiology.

ulcerative colitis   Chronic, recurrent ulceration of the colon of unknown cause. Symptoms include cramping and abdominal pain, rectal bleeding, and loose discharges of blood, pus, and mucus.

urinary incontinence   A bladder-control and elimination disorder, associated with an inability to control voiding and an increased frequency and urgency of urination.

REFERENCES

Agency for Health Care Policy and Research. (1992, March). *Urinary incontinence in adults: Clinical guidelines* (AHCPR Publication No. 92-0038). Rockville, MD: Author.

Anderson, M. (2001, August 20). An autoimmune or bacterial-related disease? *The Scientist*, pp. 22–27.

Baum, A., Gatchel, R. J., & Krantz, D. (Eds.). (1997). *An introduction to health psychology* (3rd ed.). New York: McGraw-Hill.

Blanchard, E. B. (1993). Irritable bowel syndrome. In R. J. Gatchel & E. B. Blanchard (Eds.) *Psychophysiological disorders: Research and clinical applications* (pp. 23–61). Washington, DC: American Psychological Association.

Blanchard, E. B. (2001). *Irritable bowel syndrome: Psychological assessment and treatment*. Washington, DC: American Psychological Association.

Bradley, L. A., Richter, J. E., Pulliam, T. J., Haile, J. M., Scarinci, I. C., Schan, C. A., et al. (1993). The relationship between stress and symptoms of gastroesophageal reflux: The influence of psychological factors. *American Journal of Gastroenterology, 88,* 11–19.

Drossman, D. (1998). Presidential address: Gastrointestinal illness and the biopsychosocial model. *Psychosomatic Medicine, 60,* 258–267.

Drossman, D. A., Corazziari, E., Talley, N. J., Thompson, W. G., & Whitehead, W. E. (Eds.). (2000). *Rome II, the functional gastrointestinal disorders: Diagnoses, pathophysiology, and treatment. A multinational consensus* (2nd ed.). McLean, VA: Degnon Associates.

Drossman, D. A., Creed, F. H., Olden, K. W., Sredlund, J., Jones, B. B., & Whitehead, W. E. (2000). Psychosocial aspects of the functional gastrointestinal disorders. In D. A. Drossman, E. Corazziari, N. J. Talley, W. G. Thompson, & W. E. Whitehead (Eds.), *Rome II, the functional gastrointestinal disorders: Diagnoses, pathophysiology, and treatment. A multinational consensus* (2nd ed., pp. 221–243). McLean, VA: Degnon Associates.

Drossman, D. A., Li, A., Andruzzi, E., Temple, R.D., Talley, N. J., Thompson, W. G., et al. (1993). U.S. householder survey of functional gastrointestinal disorders: Prevalence, sociodemography, and health impact. *Digest of Digestive Science, 38,* 1569–1580.

Ford, M., Miller, P., Eastwood, J., & Eastwood, M. (1987). Life events, psychiatric illness, and the irritable bowel syndrome. *Gut, 28,* 160–165.

Foxhall, K. (2001, May). APA book notes. *Monitor on Psychology,* pp. 64–65.

Gatchel, R. J. (1999). Perspectives on pain: A historical overview. In R. J. Gatchel & D. C. Turk (Eds.), *Psychosocial factors in pain: Critical perspectives* (pp. 3–17). New York: Guilford Press.

Gatchel, R. J., & Weisberg, J. N. (2000). *Personality characteristics of patients with pain.* Washington, DC: American Psychological Association.

Herschbach, P., Henrich, G., & Von Rad, M. (1999). Psychological factors in functional gastrointestinal disorders: Characteristics of the disorder or of the illness behavior? *Psychosomatic Medicine, 61,* 148–153.

Kroenke, K., & Swindle, R. (2000). Cognitive–behavioral therapy for somatization and symptom syndromes: A critical review of controlled clinical trials. *Psychotherapy and Psychosomatics, 69,* 205–215.

Lee, S., Park, M., Choi, S., Nah, Y., Abbey, S., & Rodin, G. (2000). Stress, coping, and depression in non-ulcer dyspepsia patients. *Journal of Psychosomatic Research, 49,* 93–99.

Leibbrand, R., Cuntz, V., & Hiller, W. (2002). Assessment of functional gastrointestinal disorders using the Gasto-Questionnaire. *International Journal of Behavioral Medicine, 9,* 155–172.

Maunder, R. (1998). Panic disorder associated with gastrointestinal disease: Review and hypothesis. *Journal of Psychosomatic Research, 44*(1), 91–105.

Neff, P. F., & Blanchard, E. B. (1987). A multicomponent treatment for irritable bowel syndrome. *Behavior Therapy, 18,* 70–83.

Porcelli, P., De Carne, M., & Fava, G. (2000). Assessing somatization in functional gastrointestinal disorders: Integration of different criteria. *Journal of Psychosomatic Research, 69,* 198–204.

Tries, J., & Eisman, E. (1995). Urinary incontinence: Evaluation and biofeedback treatment. In M. S. Schwartz and Associates (Eds.), *Biofeedback: A practitioner's guide* (2nd ed., pp. 597–632). New York: Guilford Press.

Tries, J., Eisman, E., & Lowery, J. P. (1995). Fecal incontinence. In M. S. Schwartz and Associates (Eds.), *Biofeedback: A practitioner's guide* (2nd ed., pp. 633–661). New York: Guilford Press.

Turk, D. C. (1996). Biopsychosocial perspective on chronic pain. In R. J. Gatchel & D. C. Turk (Eds.), *Psychological approaches to pain management* (pp. 3–32). New York: Guilford Press.

Van Dulmen, A., Fennis, J., & Bleijenberg, G. (1996). Cognitive–behavioral group therapy for irritable bowel syndrome. *Psychosomatic Medicine, 58,* 508–514.

Welgan, P., Meshkinpour, H., & Hoehler, F. (1985). The effect of stress on colon monitor and electrical activity in irritable bowel syndrome. *Psychosomatic Medicine, 47,* 139–149.

Whitehead, W., Crowell, M., Robinson, J., Heller, B., & Schuster, M. (1992). Effects of stressful life events on bowel symptoms: Subjects with irritable bowel syndrome compared with subjects without bowel dysfunction. *Gut, 33,* 825–830.

Whitehead, W., Engel, B., & Schuster, M. (1980). Irritable bowel syndrome: Physiological and psychological differences between diarrhea-predominant and constipation-predominant patients. *Digest of Digestive Science, 25,* 404–413.

Yager, J., & Weiner, H. (1970). Observations in man. *Advances in Psychosomatic Medicine, 6,* 40–55.

11

HEALTH-COMPROMISING
BEHAVIORS

Three health risk behaviors stand out among others in terms of preva-lence and potential health complications: tobacco use, alcohol abuse, and physical inactivity. Despite well-publicized health consequences, more than one quarter of the American population is at increased risk due to each of these behaviors. Furthermore, tobacco use, problem drinking, and inactivity tend to co-occur; therefore, many people have multiple risk factors for com-promised health.

Tobacco use has long been considered the leading preventable cause of death and disease in the United States (McGuiness & Foege, 1993). It is a risk factor for cancer, heart disease, stroke, respiratory disease, and high blood pressure. Furthermore, smoking is a complicating factor for individuals who are trying to manage chronic illnesses. For example, smoking may lead to pre-mature development of diabetic complications related to both microvascular and macrovascular disease (Haire-Joshu, Glasgow, & Tibbs, 1999).

Physical inactivity is an independent heart disease risk factor. In 1990, 300,000 deaths were attributed to physical inactivity and poor nutrition (Ainsworth & Macera, 1998). Physical inactivity deprives individuals of the known benefits of exercise, which include reduced risk of coronary heart disease, hypertension, colon cancer, diabetes, mental health problems, and premature mortality in general (U.S. Department of Health and Human Services [USDHHS], 1996). Heavy alcohol use has been found to increase the risks of hypertension, stroke, inflammation and cirrhosis of the liver, fetal harm during pregnancy, and cancers of the head, neck, digestive tract, and breast, as well as violence and accidental injury and death (USDHHS, 2000). Excessive alcohol use combined with smoking increases the risk of various forms of cancer beyond the risk from either smoking or alcohol use alone. For example, the National Institute on Alcohol Abuse and Alcoholism (NIAAA, 1999) reported that people who use tobacco and alcohol have a 38 times greater risk of developing mouth and throat cancer than non-smokers who are also nondrinkers. This is in contrast to the 6 and 7 times greater risk for those who only drink alcohol or only smoke, respectively.

Primary care providers are positioned to be among the first to identify unhealthy lifestyles and intervene to help patients adopt change. Physicians should assess unhealthy habits for all of their patients and strongly advise those for whom it is relevant to avoid tobacco use, drink alcohol in moderation (if they drink), and engage in regular physical activity. This advice should be given not only in response to health problems but also as a means to maintain health and prevent the onset of disease.

This chapter reviews the published guidelines used by physicians to address these three behavioral concerns. We also discuss the role a psychologist can play within the context of primary health care to help patients adopt more healthy lifestyles. Clearly, these three behaviors contribute to a broad range of health concerns. Primary care physicians and psychologists working together to address them are key to promoting health in a primary care population.

TOBACCO USE

Most people who smoke visit their physician during a typical year. This presents an ideal opportunity for health care providers to intervene to prevent a behavior that can have a major adverse impact on health. Unfortunately, surveys have indicated that this opportunity is not being utilized (Fiore et al., 2000). Approximately one third of people who currently smoke reported never having been asked about their smoking status or urged to quit by health care providers (Thorndike, Rigotti, Stafford, & Singer, 1998; Woller et al., 1995). Another study found that less than 15% of people who smoke who saw a physician in the past year were offered help to stop smoking (Goldstein et al., 1997). Given the fact that approximately 70% of people who smoke report a desire to quit using tobacco, it is clear that primary care practitioners can improve the health of their populations by improving the delivery of smoking cessation services.

The USDHHS has published a clinical practice guideline titled *Treating Tobacco Use and Dependence* (Fiore et al., 2000). This document reviews and analyzes literature published prior to January 1999 and makes recommendations for clinical interventions for tobacco cessation. These guidelines provide helpful information for psychologists working in the primary care setting.

The overarching message in the clinical guideline (Fiore et al., 2000) is that effective interventions for tobacco dependence are available and should be offered to *every* person who smokes. To accomplish this, "it is essential that clinicians and health care delivery systems (including administrators, insurers, and purchasers) institutionalize the consistent identification, documentation, and treatment of every tobacco user seen in a health care setting" (Fiore et al., 2000, p. iv). Psychologists can be instrumental in establishing a consistent method for providing smoking cessation assistance. Their role may include setting up a system for assessing smoking status and readiness to quit. Psychologists can use their expertise to teach physicians, nurses, medical technicians, and educators how to provide effective assistance to people who smoke. Additionally, they can provide direct interventions, especially to users of tobacco who are heavily dependent on smoking or who have not responded to other interventions.

Implementation of a system for assessing smoking status is the first step for addressing tobacco use in the primary care clinic's population. A meta-analysis of nine studies addressing the impact of screening systems showed that systematic screening programs markedly increased the rate at which clinicians intervened with people who smoke (Fiore et al., 2000). Methods for systemically assessing smoking status include asking about tobacco use and documenting it as part of the vital sign assessment, and using a reminder system such as stickers on medical charts or computer prompts. Although randomized clinical trials have not yet been done, the clinical guideline panel recommends additional assessment on the patient's readiness to quit. A simple question such as "Are you willing to make an attempt to quit smoking at this time?" can be asked to determine how best to proceed with intervention. Regardless of how patients answer this question, physicians should strongly advise every patient to quit smoking. Studies demonstrate that physician advice increases abstinence rates (Bien, Miller, & Tonigan, 1993). Less is known about the impact of other clinicians' (psychologists, nurses, medical technicians) advice to quit, but it is reasonable to assume that their advice would be helpful as well.

The USDHHS guideline recommends that those who are willing to make an attempt to quit smoking should be offered at least a brief intervention. Strong evidence exists that brief interventions lasting less than 3 minutes increase overall tobacco abstinence rates. Moreover, more intense interventions are more effective than less intense interventions, and the guideline recommends the former be used whenever possible. Increasing contact time up to 90 minutes increases abstinence rates; however, contact time over 90 minutes does not appear to provide added benefit. Furthermore, delivering treatment over four or more visits appears to be especially effective.

Because a high proportion of those who smoke who see their physician are not advised on strategies for smoking cessation, psychologists in primary care might need to offer training for providers in brief interventions. The USDHHS guideline suggests the use of the "5 A's" for all patients who express a willingness to quit tobacco use. These steps are presented in Exhibit 11.1. These strategies are especially applicable to the primary care setting because they are designed to take less than 3 minutes of the provider's time.

An alternative approach would be for providers to refer all willing people who smoke to the primary care psychologist for a brief intervention. The psychologist can provide the same intervention that the physician would (e.g., the 5 A's), but diverting this care can free physician time for other matters, ensure that the patient receives expert advice in behavior modification, and potentially provide more contact time with the patient. More contact time can be valuable because it has been shown to increase abstinent rates.

The USDHHS guideline strongly advocates that all patients who are willing to go through more intense intervention should be provided this care. Intensive care increases abstinence rates significantly over brief interventions. The components of an intensive intervention are listed in Exhibit 11.2. This

EXHIBIT 11.1
Components of Brief Tobacco Cessation Intervention: The "5 A's"

Ask:	Systematically identify all tobacco users at every visit.
Advise:	Strongly advise all tobacco users to quit. Advice should be clear, strong, and personalized.
Assess:	Determine willingness to make a attempt to quit.
Assist:	Aid patients' attempts to quit by establishing a plan. Patients should take the following steps: ■ Set a quit date. ■ Tell family, friends, and coworkers about quitting and request support. ■ Anticipate challenges to the planned quit attempt. ■ Remove tobacco products from their environment. Additionally, patients should be assisted with problem-solving, skills training, and social support during treatment, both within and outside the clinic. Patients should also be offered pharmacotherapy.
Arrange:	Schedule follow-up contact, preferably within the first week and again within the first month after the quit date.

Note. Source is Fiore et al., 2000.

EXHIBIT 11.2
Components of Intensive Tobacco Cessation Intervention

Types of clinicians:	Medical clinicians can deliver messages about health-related risks and benefits and also deliver pharmacological interventions. Nonmedical clinicians can deliver psychosocial and behavioral interventions.
Program intensity:	At minimum, four or more sessions lasting longer than 10 minutes should be conducted.
Program format:	Individual or group formats can be used. Proactive telephone counseling can also be incorporated.
Content:	Practical Problem-Solving Skills Training

- Recognize situations that may lead to relapse.
- Develop coping skills for danger situations such as avoiding temptation, cognitive strategies to reduce negative moods, lifestyle changes to reduce stress or increase pleasure, and strategies for coping with smoking urges.
- Understand the facts about successful quitting, including these:
  - the fact that smoking increases the chance of full relapse
  - the fact that withdrawal usually peaks 1 to 3 weeks after quitting
  - common withdrawal symptoms
  - the addictive nature of smoking.

Intratreatment Social Support

- Encourage patients in their attempts to quit; express belief that they can quit.
- Communicate caring and concern.
- Encourage patient to talk about reasons for wanting to quit, concerns about quitting, successes, and difficulties encountered.

Extratreatment Social Support

- Train patients in support solicitation skills.
- Help patients identify supportive others, including use of hotlines and help lines.
- Contact supportive others by phone or mail to help patients arrange outside support; alternatively, assign patients to be "buddies" for one another.

Pharmacotherapy

Note. Source is Fiore et al., 2000.

type of intervention can be provided individually; however, practitioners are likely to find tobacco cessation groups to be more cost effective and time efficient given the large number of people who smoke who desire to quit.

Users of tobacco who report they are unwilling to stop smoking can be given a motivational intervention intended to increase recognition of smoking as a problem and to help them move toward readiness to quit. This type of intervention uses motivational interviewing techniques (Miller & Rollnick, 2002) to examine ambivalence about continuing to use tobacco or about quitting, with specific focus on any apparent discrepancies between patients' personal values and goals and their behavior (see chapter 3, "Diabetes Mellitus," for further discussion of motivational interviewing). Although medical and psychological providers have an obligation to discuss health concerns such as tobacco use with patients, it is also important that they maintain respect for patients' rights of self-determination and choices about health-related behaviors. This is true for both ethical and practical reasons, because overly forceful confrontation can increase resistance to change. The USDHHS guideline suggests using the "5 R's" for promoting readiness to change. These are presented in Exhibit 11.3.

Pharmacotherapy is also strongly recommended by the panel (Fiore et al., 2000), except in the presence of special circumstances (i.e., those with medical complications, pregnant women or those who are breast-feeding, those smoking fewer than 10 cigarettes per day, and adolescents who smoke). Five medications have been shown to be safe and effective and are recommended as first-line smoking cessation therapies: bupropion SR (Zyban), nicotine gum, nicotine inhaler, nicotine nasal spray, and nicotine patch.

Bupropion SR (sustained release) is an antidepressant medication that blocks neural reuptake of dopamine and norepinephrine. The use of bupropion SR approximately doubles long-term abstinence rates compared to those achieved with a placebo. This medication should be prescribed 1 to 2 weeks prior to a patient's quit date. The suggested dose is 150 mg in the morning for 3 days, and then the dose is increased to 150 mg two times daily. This dose is maintained for 7 to 12 weeks following the quit date. Bupropion can be used in conjunction with nicotine substitution therapy.

Nicotine substitution therapy is administered in the form of a transdermal patch, a gum, a nasal spray, and an inhaler. All have been shown through clinical trails to be effective.

EXHIBIT 11.3
Components of a Motivational Intervention: The "5 R's"

- *Relevance:* Discuss how quitting may be relevant to patients' disease status or risk, family or social situation, health concerns, age, gender, prior experience trying to quit, and personal barriers to cessation.
- *Risks:* Ask patients to identify potential negative consequences of tobacco use, including acute risks, long-term risks, and environmental risks.
- *Rewards:* Ask patients to identify potential benefits of stopping tobacco use.
- *Roadblocks:* Ask patients to identify barriers or impediments to quitting, and discuss elements of treatment that could address these barriers.
- *Repetition:* The motivational intervention should be repeated every time an unmotivated patient visits the clinic setting.

Note. Source is Fiore et al., (2000).

Nicotine patches are available over the counter and by prescription. Use is recommended for 8 weeks. Suggested dosage depends on the brand. One brand tapers from 21 to 14 to 7 mg, whereas another brand maintains a 15-mg patch for the entire 8 weeks. Patients who smoke fewer than 10 cigarettes per day may benefit from starting with a patch containing a lower dose.

Nicotine gum is available over the counter in 2- and 4-mg pieces. It should be chewed and then held between the cheek and gum to facilitate absorption. Up to 24 pieces per day can be used to curb cravings for up to 12 weeks. The gum tends to work best when chewed on a fixed schedule (with one piece every 1 to 2 hours minimum).

Nicotine inhalers are available by prescription, and patients are instructed to take 4-mg puffs throughout the day. Inhaler therapy can be used up to 6 months.

Nicotine spray is also available only by prescription. Recommended dosage is one to two 0.5-mg sprays to each nostril every hour, with a minimum of 8 doses per day and a maximum of 40 doses per day (or 5 per hour). Therapy is recommended for 3 to 6 months.

Meta-analyses indicate that each type of nicotine substitution therapy more than doubles abstinence rates when compared to placebo intervention, with the exception of nicotine gum, which increases abstinence by 30% to 80% (Fiore et al., 2000). The USDHHS guideline notes that, for some patients, it may be appropriate to continue pharmacotherapy longer than the recommended duration because the pharmacology is healthier than a return to smoking.

Second-line pharmacotherapies, including clonidine (a benzodiazepine) and nortriptyline (an antidepressant), are sometimes used when other therapies are unhelpful or are contraindicated. Neither of these medications is FDA approved for smoking cessation.

Once a user of tobacco has made the decision to quit, it is essential that providers address relapse prevention issues. The guidelines suggest that, at a minimum, providers should engage in active discussions with patients on three topics:

- the benefits, including potential health benefits, the patient may derive from cessation
- any success the patient has had in quitting (e.g., duration of abstinence, reduction in withdrawal)
- the problems encountered or anticipated threats to maintaining abstinence, such as depression, weight gain (due to increased compensatory eating or loss of nicotine's appetite-suppressing function), alcohol use, other users of tobacco in the household, and so forth.

Additionally, every user who has quit should be congratulated on the decision to stop smoking and be encouraged to continue to abstain.

ALCOHOL

Approximately 25% of the adult population is estimated to have alcohol problems or report drinking patterns that put them at risk for problems (NIAAA, 1995). For many of these, their primary care physician will be at the front line for recognizing the problem and intervening. To assist primary care providers in meeting this responsibility, the NIAAA (1995) has published guidelines for primary care providers that addresses alcohol problems. Although the guidelines are directed toward physicians, clinical health psychologists can offer unique skills to the aid in the application of these same approaches to help meet the need in primary care.

The NIAAA guidelines recommend that physicians advise those patients who currently consume alcohol to drink in moderation. Moderate drinking is defined as no more than two drinks per day for men and one drink per day for women and for all people older than age 65. Abstinence from alcohol, however, is recommended for patients who are pregnant or considering pregnancy, patients who are taking medications that interact with alcohol, patients who have contraindicated medical conditions, and patients who are alcohol dependent.

Primary care physicians are in a position to identify alcohol problems and advise change. Treatment or rehabilitation, per se, is generally provided by referral to specialized programs. The NIAAA guidelines for primary care providers recommend four steps for screening and brief intervention:

1. ASK about alcohol use.
2. ASSESS for alcohol-related problems.
3. ADVISE appropriate action (i.e., set a drinking goal, abstain, or obtain alcohol treatment).
4. MONITOR patient progress.

We now discuss these steps in more detail.

All patients should be *asked* a general question as to whether they drink alcohol, including beer, wine, or distilled spirits. Those who do drink alcohol should be *assessed* further about their drinking patterns including number of days per week they drink and the number of drinks consumed on a typical day. It is also useful to assess the maximum number of drinks they had on any given occasion during the last month.

One of the most common alcohol assessment techniques used by primary care physicians is the CAGE (Maly, 1993). Four questions are asked:

1. Have you ever felt that you should Cut down on your drinking?
2. Have people Annoyed you by criticizing your drinking?
3. Have you ever felt bad or Guilty about your drinking?
4. Have you ever had a drink first thing in the morning to steady your nerves or get rid of a hangover (Eye opener)?

This assessment takes less than 1 minute and has good predictive validity for alcohol-related problems (Magruder-Habib, Stevens, & Alling, 1993).

A patient is considered to be at increased risk for developing alcohol-related problems if one or more of the CAGE questions are answered positively in reference to the past year. If at least one positive response is given, the NIAAA guidelines recommend further questioning about drinking patterns as well as personal or family history of alcohol-related problems. Risk is also considered higher for men if they are drinking more than 14 drinks per week or more than 4 drinks per occasion. For women, risk is higher if they drink more than 7 drinks per week or more than 3 drinks per occasion.

One or two positive responses to the CAGE questions is also an indicator that alcohol-related problems may already exist, and providers should use this as a cue to inquire further. Other evidence of alcohol-related problems includes a history of blackouts, chronic abdominal pain, depression symptoms, liver dysfunction, hypertension, sexual dysfunction, traumatic injury (e.g., from an automobile accident or fight), and sleep disorders. Laboratory tests for assessing excessive drinking include a liver function test or serum gamma-glutamyltransferase (GGT) level.

Alcohol dependence is likely if the patient has three or four positive responses to the CAGE in reference to the past year. Further assessment should look for evidence of one or more of the following symptoms:

- compulsion to drink—preoccupation with drinking
- impaired control—unable to stop drinking once started
- relief drinking—drinking to avoid withdrawal symptoms
- withdrawal—evidence of tremor, nausea, sweats, or mood disturbance
- increased tolerance—takes more alcohol than before to get "high."

Psychologists can play a key role in assessment by helping primary care physicians discriminate between problem drinking, alcohol abuse, and alcohol dependence. Recommendations can be made as to whether the individual's drinking is best addressed in primary care or is severe enough for referral to an alcohol treatment program.

The third step, *advise,* involves a specific statement of medical concern about the patient's drinking patterns and the related health risks of continuing. For some patients, complete abstinence should be recommended. The NIAAA guidelines suggest advising patients to abstain if there is evidence of alcohol dependence, if there is history of repeated failed attempts to cut down, if the patient is pregnant or trying to conceive, or if the patient has a contraindicated medical condition or is using a medication that interacts with alcohol. Patients who do not meet these criteria but whose drinking is above recommended low-risk drinking amounts are typically advised to cut down.

The NIAAA guidelines recommend providers talk with patients about a specific plan of action if the patient expresses a readiness to cut down or abstain. If patients meet the criteria for alcohol abuse, the plan should involve a referral to specialty treatment services. This level of care involves an intensity of intervention and support that cannot be provided in the primary care setting. Patients who are not alcohol dependent, however, can benefit from assistance through primary care, and the inclusion of a psychologist can likely increase the chances of success. The guidelines suggest providers make a clear recommendation for moderate consumption levels, as defined earlier. A specific goal for drinking should be negotiated and agreed on. Patients should be helped to think through their reasons for wanting to cut down and for identifying situations that trigger unhealthy drinking patterns. Educational materials that assist with these issues can be helpful.

The final step in primary care management of alcohol problems is *monitoring*. The NIAAA guidelines suggest that primary care providers monitor patient progress in the same way they manage other chronic medical problems. At each visit, the provider can support the patient's effort to change by reviewing progress to date, commending the patient for efforts made, reinforcing positive change, and assessing continued motivation. Primary care psychologists can be the ideal providers for providing this follow-up care given their expertise in behavioral analysis and modification. The guidelines also recommend that providers monitor symptoms of anxiety and depression, especially for patients who have been advised to abstain completely. These symptoms may occur following initial abstinence but often will decrease or disappear after 2 to 4 weeks. Providers are advised to monitor GGT levels as a means of assessing alcohol treatment adherence.

Intervention should also be provided for patients with a drinking problem who do not want to cut back or abstain from alcohol use. The intervention should center on motivational issues to help the patient resolve ambiguity and move toward readiness to change. The NIAAA guidelines recommend providers use the following steps to help these patients think about their drinking:

1. Restate concern for the patient's health.
2. Reinforce your willingness to help when the patient is ready.
3. Continue to monitor alcohol use at subsequent office visits.

For patients who are alcohol dependent, providers may want to consider some additional strategies:

1. Encourage the patient to consult an specialist dealing in alcohol-related problems.
2. Ask the patient to discuss the provider's recommendation with family members and schedule a follow-up visit that includes family members and significant others.

3. Recommend a trial period of abstinence, monitor for withdrawal symptoms, and review progress in a follow-up visit.

Providers must address concerns about drinking in a supportive style that does not increase patients' resistance to change. Patients are likely to respond best to an empathetic, nonconfrontational style (Miller & Rollnick, 2002). Working to understand patients' perspectives and accept their ambiguity about changing their drinking habits can help establish the rapport that is productive for change. Patients should be offered a menu of choices for making the change, and the care provider should emphasize that patients have the ultimate responsibility for changing drinking behavior. Supporting self-efficacy is also essential, so providers should clearly state their confidence in patients' abilities to decrease their drinking.

PHYSICAL INACTIVITY

Physical inactivity is among the top risk factors for poor health. The risk of developing serious health problems, such as coronary heart disease, associated with inactivity is greater than that for high cholesterol, hypertension, or cigarette smoking (American Heart Association, 2001). Unfortunately, Americans have become increasingly inactive. The Centers for Disease Control and Prevention reported (Hahn, Heath, & Chang, 1998) that between 33% and 57% of American adults (depending on race, gender, and location) are sedentary. This high prevalence of inactivity, combined with significant health risk, suggests that exercise recommendations are necessary for many patients in primary care. Unfortunately, the majority of patients do not receive physician advice to increase their physical activity level. A recent survey of more than 1,818 patients found that only 28% had received physician advice regarding exercise, and of those, only 38% received help formulating a specific plan and 42% received follow-up support (Glasgow, Eakin, Fisher, Bacak, & Brownson, 2001).

Beginning and sustaining an exercise routine can be difficult. People with health problems may experience pain, shortness of breath, or fatigue when increasing activity. Others may have difficulty incorporating time for exercise into their busy lifestyles. Still others may experience obstacles related to finances (cannot afford a fitness club), safety (neighborhood is unsafe for walking or jogging), embarrassment (uncomfortable exercising around others), or motivation (do not enjoy exercise).

Psychologists have skills for helping people identify and overcome obstacles to behavior change that can be applied to physical activity and exercise. Therefore, the psychologist in primary care can help physicians develop and implement exercise programs tailored to specific patients and can also provide follow-up. Consultations can be provided one on one or in a group format. Individualized assistance has the benefit of being tailored to the specific person, whereas groups provide the advantage of increased peer support.

When referring a patient for assistance with an exercise plan, the referring physician should provide guidance about the type of exercise that is appropriate, as well as the duration and frequency. For healthy patients, the physician's recommendation may simply be a statement that the patient has no exercise restrictions. In this case, a plan can be negotiated between the patient and the psychologists based on standard guidelines, personal preference of the patient, and environmental contingencies. For patients with medical concerns, the physician should "prescribe" specific levels and types of exercise that are appropriate for the patient's health status and do not exacerbate the medical problem. This may require the psychologist to go back to the physician to obtain specific guidance, or request the physician consult an exercise physiologist, before proceeding with a plan.

The American College of Sports Medicine (ACSM) position stand (Pollock et al., 1998) provides recommendations for improving cardiovascular fitness. The ACSM recommended aerobic exercise 3 to 5 days per week for 20 to 60 continuous minutes. Alternatively, fitness benefits can also be obtained through intermittent bouts of aerobic exercise (minimum of 10 minutes per bout) accumulated throughout the day. To obtain optimal benefits, the activity should be at sufficient intensity to keep the heart rate between 65% and 90% of the maximum heart rate for the person's age. Maximum heart rate (beats per minute) can be calculated as the person's age subtracted from 220.

Any continuous activity that uses large muscle groups and is rhythmical can be used. This includes walking, jogging, hiking, biking, rowing, dancing, stair climbing, and swimming. Selection of an activity should be based on patient preference to make it more enjoyable and enhance maintenance of the activity. Patients should be made aware that high-impact activities that involve running and jumping have higher rates of injury that can interrupt progress. Alternating activities (cross-training) can be a good strategy for avoiding boredom and for achieving a well-rounded training effect.

Resistance training for building muscle strength, as well as flexibility training, should be incorporated into an exercise program to promote overall fitness. The ACSM guideline recommends one set of 8 to 10 exercises that conditions the major muscle groups, 2 to 3 days per week, for strength training. The guideline suggests that younger people complete 8 to 12 repetitions of each exercise, whereas individuals older than age 50 years should complete 10 to 15 repetitions. Static or dynamic stretching exercises should be performed two to three times per week to maintain flexibility.

Although the ACSM recommended level of aerobic exercise is necessary to improve cardiovascular fitness, this intensity of exercise is not necessary for improving health. Studies have shown that mild to moderate exercise can have significant benefits for preventing certain chronic degenerative diseases, losing weight, and improving metabolic fitness, which in turn decreases the risk of diabetes and cardiovascular disease. This represents a change in the ACSM's position during the past two decades. The most recent position stand states, "The ACSM now views exercise/physical activity for health and fitness in the context of an exercise dose continuum. That is, there is a dose response to exercise by which benefits are derived through varying quantities of physical activity ranging from approximately 700–2000 kilocalories of effort per week. Many significant health benefits are achieved by going from a sedentary state to a minimal level of physical activity; programs involving higher intensities and/or greater frequency/ durations provide additional benefits" (Pollock et al., 1998, ¶ 12). Patients, therefore, should be encouraged and praised for *any* level of exercise they have attained.

In working with patients to increase their exercise levels, the following tips are recommended:

- Explore the types of activities the patient enjoys. Identify any past experiences in which he or she successfully sustained exercise.
- Educate the patient about the potential physical and mental benefits of exercise.
- Make exercise functional. Examples of functional exercises include gardening and yard work, housekeeping, using stairs rather than elevators, and choosing a parking space more distant from one's destination to increase walking.
- Encourage patients to take advantage of resources in their environment (e.g., parks, fitness centers, home exercise equipment).
- Prescribe type, duration, frequency, and intensity of exercise in terms of the patient's current level of conditioning. A baseline assessment can be used to determine an appropriate starting level, and increases in intensity and duration should be specified according to a predetermined schedule.
- Suggest that the patient use social support (i.e., an exercise partner) when possible to increase enjoyment and accountability.
- Assist with applying behavioral strategies to enhance success, such as targeting barriers to exercise, implementing cues, establishing behavioral contracts, and ensuring positive reinforcement.
- Prepare the client for preventing relapse by helping him or her create a plan for responding to exercise lapses.

SUMMARY

The health risks of tobacco use, alcohol abuse, and inactivity are widely known, both in the medical community and among patients. Attention to these common behavioral risk factors in the primary care clinic is essential to promoting health and preventing further complications to illness. These health risk behaviors, however, are often not the primary presenting problem for which patients seek care from their provider. Thus, physicians often struggle to find time to adequately attend to these issues. Primary care psychologists can help ensure that these important issues are addressed in busy primary care practices by collaborating on the assessment and treatment of tobacco, alcohol, and physical inactivity problems. By using the psychologist as a resource, primary care clinic physicians can increase their preventive focus and enhance the health of their patient population.

RECOMMENDED READINGS

Fiore, M. C., Baily, W. C., Cohen, S. J., Dorfman, S. F., Goldstein, M. G., Gritz, E. R., et al. (2000). *Treating tobacco use and dependence. Clinical practice guideline*. Rockville, MD: Public Health Service, U.S. Department of Health and Human Services.

National Institute on Alcohol Abuse and Alcoholism. (1995). *The physicians' guide to helping patients with alcohol problems* (Publication No. 95-3769). Retrieved September 9, 2001, from http://www.niaa.nih.gov/publications/physician.htm

Pollock, J. L., Gaesser, G. A., Butcher, J. D., Despres, J. P., Dishman, R. K., Franklin, B. A., et al. (1998). The recommended quantity and quality of exercise for developing and maintaining cardiorespiratory and muscular fitness, and flexibility in healthy adults. *Medicine and Science in Sports and Exercise, 30,* 975–991.

GLOSSARY

maximum heart rate   The peak heart rate a person should achieve while exercising. It is calculated by subtracting the person's age from 220.

moderate alcohol use   no more than two drinks per day for men and one drink per day for women and for all people older than age 65.

motivational interviewing   A strategy for helping people recognize problems and resolve ambivalence toward change.

serum gamma-glutamyltransferase (GGT) level   A test of a liver enzyme that, when elevated, may indicate long-term alcohol use.

transdermal patch   A delivery system for nicotine substitution therapy in which nicotine is absorbed through the skin.

REFERENCES

Ainsworth, B. E., & Macera, C. A. (1998). Physical inactivity. In R. C. Brownson, P. L. Remington, & J. R. Davis (Eds.), *Chronic disease epidemiology and control* (pp. 191–213). Washington, DC: American Public Health Association.

American Heart Association. (2001). *2001 heart and stroke statistical update*. Dallas, TX: Author.

Bien, T. H., Miller, W. R., & Tonigan, G. S. (1993). Brief interventions for alcohol problems: a review. *Addiction, 90*, 1118-1121.

Fiore, M. C., Baily, W. C., Cohen, S. J., Dorfman, S. F., Goldstein, M. G., Gritz, E. R., et al. (2000). *Treating tobacco use and dependence. Clinical practice guideline*. Rockville, MD: Public Health Service, U.S. Department of Health and Human Services.

Glasgow, R. E., Eakin, E. G., Fisher, E. B., Bacak, S. J., & Brownson, R. C. (2001). Physician advice and support for physical activity: Results from a national survey. *American Journal of Preventive Medicine, 21*, 189–196.

Goldstein, M. G., Niaura, R., Willey-Lessne, C., DePue, J., Eaton, C., Rakowski, W., et al. (1997). Physicians counseling smokers: A population-based survey of patients' perception of health care provider-delivered smoking cessation interventions. *Archives of Internal Medicine, 157*, 1313–1309.

Hahn, R. A., Heath, G. W., & Chang, M. H. (1998). Cardiovascular disease risk factors and preventive practices among adults—United States, 1994: A behavioral risk factor atlas. *MMWR, CDC Surveillance Summaries, 45*, 35–69.

Haire-Joshu, D., Glasgow, R. E., & Tibbs, T. L. (1999). Smoking and diabetes. *Diabetes Care, 22*, 1887–1898.

Magruder-Habib, K., Stevens, H. A., & Alling, W. C. (1993). Relative performance of the MAST, VAST, and CAGE versus DSM-III-R criteria for alcohol dependence. *Journal of Clinical Epidemiology, 46*, 435–441.

Maly, R. C. (1993). Early recognition of chemical dependence. *Primary Care, 20*, 33–50.

McGuiness, J. M., & Foege, W. H. (1993). Actual causes of death in the United States. *Journal of the American Medical Association, 270*, 2207–2212.

Miller, W. S., & Rollnick, S. (2002). *Motivational interviewing* (2nd ed.). New York: Guilford Press.

National Institute on Alcohol Abuse and Alcoholism. (1995). *The physicians' guide to helping patients with alcohol problems* (Publication No. 95-3769). Retrieved September 9, 2001, from http://www.niaaa.nih.gov/publications/physician.htm

National Institute on Alcohol Abuse and Alcoholism. (1999). Alcohol and tobacco. *Alcohol Alert, 39*. Retrieved July 3, 2001, from http://www.niaaa.nih.gov/publications/aa39.htm

Pollock, J. L., Gaesser, G. A., Butcher, J D., Despres, J. P., Dishman, R. K., Franklin, B. A., et al. (1998). The recommended quantity and quality of exercise for developing and maintaining cardiorespiratory and muscular fitness, and flexibility in healthy adults [Electronic version]. *Medicine and Science in Sports and Exercise, 30,* 975–991.

Thorndike, A. N., Rigotti, N. A., Stafford, R. S., & Singer, D. E. (1998). National patterns in the treatment of smokers by physicians. *Journal of the American Medical Association, 279,* 604–608.

U.S. Department of Health and Human Services. (1996). *Physical activity and health: A report of the surgeon general.* Atlanta, GA: Author.

U.S. Department of Health and Human Services. (2000). *10th Special report to the U.S. Congress on alcohol and health.* Atlanta, GA: Author.

Woller, S. C., Smith, S. S., Piasecki, T. M., Jorenby, D. E., Belberg, C. P., Love, R. R., et al. (1995). Are clinicians intervening with their patients who smoke? A "real-world" assessment of 45 clinics in the upper Midwest. *Western Medical Journal, 94,* 266–272.

12

HIGH UTILIZERS
OF PRIMARY CARE SERVICES

Every primary care practice has a small percentage of patients who use a disproportionate percentage of the available appointment slots. These patients are referred to as *high utilizers* or *frequent consulters*. One analysis of utilization at a large health maintenance organization found that patients in the top 10% of the utilization distribution used 29% of the primary care visits, even when patients with pregnancy, terminal illness, or physical illness *requiring* frequent care were excluded (Katon et al., 1990). Other studies have reported that 8.8% of older patients used 34.9% of the consultations (Roos & Shapiro, 1981) and that 5% of families in a prepaid health plan used 12.3% of the visits (Schor, Starfield, Stidley, & Hankin, 1987). Some high utilizers visit frequently because their provider recommended they do so. Others, however, visit much more often than is medically necessary. This latter group is the focus of this chapter.

Primary care providers tend to be highly frustrated with a sizable proportion of these patients who are high utilizers (Lin et al., 1991). A number of factors likely contribute to this frustration. One reason is that many people persist in seeking care despite a failure to benefit from the treatment that is provided. Additionally, some of the high utilizers consistently overuse walk-in services and telephone consultation, thereby putting strain on the practice's scheduling system. The patients whom physicians find most frustrating tend to view their own health status less favorably, and report more somatic symptoms, than do other high utilizers whom physicians find less frustrating (Lin et al., 1991). Further adding to frustration, some of these patients are highly demanding and chronically dissatisfied with the care they are receiving. Not infrequently, physicians find some of their most frequent consulters not complying with self-management or medication recommendations. Finally, in some situations, the patients have chronic conditions, yet they persist in demanding a cure, rejecting any attempt by the provider to help them adapt to their conditions or manage their symptoms.

Physicians are trained to diagnose and treat disease, and advancements in medical technology have led physicians to expect reasonable success in a high proportion of cases. Therefore, when patients visit the clinic frequently, without signs of progress, many physicians feel unprepared to handle them. The training and expertise of a clinical health psychologist can be invaluable to physicians for working with these high utilizers. Many of these patients display physical symptoms that are rooted in psychosocial stress or emotional distress (Katon et al., 1990). However, they usually do not view themselves as having psychiatric problems (Karlsson, Lehtinen, & Joukamaa, 1994) and, therefore, will often refuse a referral to specialty mental health care.

The needs of these patients, and the frustrations of their physicians, point to the benefits of integrating behavioral health care (and specifically, a clinical health psychologist) into the primary care team. Offering behavioral health care in the primary care clinic, when appropriate, provides the physician with a specialized resource for addressing patients' psychosocial or psychological concerns, and it does so in a way that is more acceptable to patients than a referral to specialty mental health services. These patients, however, who are often dissatisfied with their care already, must not be given the perception that they are being "dumped" on a mental health provider. Furthermore, integrated primary care enhances the collaboration between physician and psychologist.

WHO ARE THE HIGH-UTILIZING PATIENTS?

Gill and Sharpe (1999) reviewed the literature on frequent consulters in general medical practices to better understand why some patients consult their doctors more frequently than others. They found 34 studies, published between 1954 and 1997, and conducted primarily in the United Kingdom, the United States, and Scandinavia. These studies defined *frequent consulter* or *high utilizer* in a variety of ways. Some set a cutoff in the distribution of consultation rates, usually either the top 10% or 25%. Other studies used a minimum number of visits in a given year to define a frequent consulter.

Criteria ranged from 6 to 20 visits per year, although most studies used a minimum of between 9 and 14 visits per year.

This review (Gill & Sharpe, 1999) demonstrated that several demographic variables are associated with high utilization rates. Women tend to be frequent consulters more often than men in the majority of the studies. Children and older people also have higher consultation rates than the general population. When children or older populations are analyzed separately, however, the proportion of frequent consulters is similar to that of other age groups. Gill and Sharpe also reported evidence for associations between high medical utilization and characteristics such as low income, being single, marital breakdown, and unemployment.

Most notable in this review is the finding that the rates of physical disease were much higher among high utilizers than among patients with average consultation rates. Some of the common medical conditions among high utilizers are cardiovascular disease, chronic pain, cancer, and respiratory disease. Studies that reviewed medical records found the rates of physical disease among high utilizers to be 40% to 50%. Gill and Sharpe (1999) reported that no studies existed to contradict this outcome. This finding is in contrast to the traditional view that high utilizers typically do not have "real" physiological conditions. The review also found, however, that about 50% of high-utilizing patients were psychologically distressed or were likely to have a psychiatric disorder. The most frequent conditions observed were depressive disorders, anxiety disorders, and somatization disorder; however, as noted earlier, most of these patients do not view themselves as psychiatrically ill (Karlsson, Lehtinen, & Joukamaa, 1994). Other common characteristics among frequent utilizers of health care include poor perception of health, a tendency to view common bodily sensations as abnormal, an *external locus of control*, and negative mood from intrinsic causes.

We should note here that many high-utilizing patients may be best managed by regular physician visits and, thus, frequent consulting is not inappropriate. This would include patients with chronic diseases who are benefiting from treatment, as well as those with acute conditions, such as pregnancy. Care for these patients is likely to be well incorporated into the standard primary care practice. The 50% of high utilizers who can be classified as "distressed" (Katon et al., 1990) may include most of the patients who do not respond well to biologically based medical care, and they may be the patients most in need of collaborative care from a health psychologist.

ROLE OF THE HEALTH PSYCHOLOGIST WITH HIGH-UTILIZING PATIENTS

Substantial evidence suggests that treatments targeting distress and psychosocial concerns among high-utilizing patients can not only reduce distress but can also decrease utilization. In fact, Strosahl (1998) listed "limiting unnecessary medical utilization" as one of the three primary outcome arenas for integrated care. A clinical health psychologist is likely to be the most qualified person on the primary care team to provide the necessary treatment.

Assessing and treating depression is one area in which health psychologists can make a significant impact among high-utilizing patients. Studies have demonstrated that depressed patients use medical care at a significantly higher rate, and have significantly greater total medical costs, than do nondepressed patients (Callahan, Hui, Nienaber, Musick, & Tierney, 1994; Levenson, Hamer, & Rossiter, 1990). Likewise, a large percentage of patients who are high utilizers also experience active depression that is either not recognized or not being treated successfully (Pearson et al., 1999). Two recent studies provided systematic treatment to high utilizers with depression, and they have shown significant clinical improvement (Katzelnick et al., 2000; Simon et al., 2001). Although these studies did not evaluate the impact of treatment on utilization rates, they do indicate that high utilizers, as a group, can be clinically responsive to mental health interventions. A number of studies, however, have also demonstrated that treatment of depression can reduce overall medical utilization. This literature has been reviewed extensively by Simon and Katzelnick (1997).

As noted in other chapters, depression can be effectively treated in primary care using a number of formats. Psychologists can help primary care providers recognize depression through screening programs and through consultative evaluations. They can recommend antidepressant medications, when indicated, and provide brief cognitive–behavioral therapy. Bibliotherapy (Jamison & Scogin, 1995) and group treatment (Peterson & Halstead, 1998) are other avenues that might be applied for treating depression in high-utilizing patients.

Although direct mental health treatment has been shown to be effective, psychiatric consultation to general physicians has been less successful with this population. Katon and colleagues (1992) studied the impact of psychiatric consultation on physicians in their work with distressed high utilizers. In the 12 months after consultations, they found increased prescription rates by the physicians who received the consultations; however, no significant differences were seen among intervention patients and controls in psychiatric distress, functional disability, or utilization of health care at 6 and 12 months.

Olbrisch (1981) evaluated the impact of a brief stress management program on high-utilizing patients. The 1-hour education program was designed to increase patients' awareness of psychological and social factors that make people prone to illness and to inappropriate use of medical resources. The program resulted in reduced utilization for a short time, but the effect dissipated over time.

Evidence also suggests that high-utilizing patients may be helped by focused efforts to assist them in knowing when it is appropriate to consult with their primary care physicians. Environmental contingencies, faulty beliefs about symptoms and medical care, and past modeling may contribute to frequent unnecessary medical visits. Education that targets these factors can reduce unnecessary visits. One study applied an educational intervention to high-utilizing patients that addressed personal decision making about the use of medical care (Vickery et al., 1983). Patients given the materials in the form of written communication had significant decreases in total medical visits (17%) and minor illness visits (35%) compared to a control group. Although a telephone information service was also offered, many patients did not use it.

FORMATS FOR WORKING WITH HIGH-UTILIZING PATIENTS

Patients who seek "unnecessary" medical care on a frequent basis clearly have needs that should be attended to. The frustrations felt by primary care providers and their frequently consulting patients may stem largely from the fact that traditional primary care services do not "fit" the needs of these patients. Primary care physicians' training and practice focus on biological medicine, whereas these patients often have significant psychosocial needs. Initiatives that are aimed at high-utilizing patients must help patients shift to care that allows their psychosocial needs to be met through more frequent, but less costly, services than can be provided through traditional primary care appointments (Strosahl, 1998).

Two pilot programs initiated by Kaiser Permanente Medical Group are potential mechanisms for meeting high-utilizing patients' needs for regular clinic contact within a busy primary care practice. *Drop-in group medical appointments,* or DIGMAs, involve group-setting medical visits that are available on a weekly basis ("DIGMAs," 2001). The groups are led by a behavioral health provider and a physician, and they last for 90 minutes. DIGMAs were originally designed to improve access to appointments, but they also are an efficient way to manage patients who require frequent visits. Furthermore, the group setting provides social support that might otherwise be unavailable to many patients. The sessions generally begin with the behavioral health provider giving a brief summary of the DIGMA concept and setting the ground rules for the meeting. Next, each patient has an opportunity to state what he or she needs during that appointment. A list of names and problems is created from this initial go-round, and the two providers decide on how best to approach the agenda for that particular session. Each patient, in turn, then discusses his or her particular needs. The physician covers medication issues, individualized for each patient, while the behavioral health provider leads a discussion on things patients can do to manage health in each topic area that arises. The physician sits at the computer and documents in each patient's chart during the course of the group session. The pilot project, conducted at four Kaiser Permanente clinics, has demonstrated high levels of satisfaction among patients and their providers and has improved access to the clinic dramatically.

A second initiative developed at Kaiser Permanente is called the *cooperative health care clinic* (CHCC; Scott, Gade, McKenzie, & Venohr, 1998). This program was initially developed specifically for high-utilizing older patients, but has also been used with a variety of special populations, such as for well-baby checks and disease management programs. With the CHCC concept, groups of 20 consistent members meet on a monthly basis. New members are recruited and added if numbers drop off due to death or members choosing to discontinue. Each session includes 15 minutes of warm-up and socialization, 30 minutes of education, 30 to 40 minutes of interactive time with nurses and physicians (including blood pressure checks, routine injections, and physical exams), 10 minutes for a question-and-answer period, and 5 minutes for planning the next meeting. After the group session, 60 minutes of provider time are set aside for patients to meet privately with the physician, as needed. During the group time, members are encouraged to interact with each other, providing ideas, feedback, and support. Furthermore, the CHCC group is consistently focused on helping patients be participants in the process of health care decision making; members are encouraged not to be passive recipients of care. Results of the pilot evaluation at Kaiser showed increased satisfaction for patients and their providers, improved quality of care, and cost savings in the areas of hospitalization, emergency room visits, nursing home stays, and referrals to subspecialties (Scott et al., 1998).

Scott and colleagues (1998) emphasized that the premise of the CHCC group is to offer quality, cost-effective care that is provided by the most appropriate member of the primary care team. Although the Kaiser CHCC groups did not use psychologists, integrated primary care clinics would most likely find the clinical health psychologist to be ideal for this role. The health psychologist can play key roles in group facilitation (a skill in which most physicians have little formal training), education on the role of biopsychosocial factors in health and illness, and application of self-management strategies. Additionally, the psychologist can offer brief, private consultations to patients following the group session, similar to that provided by the physician, to better meet the psychosocial needs of the patients.

A final approach for meeting the needs of high-utilizing patients is through regular individual consultation. Strosahl (1998) referred to this as *specialty consultation* and suggested that it should consume approximately 10% of a primary mental health provider's time. In this model, the physician refers high-utilizing patients who have psychosocial or behavioral health needs to the psychologist for comanagement. Patients are seen by the psychologist at regularly scheduled intervals, although appointments are relatively infrequent (e.g., monthly or quarterly). This type of care may be continued for months or even years with an individual patient. This strategy diverts nonmedical aspects of care away from the physician, whose appointments are more expensive and more in demand, while providing the patient with skills for coping and self-management, as well as addressing psychosocial concerns.

SUMMARY

A small percentage of patients utilize a significant proportion of appointments in most primary care practices. Although some of these patients have a higher than average number of appointments due to the acuity of their medical problems, others use care frequently due to psychosocial problems that are manifesting as physical symptoms. To decrease suffering and reduce unnecessary utilization, these individuals should receive care focused on their true needs, and, in many instances, these patients need more than biologically based medical care. Integrated psychologists can help ensure that this occurs and, in many cases, they are the best providers to deliver this type of care. Some patients will require frequent contact to meet their needs, and a variety of formats can be used to facilitate these contacts, including individual consultation and group medical appointments. Such services will help ensure that high-quality care is provided to some of the clinic's neediest patients in a way that is least disruptive to the functioning of the practice.

RECOMMENDED READING

Gill, D., & Sharpe, M. (1999). Frequent consulters in general medical practice: A systematic review of studies of prevalence, associations, and outcome. *Journal of Psychosomatic Research, 47,* 115–130.

GLOSSARY

cooperative health care clinics   A format for seeing patients at regular intervals for medical care, education, and support. Groups of patients, with consistent membership, meet monthly. Patients are encouraged to be active participants in health care decision making.

drop-in group medical appointments (DIGMAs)   A group format for providing medical care to patients who require frequent visits. The group is cofacilitated by a behavioral health provider and a physician.

external locus of control The perception that control in one's life is mediated by factors outside of oneself.

somatization The manifestation of psychosocial stress or psychological issues in the form of physical symptoms.

specialty consultation A model for meeting the needs of high-utilizing patients in which a primary care psychology consultant sees patients for brief, regularly scheduled visits on an infrequent basis. Care is comanaged by the psychologist and the physician. The goal is to divert nonmedical aspects of care away from the physician.

REFERENCES

Callahan, C., Hui, S. L., Nienaber, N. A., Musick. B. S., & Tierney, W. M. (1994). Longitudinal study of depression and health services use among elderly primary care patients. *Journal of the American Geriatric Society, 42,* 833–838.

DIGMAs: Satisfaction Rx for doctors and patients. (2001, June). *Hospital Peer Review, 26,* 81–82.

Gill, D., & Sharpe, M. (1999). Frequent consulters in general medical practice: A systematic review of studies of prevalence, associations, and outcome. *Journal of Psychosomatic Research, 47,* 115–130.

Jamison, C., & Scogin, F. (1995). The outcome of cognitive bibliotherapy with depressed adults. *Journal of Consulting and Clinical Psychology, 63,* 644–650.

Karlsson, H., Lehtinen, V., & Joukamaa, M. (1994). Frequent attenders of Finnish public primary health care: Sociodemographic characteristics and physical morbidity. *Family Practice, 11,* 424–430.

Katon, W., Von Korff, M., Lin, E., Bush, T., Russo, J., Lipscomb, P., et al. (1992). A randomized trial of psychiatric consultation with distressed high utilizers. *General Hospital Psychiatry, 14,* 83–85.

Katon, W., Von Korff, M., Lin, E., Lipscomb, P., Russo, J., Wagner, E., et al. (1990). Distressed high utilizers of medical care. DSM-III-R diagnoses and treatment needs. *General Hospital Psychiatry, 12,* 355–362.

Katzelnick, D. J., Simon, G. E., Pearson, S. D., Manning, W. G., Helstad, C. S., Henk, H. J., et al. (2000). Randomized trial of a depression management program in high utilizers of medical care. *Archives of Family Medicine, 9,* 345–351.

Levenson, J., Hamer, R. M., & Rossiter, L. F. (1990). Relation of psychopathology in general medical inpatients to use and cost of services. *American Journal of Psychiatry, 147,* 1498–1503.

Lin, E. H., Katon, W., Von Korff, M., Bush, T., Lipscomb, P., Russo, J., et al. (1991). Frustrating patients: Physician and patient perspectives among distressed high users of medical services. *Journal of General Internal Medicine, 6,* 259–260.

Olbrisch, M. E. (1981). Evaluation of a stress management program for high utilizers of a prepaid university health service. *Medical Care, 19,* 153–159.

Pearson, S. D., Katzelnick, D. J., Simon, G. E., Manning, W. G., Helstad, C. P., & Henk, H. J. (1999). Depression among high utilizers of medical care. *Journal of Internal Medicine, 14,* 461–468.

Peterson, A. L., & Halstead, T. S. (1998). Group cognitive behavior therapy for depression in a community setting: A clinical replication series. *Behavior Therapy, 29,* 3–18.

Roos, N. P., & Shapiro, E. (1981). The Manitoba longitudinal study on aging: Preliminary findings on health care utilization by the elderly. *Medical Care, 19,* 644–657.

Schor, E., Starfield, B., Stidley, C., & Hankin, J. (1987). Family health: Utilization and effects of family membership. *Medical Care, 25,* 616–626.

Scott, J., Gade, G., McKenzie, M., & Venohr, I. (1998). Cooperative health care clinics: A group approach to individual care. *Geriatrics, 53,* 68–81.

Simon, G. E., & Katzelnick, D. J. (1997). Depression, use of medical services, and cost-offset effects. *Journal of Psychosomatic Research, 42,* 333–344.

Simon, G. E., Manning, W. G., Katzelnick, D. J., Pearson, S. D., Henk, H. J., & Helstad, C. S. (2001). Cost-effectiveness of systemic depression treatment for high utilizers of general medical care. *Archives of General Psychiatry, 58,* 181–187.

Strosahl, K. (1998). Integrating behavioral health and primary care services: The primary mental health care model. In A. Blount (Ed.), *Integrated primary care: The future of medical and mental health collaboration* (pp. 139–166). New York: W. W. Norton.

Vickery, D. M., Kalmer, H., Lowry, D., Constantine, M., Wright, E., & Loren, W. (1983). Effect of a self-care education program on medical visits. *Journal of the American Medical Association, 250,* 2952–2956.

13

COPING WITH CHRONIC
OR TERMINAL ILLNESS

Coping with chronic illness is one of the most challenging areas in the field of medicine (Baum, Gatchel, & Krantz, 1997). Many of the diseases discussed in this book, such as diabetes, hypertension, and gastrointestinal disorders, are not illnesses that one can completely get over or forget. That is to say, such diseases are usually not cured by a specific treatment. For example, diabetes and hypertension are essentially lifetime diseases that are controlled rather than cured. The use of insulin, pain-reducing analgesics, dietary restrictions, and so on, often allow individuals with these diseases to live normal lives, even though the underlying conditions remain with them. These diseases require special coping skills and health care (Baum et al., 1997). Patients must often learn to cope with pain, various symptoms that may produce discomfort, physical impairment, and changes in activities of daily living associated with their disease and its treatment. Some forms of treatment, such as pharmacotherapy, often have various side effects that may be as uncomfortable and disruptive as the actual symptoms of the disease.

Thus, coping with chronic illness requires dealing with all of the preceding factors. Activities of daily living often change because individuals' former ways of doing things usually are disrupted or need to be abandoned. At the same time, new fears are present (such as fear of progression of the disease),

213

and plans for the future may also need to be changed. Patients and their health care providers often face formidable difficulties associated with chronic illness and treatment. As discussed in the next section, many important coping issues are common to a broad range of diseases, and a number of psychosocial factors (such as control, denial, and social support) are important in coping with a variety of chronic diseases. Later in this chapter, we discuss pain-related symptoms, recovery from heart attack, and coping with cancer and acquired immune deficiency syndrome (AIDS) as examples of the major variables and processes associated with chronic disease. Indeed, many researchers have examined how patients cope with diseases such as cancer, diabetes, arthritis, kidney disease, AIDS, and chronic lung disease (Antonucci, Ajrouch, & Janevic, 1999; Cox & Gonder-Frederick, 1992; Zautra & Manne, 1992).

COPING MECHANISMS: AN OVERVIEW

As Boothby, Thorn, Stroud, and Jensen (1996) have noted, the most heuristic and common theoretical framework utilized to conceptualize coping is the *transactional model of stress*. This transactional model of stress was originally introduced by Lazarus and Folkman (1984), and it highlights a number of important factors and processes involved in coping with stress, such as those associated with chronic illness. These factors and processes include the following:

- Individual or dispositional variables, such as one's personality, social roles, or biobehavioral characteristics, can affect an individual's response to a stressor such as chronic illness.
- Individuals often engage in an array of ever-changing and evolving appraisal processes that may influence their emotional responses to the chronic illness, including the potential coping responses.
- There are basically three types of stressful appraisals: those that suggest that the chronic disease poses a threat; those that suggest that the chronic disease poses a challenge; or those that suggest that the chronic disease will result in possible harm or loss.
- Beliefs about possible coping options, and their potential effectiveness, are frequently referred to as *secondary appraisals*.
- The actual coping responses utilized by patients to manage specific external or internal demands of a chronic disease will ultimately affect important adaptation outcomes, such as mental and physical health, social functioning, morale, and quality of life.

A number of specific coping strategies, and subsequent attempts at adjustment to chronic illnesses, have been examined in the clinical research literature. Issues related to coping with chronic and terminal illness are reviewed in Exhibit 13.1.

TRADITIONAL MEDICAL TREATMENT APPROACHES AND PHYSICIAN RECOMMENDATIONS

Health care providers tend to withhold or overly simplify information about chronic illnesses and their implications when interacting with patients. This tendency negatively affects attempts by patients to cope

---

EXHIBIT 13.1
Coping and Adjustment Issues Related to Chronic or Terminal Illness

- *Perceived lack of control and helplessness:* Consistent clinical research has demonstrated that a perceived lack of control over important events, and the resultant feelings of helplessness, is a potent stressor and results in reduced motivation and emotional distress such as anxiety and depression. It also negatively affects health outcomes.
- *Catastrophizing:* Related to helplessness, this is defined as one's use of excessive and exaggerated negative self-statements when faced with negative events (such as a chronic illness). Catastrophizing has been associated with higher levels of psychosocial distress and dysfunction, poorer physical functioning and disability, frequent reports of pain interference in daily activities, and lower levels of general activity.
- *Hardiness:* This is a very different coping style compared to the previous two. Hardiness refers to the belief that one has control over what happens to oneself, a strong sense of purpose or commitment to achieve a particular goal, and an enduring "zest" for challenge.
- *Optimism:* This reflects a fundamental bias to view the world as benign and controllable, and a general expectation of positive outcomes. It is related to perceived control and self-efficacy, and has also been associated with more positive health outcomes.
- *Praying/hoping:* Many individuals use prayer as a method to help them overcome poor health and suffering or to have a positive response such as "I have faith in my doctors to cure my illness." Unfortunately, these passive coping methods have not been found to be very adaptive in helping to adjust and deal with chronic illnesses, such as chronic pain.
- *Distraction/diverting attention:* The ability to regularly engage in distracting activities allows less time for individuals to overly ruminate or catastrophize about their chronic illnesses. This type of coping results in a more positive mood. Moreover, it increases the probability of more interaction with others, thus enhancing the positive effects of social support.
- *Positive coping self-statements:* Numerous studies have found that positive self-statements are often associated with more adaptive functioning in the face of adversity. Many cognitive–behavioral treatment techniques include training in positive self-statements as an integral component of the overall treatment strategy.

---

effectively. For example, some physicians do not always inform patients that they have cancer or some other fatal disease when the prognosis is not good (Baum et al., 1997). One reason for this is the fear that patients may become depressed or even suicidal. Mount, Jones, and Patterson (1974) documented the reluctance of physicians to disclose information fully to patients. Fortunately, this tendency to withhold information has diminished somewhat since the 1970s. In fact, many physicians now inform some, or all, of their patients about their cancer diagnoses (Greenwald & Nevitt, 1982). Nevertheless, some information is still frequently withheld, and this can pose problems for patients who are not given the opportunity to engage in appropriate methods of coping with the potential negative consequences of their disease (Bedell & Delbanco, 1984).

As discussed later, health care providers can provide guidance to stimulate an appropriate coping mechanism in patients, and this can have a very positive therapeutic impact on the chronic disease state. As we reviewed in Exhibit 13.1, inappropriate coping strategies, which patients may automatically engage in if not provided this type of guidance, can have a major negative impact. More positive coping mechanisms, as we will see, can have quite a positive impact on the disease-related functioning of patients.

Finally, medical providers can empower patients to play a larger role in their health care. Empowering patients is often quite beneficial in increasing adherence and decreasing medical errors. Indeed, in 2000, the U.S. Institute of Medicine published a report on patient safety, entitled *To Err Is Human* (Kohn, Corrigan, & Donaldson, 2000). Together with the U.S. Agency for Healthcare Research and Quality, a number of important recommendations have been made concerning what patients should know. These are presented in Exhibit 13.2.

CHRONIC PATIENT MANAGEMENT ISSUES

Quite often, the treatment management of patients with chronic illnesses can be quite challenging. A method to help practitioners anticipate patient management issues has been developed. The Millon Behavioral Health Inventory (MBHI) was originally designed for patients undergoing evaluation or treatment in medical settings for physical disorders (Millon, Greer, & Meagher, 1982).

The major intent of the MBHI is to provide relevant information for making treatment decisions for patients with physical problems. Such information involves factors such as the patient's style of relating to health care personnel and probable responses to illness and treatment interventions. The MBHI can be especially valuable for health care professionals in deciding the best patient-management philosophy for each patient, especially those with chronic illnesses. It can be quite useful for primary care physi-

EXHIBIT 13.2
Recommendations to Patients for Improving Medical Safety and Quality of Care

- Patients should be involved in their health care (e.g., question anyone who is involved in their health care). Also, they should learn about their conditions and treatments by asking their doctors and nurses and by using other reliable sources.
- Patients should ensure that all of their doctors know about all medications and dietary supplements they are taking, as well as any allergies or adverse reactions they have to medicines.
- When patients' physicians write a prescription, patients need to be certain that they can read it and clearly understand when it should be taken. Also, patients should ask for information about the medication in terms they can understand (e.g., What is it for? Is the medicine safe to take with other medicines?)
- Patients should ask for written information about any side effects the medicine may cause.
- Patients who are having surgery should ensure that they, their doctors, and their surgeons all agree about and understand exactly what will be done.
- If patients have a choice, they should select a hospital that specializes in the procedure or surgery needed.
- Patients should always speak up if they have any questions or concerns.
- Patients should ensure that all health professionals involved in their care have all of the important information they need about the patients' health.
- If patients have a test conducted, they should not assume that "no news is good news." Patients should ask about the results and what they mean.

cians in their treatment of patients with chronic illnesses. It provides a "thumbnail" sketch of some important patient characteristics that may be quite useful in better managing these patients because it helps health care professionals better understand the potential issues and psychological strengths and weaknesses of their patients.

Millon and colleagues have recently developed a new scale—the Millon Behavioral Medicine Diagnostic—that expands the MBHI and includes more information on the presence of psychiatric indices. However, it is still in its "adolescent" stage of development (Bockian, Meagher, & Millon, 2000) and, therefore, is not discussed here.

The MBHI is a 150-item self-report inventory, and it provides 20 clinical scales organized into four broad categories:

1. *Personality and Basic Coping Styles:* This basic category assesses general personality traits and the manner in which a patient is likely to relate to health care personnel, services, and medical regimens.

2. *Psychogenic Attitudes Scales:* These scales are meant to reflect psychosocial stressors found to be important in precipitating or exacerbating physical illness. The scales reflect unique personal feelings and perceptions of the patient concerning

various aspects of psychological stress that increase susceptibility to psychophysiological disorders or aggravate the course of the current disease.

3. *Psychosomatic Correlates Scales:* These scales were designed for use with only those patients who have one of a number of specific disease syndromes: allergic inclination, gastrointestinal susceptibility, and cardiovascular tendency. These scales were developed to assess the degree to which emotional factors complicate the course of a particular ailment or whether the disorder has a significant psychosocial component contributing to it.

4. *Prognostic Indices Scales:* These scales are meant to predict psychological complications or difficulties associated with the course of a patient's illness.

THE SIGNIFICANT ROLE OF SOCIAL SUPPORT IN COPING WITH CHRONIC OR TERMINAL ILLNESS

Social support appears to be an important resource that can have a profound effect on the general well-being of any individual. More importantly, when that individual is ill, the significance and ramifications of social support increase dramatically. By physically helping patients to meet the demands of treatment or by providing emotional support, this assistance seems to be invaluable. Regardless of the type of disease, illness has an effect on the individual and on his or her social support network. Chronic and terminal diseases have a profound and long-term impact on the lifestyle and well-being of a person.

Social Support Hypotheses

A number of hypotheses have been proposed concerning the effects of social support on health and physical well-being. The *stress-buffering hypothesis* of social support is one of the most widely accepted regarding this effect. According to this hypothesis, social support offers a "buffer," or protection, against the negative effects of stressful events and situations. This protection serves to provide the individual with an illness with coping resources that they can utilize. Thus, the stress response to the illness can be significantly decreased (Koopman et al., 2000). For example, research has indicated that emotional support from friends and family is quite protective and is associated with longer survival in cancer patients (Ell, Nishimoto, Mediansky, & Mantell, 1992). Moreover, research has shown that support from the family makes adjustment to having cancer easier, and the loss of such support can be quite devastating (Lichtman & Taylor, 1988).

Cobb (1976) was one of the first clinical researchers to point out the fact that social support is one of the most important and well-studied mediators of stress. He defined social support as the feeling that an individual is cared about and valued by other people, and that he or she belongs to a social network. Subsequently, Cohen and Wills (1985) provided a more systematic review of the different types and mechanisms of social support. They pointed out that measures of perceived social support could tap into the feelings of adequacy and usefulness of such social support, as well as ratings of the availability of different kinds of support. In discussing social support, we need to be aware that individuals derive many kinds of support from others, as delineated here:

- *Esteem* support refers to the effects of other individuals increasing our feelings of self-esteem. For example, people may feel better about themselves if a group of friends and acquaintances think well of them.
- *Informational* support refers to the ability to get important and necessary information about treatment and disease-related questions from social interaction with others.
- *Social companionship* refers to the support derived from social activities. This helps to prevent social isolation and inactivity.
- *Instrumental* support refers to the actual physical help individuals can get from friends. For example, friends may be able to take patients to doctor's appointments if the patients are unable to get there by themselves.

As an example of the preceding four types of support, Baum et al. (1997) provided the following analogy: "If your car breaks down, your friends may bolster your self-esteem by assuring you that it is not your fault (esteem support), providing information about how to get it repaired (informational support), taking you with them to a party (companionship), or giving you a ride to the garage to get your car towed (instrumental support)" (pp. 82–83).

Numerous studies have demonstrated the positive effects of social support on coping with many chronic or terminal illnesses. Social support has been found to be helpful for people with advanced melanoma cancer (Fawzy et al., 1993), cardiovascular disease (Von Dras, Siegler, Barfoot, Williams, & Mark, 2000), heart failure (Jaarsma et al., 1999), stroke recovery (Mant, Carter, Wade, & Winner, 2000), breast cancer (Spiegel, Bloom, Kraemer, & Gottheil, 1989), cancer (Ell et al., 1992), human immunodeficiency virus (HIV; Fleishman et al., 2000), and progression from HIV to AIDS (Leserman et al., 2000).

How Can Health Care Providers Stimulate Support?

We have stressed the importance of social support for patients. However, the important question is that of how a health care provider can stimulate such support. This can be done in a number of ways, as summarized here:

- Get family members and significant others involved in the treatment process. Meeting with such individuals on a regular basis, along with the patient, will keep "everyone in the loop" and stimulate the acceptance of a team approach to the patient's care. This will further reinforce the importance of social support.
- Numerous support groups for specific diseases can be readily accessed on Web sites. Health care professionals should be current on such support groups and even have a list available for patients to stimulate participation in such groups.
- For patients who are isolated or hesitant to participate in such groups, the next strategy would be to refer them for individual counseling. Such counseling will help patients identify and express feelings about their medical conditions, as well as work through important emotional issues associated with chronic disease. Very effective cognitive–behavioral counseling techniques can be utilized (e.g., O'Donohue, Fisher, & Hayes, in press). Such individual counseling may serve as a "spring board" for getting involved in a broader treatment or social support group. Of course, again, the health care provider will need to have a list of appropriate referral sources of counselors in the area that can be given to patients.

THE IMPORTANT ISSUE OF QUALITY OF LIFE

In recent years, the health care community has become more responsive to taking into account not only how medical treatments affect physical health status and survival, but also how they may have a significant impact on the *quality of life* of patients and their ability to function on a daily basis (Kaplan, 1994). Physicians now accept that the two major goals of health care are (1) to help individuals live for a longer period of time and (2) to improve the quality of their lives before death. The concept of quality of life has been conceptualized along a number of dimensions (Baum et al., 1997) and includes the following:

- physical symptoms that a patient experiences
- functional status of an individual (i.e., one's ability to take care of oneself and to engage in activities of daily living)
- role activities, or the ability to work, at one's job or at home
- social functioning of an individual, including interpersonal relationships and intimacy

- emotional status of the individual, such as anxiety, stress, and depression
- cognitive and intellectual functioning of the individual
- general energy level and vitality of the individual
- general satisfaction with one's life.

A useful approach has been developed by Kaplan (1994) to incorporate quality-of-life assessments into the evaluation of health care outcomes. It combines weighted measures of symptoms and function to derive a numerical assessment of a patient's well-being for a particular point in time—the quality-adjusted life year (QALY). The treatment of prostate cancer in elderly men was given as an example. Three major treatment options are available for this disorder: surgical removal of the prostate, radiation therapy, and "watchful waiting" in which there is regular evaluation and supervision by the physician. The first two aggressive treatments are associated with risk of complications, such as impotence and incontinence, which may reduce subsequent life satisfaction. This is in contrast to the more passive "watchful waiting" approach. In utilizing the QALY as a treatment option index, Fleming, Wasson, Albertsen, Barry, and Wennberg (1993) were able to balance the risk of the cancer possibly metastasizing using the "watchful waiting" approach against the potential quality-of-life consequences of more aggressive treatment. When the QALY approach was applied to such patients, these investigators found that the three treatment options were essentially identical in their expected results and, therefore, should be a matter of the patient's preference. Therefore, it was concluded that waiting, rather than aggressive treatment of prostate tumors, is a legitimate option for elderly men with prostate cancer. Using such an approach empowers patients to become legitimate partners in the decision-making process with their physicians. This, in and of itself, can be quite therapeutic for patients and can help establish a better patient–doctor relationship that can have an important impact on subsequent adherence to medical recommendations.

Another widely used quality-of-life measure developed for patients with a medical illness is the Medical Outcomes Study (MOS) 36-Item Short Form Health Survey (SF-36; Ware, Snow, Kosinski, & Gandek, 1993). The SF-36 is a 36-item questionnaire that can be easily utilized in a busy medical clinic. It assesses health-related quality-of-life issues from the health care recipient's point of view and evaluates both physical and mental health aspects. The SF-36 has eight separate scales: Physical Functioning, Role Disability (Physical), Bodily Pain, General Health Perceptions, Vitality, Social Functioning, Role Disability (Emotional), and General Mental Health. It also has two standardized summary scales: the Mental Component Scale and the Physical Component Scale. The SF-36 is now being widely used in health outcomes research. Most importantly, excellent norms for various medical populations, against which to compare patient samples, are published in the SF-36 manual.

COPING WITH CHRONIC OR TERMINAL ILLNESS: APPLICATION TO FOUR CONDITIONS

In this section, to illustrate how coping processes and variables can affect chronic or terminal illness, we discuss four medical conditions that range from chronic to a more terminal end stage: pain, recovery from heart attack, cancer, and AIDS. In all of these medical conditions, we demonstrate how a clinical health psychologist's aid is invaluable in providing important interventions and guidance to primary care physicians.

Pain

Boothby et al. (1999) have a provided an excellent review of the research literature on the effects of coping on patients with pain. This review included pain related to chronic illnesses and procedures, such as rheumatoid arthritis, sickle cell disease, fibromyalgia, knee-replacement surgery, breast cancer surgery, temporomandibular disorders, headache, and low back pain. On the basis of their comprehensive review of the empirical literature, Boothby and colleagues reached a number of general conclusions that have practical and clinical implications:

- The association between passive coping strategies (such as wishful thinking and praying/hoping) and positive adaptation appears to be negative. Such passive strategies have the potential to interfere with improvement. Therefore, chronic pain management should include encouraging patients to take a very active role in their recovery.
- Other passive coping strategies such as the use of pain-contingent rest, guarding or bracing behaviors to avoid injury, and the use of sedatives or hypnotic medication for dealing with *chronic* pain, should be discouraged. Although these strategies may produce short-term reductions in discomfort and pain, they have the strong potential to reduce physical functioning and result in the weakening of muscles and tendons that, in the long run, will lead to more discomfort and pain.
- Discouraging *specific* passive strategies (such as rest and catastrophizing) may be more appropriate than telling patients to avoid *all* passive strategies. A compromise might need to be made between combinations of *both* passive and more active coping strategies.
- Health care practitioners may find it practical to teach and encourage specific active coping strategies, such as relaxation, stress management, and cognitive restructuring. This can be done on an individual or group basis.

Recovering From a Heart Attack

Recovering from a heart attack, which subsequently involves a lifetime effort to avoid a recurrent heart attack, is a biopsychosocial process in which the recovery outcome depends on the biological status of the patient and on the patient's interpretation of the illness and the success or failure of personal psychological coping mechanisms. Rehabilitation programs that focus on reducing emotional distress and facilitate adjustment after a heart attack are associated with reduced mortality and improved quality of life (Lewin, Robertson, Cay, Irving, & Campbell, 1992). As Baum et al. (1997) have discussed, the process of recovery from heart disease is usually divided into two phases: an acute phase (in the hospital) and a convalescent phase (after release from the hospital).

The three main concerns patients recovering from heart attacks usually expressed after release from the hospital are the following: survival issues, such as fear of death and recurrence of the disease; the effects of the illness on the ability to resume work activities; and the effects of the illness on sexual functioning. Indeed, the onset of a heart attack, and the subsequent recovery from it, is a very stressful and potentially uncontrollable crisis for most patients. This is because those patients, in addition to physical pain and fear of death, are confronted with uncertainties about employment and family activities. Many restrictions of lifestyle and some fear and uncertainty may well persist for months or even years beyond the acute phase of illness. For example, depression is considered to be one of the major problems in cardiac convalescence and rehabilitation (Carney, Freedland, Rich, & Jaffe, 1995). In addition, after the period of hospitalization, many patients are reluctant to resume normal activities or to return to work, often to the extent that it is not justified by their medical disability. One common characteristic of this group of patients is called *cardiac invalidism*. This is characterized by excessive dependency, helplessness, and restriction of activity.

In terms of coping strategies that can play an important role in positively influencing the course of cardiac patients' recovery and rehabilitation, a number of empirical findings have been reported:

- The family can play an important role. Because most patients with coronary problems are middle-aged men, special emphasis has been placed on how the wife can affect the way in which the husband copes with his disease. Conflicts between husband and wife, and overprotectiveness on the part of the spouse, can significantly interfere with the recovery process. Therefore, efforts must be made to help the spouses work as a team in coping with the aftermath of the distress and uncertainty caused by the heart attack.

- Patients who feel relatively less depressed, more confident, and less threatened during the acute phase of the illness have been found to fare better, on an overall biopsychosocial basis, at a later point in the recovery process. Thus, coping techniques that enhance the patient's behavioral control (such as encouraging participation in the rehabilitation process decision making and providing rehabilitation programs from which to select), as well as cognitive control (such as providing information and increasing predictability of possible environmental triggers of post–heart attack symptoms), will facilitate recovery.
- A sense of consistency in the physician/nurse team assigned to patients during their stay in the coronary care unit, and during subsequent transfer to a rehabilitation program, is important in terms of consistent information being delivered to patients and of patients' perception of a greater sense of medical support.
- The importance of reducing post–heart attack stress has been found to be important in promoting maximal recovery. Thus, coping skills to reduce stress are important for patients to learn.
- Social isolation has also been found to be related to a greater likelihood of dying from a heart attack. Thus, again, social support is extremely important in recovering from this disease.

Cancer

Besides being a frightening and painful disease, the various aversive treatments for cancer make it particularly difficult to cope with. Adaptation to life with cancer is difficult because it is often life threatening, sometimes painful, and is an unusually unpleasant, fatigue-causing disease. Treatments such as surgery, radiation, chemotherapy, and some of the more recent immunotherapies are frequently difficult to endure because of many unpleasant side effects. In addition, cancer treatment and surveillance are long-term commitments and usually cause a great deal of disruption and worry as the patient adjusts to being healthy again. Obviously, such factors cause emotional distress. An individual's ability to cope with these stressors is important in determining quality of life among patients with cancer and their families (e.g., Cooper & Faragher, 1993). How well a patient copes with stress is related to anxiety, depression, hostility, and self-esteem among patients with cancer (Katz, 1994). Baum and colleagues (1997) have summarized the following relationships between coping and cancer:

- More stoic, nonexpressive styles of coping are not positively related to cancer occurrence or survival, especially when combined with avoiding social support.
- Men and women appear to cope differently when faced with a major stressor such as cancer, with women appearing to be more adaptive to this medical condition and to be most helped by social support.
- Among parents of children with cancer, both fathers and mothers appear to adjust well to the situation and to use similar means to deal with family disruption and worry.
- The coping skills of family members are very important because the general health and well-being of the family can significantly affect the mood and well-being of the patient.
- Once again, social support appears to be a very important resource for people dealing with the stress associated with cancer. Support from the family makes adjustment to having cancer quite a bit easier; the loss of such support can be devastating.
- The primary source of support for cancer patients is the spouse or significant other in a relationship. When these partners are perceived as being supportive, and the patient is satisfied with their assistance, the patient's well-being is enhanced.

Finally, a very important psychosocial development in the treatment of cancer has been the use of groups to provide support and psychotherapy for patients with cancer. Indeed, a study of patients with cancer revealed that women with little social support or contact with others were more likely to die from cancer (Reynolds & Kaplan, 1990). In addition, studies also suggest that patients with cancer who are married survive longer than do patients who are unmarried (Goodwin, Hunt, Key, & Samet, 1987). A hallmark study by Spiegel et al. (1989) demonstrated that a 1-year group psychotherapy intervention for women with metastatic breast cancer resulted in these women living an average of 18 months longer than women given standard care. Moreover, the group intervention was associated with better mood, more effective coping, less pain, and better mental health. A meta-analysis of such psychosocial interventions, in which 45 studies of treatment–control group comparisons were made, concluded that the emotional adjustment was improved, and the treatment and disease-related symptoms decreased, among patients given these special psychosocial treatments (Meyer, 1995). Thus, again, a comprehensive biopsychosocial approach to this disease is effective, reinforcing the overall clinical efficacy of such an approach with the other diseases we have discussed in this book.

Acquired Immune Deficiency Syndrome

AIDS is a disease caused by HIV that weakens the immune system and causes individuals to develop opportunistic infections. Since its "discovery" in the early 1980s, AIDS has become one of the most deadly and feared diseases in the world. We are experiencing a global epidemic of AIDS, with 20 million people having already died from it, and another 30 million currently infected with it. Because AIDS is a recently recognized disease, we still have a great deal to learn about it. This illness is best viewed as a spectrum from one extreme to the other, that is, from someone who has just been infected by the virus to someone who has actually developed AIDS. Some people who are exposed do not immediately develop AIDS, and the rate of progression of HIV disease to AIDS is not well understood. Approximately 50% of those who are infected with HIV subsequently develop AIDS within 10 years (Friedland, 1990). Much uncertainty remains concerning this disease, which can severely affect the coping skills of patients who have been infected.

In terms of treatment, the U.S. Food and Drug Administration has approved a number of drugs for the treatment of AIDS. One of the most widely known drugs prescribed for AIDS is AZT. This drug appears to inhibit the spread of the virus; however, it is not clear whether it improves the immune functioning of the individual. Dideoxyinosine (DDI), like AZT, appears to combat the HIV virus itself. In addition, various other medications to help treat the secondary infections that are caused by AIDS are being developed. However, keep in mind that the available drugs *do not cure* AIDS; they only help to treat opportunistic infections that are the result of AIDS. One of the most common and deadly of the opportunistic infections is *Pneumocystis carinii* pneumonia. Patients with AIDS must be given drugs for the rest of their lives to prevent the occurrence and reoccurrence of such infections. These medications also often cause neuropsychiatric side effects, such as confusion, visual hallucinations, delirium, depression, loss of appetite, and headache. Therefore, the mental status of these patients must be carefully considered in addition to prescribing methods to deal with any unwanted side effects. Combinations of various drugs have also shown great promise.

Besides the medical treatment required for dealing with this disease, stress and its resultant psychosocial sequelae are important components in dealing with patients with AIDS. Indeed, comprehensive treatment and counseling programs have been developed that include coping techniques such as stress management and support groups. The support groups focus primarily on the management of emotional distress issues such as anger, feelings of helplessness and depression, grief, fear of dying, and related issues. A review of such programs has been provided by Baum et al. (1997). For example, Auerbach, Oleson, and Solomon (1992) evaluated intervention that combined biofeedback, guided imagery, and hypnosis and compared this intervention to a no-treatment control group. The results of the intervention suggested a decrease in physical symptoms, along with an increase in vigor and hardiness. In addition, programs that involve multiple components such as active coping, social support, and interventions using relaxation exercises can also determine how well people adjust (e.g., Lutgendorf, Antoni, Kumar, & Schneiderman, (1994).

Finally, note that AIDS was originally considered a disease of the gay population, particularly a white gay male disease. However, during the past decade, both the highest incidence and greatest number of new cases of HIV infection in the United States have been within ethnic minority populations, particularly among Black Americans and Hispanics (Mays et al., 2001). For example, the prevalence of HIV infection has been estimated to be from 3.3 to 4.9 per 1,000 among White American men, but from 16.8 to 22.5 among Black American men and from 9.0 to 13.0 among Hispanic men. Comparable patterns are also found for women. In fact, about one half of all new infections occur in women. (Sex between men and women is the main way AIDS is being spread.) Unfortunately, much of the research on AIDS continues to be conducted using White American male participants. This can be problematic because there is evidence in various areas of medicine that racial, ethnic, and gender differences in disease susceptibility and drug response do exist (Mays et al., 2001). Therefore, failure to consider these differences while attempting to develop new methods of treatment has potential significant public health implications, particularly for ethnic minority and female Americans. Indeed, AIDS is now a major health problem for women in the United States, being the third leading cause of death among women between ages 25 and 44 (Ickovics, Thayaparan, & Ethier, 2001). Again, a troubling question is whether the current research using White American men will translate effectively to women in developing new treatment and drug approaches.

END-OF-LIFE ISSUES

Finally, another component of care for patients with chronic illnesses that often cannot be avoided is the sometimes inevitable issue of end of life. In terms of cancer, for example, Powazki, Palcisco, Richardson, and Stagno (2000) have reviewed important variables that need to be considered related to this issue. Of course, end of life is a delicate issue that should be handled with the utmost respect and sensitivity. It is usually wise to work on this issue with patients who have a potentially life-threatening disease *only* when they themselves have come to terms with death and are able and willing to talk about it. A growing hospice movement is increasingly available to aid patients and their families during this stressful period. Such programs have specialists trained to provide home care for those who plan to die at home. Indeed, the hospice care approach, which originated in Great Britain, has been shown to produce better quality of life for the dying patient (e.g., Viney, Walker, Robertson, Lilley, & Eivan, 1994). It involves a medical and social support system, focused on enriching quality of life, through medical, psychosocial, and spiritual care for both terminally ill patients and their families. In this approach, patients and their families are considered to be a "unit of care." As such, these people are viewed as forming a system, with each person affecting the others, and each needing hospice attention and care. Saunders (1986) has delineated the basic components of the hospice approach.

We should also point out that a number of articles have been written about the topic of death and dying. The most popular one is Kübler-Ross's five-stage theory, which suggests that individuals pass through five predictable stages as they adjust to the prospect of dying (Kübler-Ross, 1975). These include the following, as discussed next: denial, anger, bargaining, depression, and acceptance.

1. *Denial:* This first stage is viewed as the individual's initial reaction to learning about the diagnosis of a terminal illness. The reaction may be that a medical mistake was made because of a misdiagnosis or a "mixup" of one's own examination with that of another patient, and that this mistake will soon be rectified. For the vast majority of people, this denial and shock that anything is wrong last only a few days. When this situation lasts more than a brief period, it may require some psychological intervention.

2. *Anger:* When the denial stage ends, issues arise that need to be dealt with, such as future treatment and who will help during the process. At this point, the anger stage sets in, with the angry patient asking "Why me?" The patient may now display resentment toward anyone who is healthy, such as family members, friends, and health care providers. This emotion is often difficult for family and friends to deal with, and these individuals may need to work with a therapist to understand that the patient is not really angry with them, but at fate in general.

3. *Bargaining:* During this stage, anger is usually abandoned, and a different coping strategy is employed: the assumption that one can trade good behavior for good health. This behavior usually takes the form of doing charitable work, religious activity, and uncharacteristically pleasant behavior.

4. *Depression:* Once patients realize that bargaining had no impact on their illness, depression usually begins to set in. Kübler-Ross views this as the stage when patients begin to

come to terms with their lack of control over their terminal illness. "Anticipatory grief" begins, when patients begin to mourn the prospect of their own deaths. There appear to be two stages: when the patient initially comes to grips with the loss of past important activities and friends; and coming to grips with the future loss of relationships and activities. This stage of depression may be important to go through. Of course, care must be taken such that the depression is not allowed to become overwhelming. The risk of suicide is substantially increased in patients experiencing this stage. Social support and therapeutic intervention may be helpful at this time.

5. *Acceptance*: At this stage, patients become resigned to the prospect of their deaths, often being too weak to be angry and too accustomed to the thought of dying to be depressed. Many patients use this time to make final preparations and "get things in order."

SUMMARY

As we have discussed in this chapter, coping with chronic illnesses is one of the most challenging areas in the field of medicine today. In this chapter, we have discussed many of the coping issues that are common to a broad range of chronic diseases. As we reviewed, clinical health psychologists are invaluable in providing important interventions and guidance to help primary care physicians with patients who are chronically ill. We paid special attention to the most common theoretical framework utilized to conceptualize coping: the transactional model of stress. This model highlights the important individual depositional variables and processes involved in coping with chronic illness. Such coping responses ultimately affect important adaptation outcomes, such as mental and physical health, social functioning, morale, and quality of life.

The treatment and management of patients with chronic illnesses can be quite challenging. Moreover, social support appears to be an important resource that can have a profound effect on the general well-being of individuals. The quality of life of patients, and their ability to function on a daily basis, is important to keep in mind when treating patients with chronic medical conditions. Another important component in the treatment of patients with chronic illnesses is that of end-of-life care. Kübler-Ross's five-stage theory suggests that individuals pass through five predictable stages as they adjust to the prospect of dying. This is a useful model to utilize in counseling patients who are faced with end-of-life issues.

RECOMMENDED READINGS

Antonucci, T. C., Ajrouch, K. J., & Janevic, M. (1999). Socioeconomic status, social support, age, and health. *Annals of the New York Academy of Sciences, 896*, 390–392.

Goodheart, C. D., & Lasing, M. H. (1997). *Treating people with chronic disease. A psychological guide*. Washington, DC: American Psychological Association.

Kübler-Ross, E. (1975). *Death: The final stage of growth*. Upper Saddle River, NJ: Prentice Hall.

GLOSSARY

acquired immune deficiency syndrome (AIDS)   A disease caused by the human immunodeficiency virus that weakens the immune system and causes individuals to develop opportunistic infections.

cardiac invalidism   A common characteristic of patients recovering from a heart attack, characterized by excessive dependency, helplessness, and restriction of activity.

hospice care   An approach used to produce better quality of life for patients who are dying. It involves providing medical, psychosocial, and spiritual care for patients who are terminally ill and their families.

Millon Behavioral Health Inventory (MBHI)   An inventory designed to provide relevant information for treatment decisions for patients who have physical problems.

opportunistic infections   Infections caused by microorganisms capable of adapting to a tissue or host other than the normal one. These infections often occur when the immune system is compromised.

***Pneumocystis carinii* pneumonia (PCP)**   One of the most common and deadly opportunistic infections experienced by patients with AIDS.

QALY   The quality-adjusted life year index, which combines weighted measures of symptoms and function to derive a numerical assessment of a patient's well-being for a particular point in time. It is used to incorporate quality-of-life assessments into the evaluation of health care decisions.

SF-36   A quality-of-life measure developed for patients with medical illnesses. It has eight separate scales and two standardized summary scales.

stress-buffering hypothesis of social support   The hypothesis that social support offers a "buffer," or protection, against the negative effects of stressful events and situations.

transactional model of stress   A general model of stress that highlights a number of important psychosocial factors and processes involved in coping with stress.

REFERENCES

Antonucci, T. C., Ajrouch, K. J., & Janevic, M. (1999). Socioeconomic status, social support, age, and health. *Annals of the New York Academy of Sciences, 896,* 390–392.

Auerbach, J. E., Oleson, T. D., & Solomon, G. F. (1992). A behavioral medicine intervention as an adjunctive treatment for HIV-related illness. *Psychology and Health, 6,* 325–334.

Baum, A., Gatchel, R. J., & Krantz, D. (1997). *An introduction to health psychology.* New York: McGraw-Hill.

Bedell, S., & Delbanco, T. L. (1984). Choices about cardiopulmonary resuscitation in the hospital—When do physicians talk with patients? *New England Journal of Medicine, 310,* 1089–1093.

Bockian, N., Meagher, S., & Millon, T. (2000). Assessing personality with the Millon Behavioral Health Inventory, the Millon Behavioral Medicine Diagnostic, and the Millon Clinical Multiaxial Inventory. In R. J. Gatchel & J. N. Weisberg (Eds.). *Personality characteristics of patients with pain* (pp. 61–88). Washington, DC: American Psychological Association.

Boothby, J. L., Thorn, B. E., Stroud, M. W., & Jensen, M. P. (1999). Coping with pain. In R. J. Gatchel & D. C. Turk (Eds.), *Psychological factors in pain: Critical perspectives* (pp. 343–359). New York: Guilford Press.

Carney, R. M., Freedland, K. E., Rich, M. W., & Jaffe, A. S. (1995). Depression as a risk factor for cardiac events in established coronary heart disease: A review of possible mechanisms. *Annals of Behavioral Medicine, 17,* 142–149.

Cobb, S. (1976). Social support as a moderator of life stress. *Psychosomatic Medicine, 38,* 300–314.

Cohen, S., & Wills, T. A. (1985). Stress, social support, and the buffering hypothesis: A critical review. *Psychological Bulletin, 98,* 310–357.

Cooper, C. L., & Faragher, E. B. (1993). Psychosocial stress and breast cancer: The interrelationship between stress events, coping strategies and personality. *Psychosomatic Medicine, 23,* 653–662.

Cox, D. J., & Gonder-Frederick, L. (1992). Major developments in behavioral diabetes research. *Journal of Consulting and Clinical Psychology, 60,* 628–638.

Ell, K., Nishimoto, R., Mediansky, L., & Mantell J. (1992). Social relations, social support and survival among patients with cancer. *Journal of Psychosomatic Research, 36* (6), 531–541.

Fawzy, F. I., Fawzy, N. W., Hyun, C. S., Elashoff, R., Guthrie, D., Fahey, J. L., et al. (1993). Malignant melanoma: Effects of an early structured psychiatric intervention, coping, and affective state on recurrence and survival 6 years later. *Archives of General Psychiatry, 50,* 681–689.

Fleishman, J. A., Sherbourne, C. D., Crystal, S., Collins, R. L., Marshall, G. N., Kelly, M., et al. (2000). Coping, conflictual social interaction, social support, and mood among HIV-infected persons. *American Journal of Community Psychology, 28,* 421–453.

Fleming, I. C., Wasson, J. H., Albertsen, P. C., Barry, M. J., Wennberg, J. E., et al. (1993). A decision analysis of alternative treatment strategies for clinically localized prostate cancer. *Journal of the American Medical Association, 269,* 2650–2658.

Friedland, G. H. (1990). Early treatment for HIV: The time has come. *New England Journal of Medicine, 322,* 1000–1002.

Goodwin, J. S., Hunt, W. C., Key, C. R., & Samet, J. M. (1987). The effect of marital status on stage, treatment and survival of cancer patients. *Journal of the American Medical Association, 258,* 3125–3130.

Greenwald, H. P., & Nevitt, M. C. (1982). Physician attitudes toward communication with cancer patients. *Social Science and Medicine, 16,* 591–594.

Ickovics, J. R., Thayaparan, B., & Ethier, K. A. (2001). Women and AIDS: A contextual context. In A. Baum, J. D. Reverson, & J. E. Singer (Eds.), *Handbook of health psychology* (pp. 817–840). Mahwah, NJ: Lawrence Erlbaum Associates.

Jaarsma, T., Halfens, R., Huijer, A. H., Dracup, K., Gorgels, T., Van Ree, J., et al. (1999). Effects of education and support on self-care and resource utilization in patients with heart failure. *European Heart Journal, 20,* 673–682.

Kaplan, R. M. (1994). Value judgment in the Oregon Medicaid experiment. *Medical Care, 32,* 975–988.

Katz, I. R. (1994). Prevention of depression, recurrence, and complications in late life. Symposium: Disease prevention research at NIH: An agenda for all. *Preventive Medicine, 23,* 743–750.

Kohn, L. T., Corrigan, J. M., & Donaldson, M. S. (Eds.). (2000). *To err is human. Building a safer health system.* Washington, DC: National Academy Press.

Koopman, C., Gore-Felton, C., Marouf, F., Butler, I. D., Field, N., Gil, M., et al. (2000). Relationships of perceived stress to coping, attachment, and social support among HIV-positive persons. *AIDS Care, 12,* 663–672.

Kübler-Ross, E. (1975). *Death: The final stage of growth.* Upper Saddle River, NJ: Prentice Hall.

Lazarus, R. S., & Folkman, S. (1984). *Stress, appraisal and coping.* New York: Springer Verlag.

Leserman, J., Petitto, J. M., Golden, R. N., Gaynes, B. N., Gu, H., Perkins, D. O., et al. (2000). Impact of stressful life events, depression, social support, coping, and cortisol on progression to AIDS. *American Journal of Psychiatry, 157,* 1221–1228.

Lewin, B., Robertson, J. H., Cay E. L., Irving, J. B., & Campbell, M. et al. (1992). Effects of self-help post-myocardial-infarction rehabilitation on psychological adjustment and use of health services. *Lancet, 339,* 1036–1040.

Lichtman, R. R., & Taylor, S. E. (1988). Close relationships and the female cancer patient. Women with cancer: Psychological perspectives. In B. L. Anderson (Ed.), *Contributions to psychology and medicine* (pp. 233–256). New York: Springer Verlag.

Lutgendorf, S. K., Antonio, M. H., Kumar, M., & Schneiderman, N. (1994). Changes in cognitive coping strategies predict EBV-antibody titer change following a stressor disclosure induction. *Journal of Psychosomatic Research, 38,* 63–78.

Mant, J., Carter, J., Wade, D. T., & Winner, S. (2000). Family support for stroke: A randomized controlled trail. *The Lancet, 356,* 808–813.

Mays, V. M., So, B. T., Cochrane, S. D., Detels, R., Benjamin, R., Allen, E., et al. (2001). HIV disease in ethnic minorities: Implications of racial/ethnic differences in disease susceptibility and drug dosage response for HIV infection and treatment. In A. Baum, J. D. Reverson, & J. E. Singer (Eds.), *Handbook of health psychology* (pp. 801–816). Mahwah, NJ: Lawrence Erlbaum Associates.

Meyer, T. J. (1995). Effects of psychosocial interventions with adult cancer patients: A meta-analysis of randomized experiments. *Health Psychology, 14,* 101–108.

Millon, T., Green, C., & Meagher, R. (1982). *The Millon Behavioral Health Inventory manual.* Minneapolis: National Computer Systems.

Mount, B. M., Jones, A., & Patterson, A. (1974). A death and dying attitude in a teaching hospital. *Urology, 4,* 741–748.

O'Donohue, W., Fisher, J., & Hayes, S. (in press). *Empirical supported techniques for cognitive behavior therapy: A step by step guide for clinicians.* New York: Wiley.

Powazki, R. D., Palcisco, C., Richardson, M., & Stagno, S. J. (2000). Psychosocial care in advanced cancer. *Seminars in Oncology, 27,* 101–108.

Reynolds, P., & Kaplan, G. A. (1990). Social connections and risk for cancer: Prospective evidence from the Alameda County Study. *Behavioral Medicine, 16,* 101–110.

Saunders, C. (1986). A philosophy of terminal care. In M. J. Christre & P. G. Mellett (Eds.), *The psychosomatic approach: Contemporary practice of whole-person care* (pp. 201–250). New York: Wiley.

Spiegel, D., Bloom, J. R., Kraemer, H. C., & Gottheil, E. (1989). Effects of psychosocial treatment on survival of patients with metastatic breast cancer. *Lancet, 2,* 888–891.

Viney, L. L., Walker, B. M., Robertson, T., Lilley, B., & Eivan, C. (1994). Dying in palliative care units and in the hospital: A comparison of the quality of life of terminal cancer patients. *Journal of Consulting and Clinical Psychology, 62,* 157–164.

Von Dras, D. D., Siegler, I. C., Barfoot, J. C., Williams, R. B., & Mark, D. B. (2000). Coronary catheterization patient and wife's perceptions of social support: Effects due to characteristics of recipient, provider, and their interaction. *International Journal of Aging and Human Development, 50,* 97–125.

Ware, J. E., Snow, K. K., Kosinski, M., & Gandek, B. (1993). *SF-36 health survey: Manual and interpretation guide.* Boston: The Health Institute, New England Medial Center.

Zautra, A. J., & Manne, S. L. (1992). Coping with rheumatoid arthritis. A review of a decade of research. *Annals of Behavioral Medicine, 14,* 31–39.

14

FUTURE TRENDS
AND OPPORTUNITIES

As reviewed elsewhere (e.g., Gatchel, 1999), many historical changes have occurred in medicine during the past centuries. During the Renaissance, the perspective that the mind (or the soul) influenced the body was regarded as unscientific. The goal of understanding the mind and soul was viewed as the purview of religion and philosophy; the understanding of the body was viewed as a separate realm of the growing field of physical medicine. This was a result of the new approach to the investigation of physical phenomena that emerged during this period. Work based on dissection of the human body, and associated experimentation, stimulated a revolution aimed at gaining more knowledge through careful observation, experimentation, and objective quantification, rather than relying on common sense, mythology, or outdated dogma. A number of revolutionary works and textbooks on anatomy and physiology also appeared that marked the advancement of the view that the body can be explained by its own mechanisms. This viewpoint initiated the trend toward a *biomedical reductionism* approach, which argued that concepts such as the mind and the soul were not needed to explain physical functioning or behavior. It also stimulated a great revolution in knowledge, with sciences such as anatomy, biology, physiology, and physics evolving simultaneously, all of which were based on the principles of scientific investigation.

Unfortunately, this new mechanistic approach to the study of human anatomy and physiology also fostered a "dualistic" viewpoint that mind and body function separately and independently. The individual usually viewed as popularizing and solidifying this dualistic viewpoint was the 17th-century French philosopher René Descartes (1596–1650). Descartes argued that the mind or soul was a separate entity parallel to—and incapable of affecting— physical matter or somatic processes in any significant or direct way. Such a dualistic viewpoint gained additional acceptance during the 19th century with the discovery that microorganisms caused certain diseases. This new biomedical reductionism philosophy of medicine became the only acceptable basis for explaining disease through understanding mechanical laws and physiological principles.

The influence of this strict mechanistic, dualistic approach to medicine began to subside during the late 19th and early 20th centuries. Influential writings began to appear that emphasized the importance of taking an integrated, more holistic approach to health and illness. A more comprehensive *biopsychosocial model* of illness was proposed that emphasized the unique interaction of biological, physiological, and psychosocial factors that needs to be taken into account for the better understanding of health and illness. Of course, conventional medicine has always been slow to change, and it is only now that this biopsychosocial perspective is gaining greater acceptance in the medical community. One of the reasons for this increasing acceptance of such a biopsychosocial perspective has been the increasing prevalence of chronic medical disorders in the United States. Indeed, with the increase in size of the aging population in this country, the prevalence of chronic medical conditions can be expected to continue to rise. As of 2001, approximately 35 million Americans, age 65 years or older, accounted for 12.4% of the total population (U.S. Census Bureau, 2001). By the year 2030, it has been projected that about 20% of the population will be 65 years or older (U.S. Census Bureau, 2000). Awareness of these population trends is contributing to increased concern about health care for older adults, because these older individuals are likely to have a high prevalence of chronic medical problems.

As discussed throughout this book, chronic medical conditions require a comprehensive biopsychosocial approach to assessment and treatment. Moreover, chronic conditions usually cannot be *cured;* instead they are merely *treated.* In addition, the medical community is beginning to realize that, to prevent such chronic diseases, health care providers will need to take a more active preventive approach and to be more proactive in dealing with acute problems in primary care settings. As such, many lifestyle habits, such as avoiding smoking, avoiding overeating, and exercising regularly, are being viewed as extremely important in preventing the onset of disease states and in arresting the development of more chronic stages of these diseases if they do occur. This is a major challenge in today's health care system, especially in light of the rising costs of health care in the United States. In the future, attention will need to be given to *quality of care* in the primary care setting. This is where cost containment can be initiated—by preventing the development of chronic medical problems—and this is where clinical health psychologists can be quite proactive in helping to change the behaviors that contribute to the development of chronic disease states.

CHANGES IN MEDICAL EDUCATION

The medical community is now poised to give health psychology a higher profile in the education of new physicians in the United States. Indeed, "We know that at least half of all deaths in the United States have behavioral and social factors as significant causes, from smoking to adherence to physicians' recommendations for treatment, to social and cultural factors that influence the interaction between a patient and the health-care system. . . . If we expect physicians to do their best in providing medical care, they have to understand the roles these factors play in disease and health" (Kington, as cited in Carpenter, 2001, pp. 78–79). To enhance such an understanding, a move has begun to provide medical students with better education about health psychology and behavioral medicine principles. As Carpenter (2001) has reported, the University of California at San Francisco started classes in fall 2001 that integrate behavioral science, social science, and culture into all aspects of instruction—from students' first day of classes to the last clinical rotation. The goal of this new integrated curriculum is to "ensure that medical students recognize that there is a basic science to understanding behavior, so that when they go out into practice, they can think about it and keep up with the behavioral medicine literature, just as they do with the biological sciences" (Adler, as cited in Carpenter, 2001, p. 78).

This new curriculum should be adopted in medical schools throughout the United States, so that all doctors of the future will be able to think in a more holistic manner about patients' medical problems, including the psychosocial and behavioral factors that potentially contribute to them (i.e., embracing a biopsychosocial perspective). As an example, Carpenter (2001) indicated that in such a curriculum, when students are learning about organ systems, they will not only learn about the biological principles of, say, cardiac, pulmonary, and renal health, but will also learn about behavioral and social factors that can affect these organ systems, such as diet, depression, exercise, relaxation, and social support.

This change marks a major revolution in the integration of heath psychology and medicine because the theoretical and practical communication barriers between physicians and clinical health psychologists will be gone. This will be particularly important in the primary care setting, where educating patients about a holistic approach to health through medical and behavioral lifestyle prevention strategies can be routinely taught. A consistent message regarding prevention strategies will go a long way toward better indoctrinating the general public about the important fact that one cannot separate maladaptive lifestyle habits and the onset and further development of disease states. Patients need to learn that medicine cannot *cure* all diseases. Instead, most diseases must be *treated* over a long period of time, which will require patients to take a more active role in the treatment process. Educating patients about their need to play a more active role in their care and to embrace an interactive patient–doctor relationship is an area in which a clinical health psychologist can provide an invaluable service. Of course, concurrent training of clinical health psychologists in comprehensive biopsychosocial-oriented programs will also be essential for providing such important services (Committee on Education and Training, Division 38, 1999).

PSYCHOEDUCATIONAL PROGRAMS AND HEALTHY LIFESTYLES

Clinical health psychologists have, during the last three decades, developed numerous techniques to promote healthy lifestyles so as to prevent the onset of disease. We have discussed many of these methods throughout this book. One particular area that shows great promise, in terms of cost containment, is the use of psychoeducational programs in integrated primary care. As Cummings (2000) noted, such psychoeducational programs have various elements in common. Exhibit 14.1 lists such elements, but note that not all psychoeducational protocols contain every one of the elements listed. Such programs can be taught on a group basis, thus reducing the higher costs associated with one-on-one treatment. Moreover, one added benefit of group education is the social support provided by such groups. Again, throughout this book, we have reviewed the therapeutic benefits of social support for many disorders.

RECENT ALTERNATIVE OR COMPLEMENTARY MEDICINE APPROACHES

The general population is beginning to more widely utilize various alternative or complementary medicine approaches. Such approaches can be defined as medical interventions that are not usually taught widely in U.S. medical schools and that are not generally available in hospitals.

EXHIBIT 14.1
Basic Elements of Psychoeducational Protocols

- *Educational component:* This teaches patients about the medical condition, as well as the interaction between the patients' bodies and their emotional states.
- *Pain management:* For those patients with chronic pain, help is provided to reduce unnecessary reliance on pain medication and to address potential problems associated with iatrogenic addiction.
- *Relaxation techniques:* Patients can be taught meditation and the use of guided imagery as relaxation strategies.
- *Stress management:* Patients can be taught stress management techniques that are tailored to specific medical conditions and populations.
- *Social support:* Social support can be provided, not only in a group milieu, but also in the presence of "veteran patients" who have gone through a particular program.
- *Self-evaluation:* This component of education teaches patients to evaluate how well they are doing and teaches them to monitor vital signs such as blood pressure, diet, insulin, and other signs that are important in chronic illness.
- *Self-efficacy:* By taking a more active role in their treatment, patients learn to believe that they can perform specific actions to help in the treatment process. This increases patients' ability to cope with sudden exacerbations of their medical conditions.
- *Modular formatting:* This refers to the fact that psychoeducational protocols are structured to serve different but similar populations and conditions, by inserting or substituting condition-specific modules.

Note. Source is Cummings (2000).

Examples of such approaches include acupuncture, massage, chiropractic, and various herbal remedies. In a survey study on the use of such approaches in the United States, Eisenberg et al. (1993) found that an estimated 60 million Americans used such alternative medical therapies in 1990, at an estimated cost of $13.7 billion. In addition, the estimated number of annual visits to providers of alternative medicine amounted to 425 million visits, which far exceeded the number of visits to all primary care physicians in the United States (388 million visits). Another important finding was that 70% of patients who acknowledged using alternative therapy never mentioned it to their physicians. These data stimulated a great deal of attention and debate considering this "invisible mainstream" that exists within the U.S. health care system.

Many misconceptions remain about alternative or complementary medicine. In the past, it has often been viewed as some sort of "fringe" medicine. This, however, is far from the truth. Alternative or complementary medicine is an important area within medicine. It is simply a continuation of the tradition of medicine that incorporates new approaches that have been demonstrated to be efficacious based on scientific research. For example, therapies based on herbs have been used to treat various medical problems for hundreds of years. The Chinese practice of acupuncture also has a long history. In fact, the National Institutes of Health now has an Office of Alternative Medicine, which focuses on helping to stimulate new research in this area of medicine. As mentioned earlier, conventional medicine has been historically slow to embrace new concepts and treatment approaches. Alternative or complementary medicine is an example of a new area of medicine that is slowly being embraced. Indeed, a national trend has developed in which some third-party payers authorize alternative therapies in the form of "expanded benefits" (Eisenberg, 1997).

As noted earlier, one of the striking findings of the Eisenberg et al. (1993) study was the fact that 70% of patients who were using alternative or complementary therapies never mentioned it to their physicians. This has created a potential medical problem because, for example, certain over-the-counter herbal remedies can duplicate medically prescribed drugs. As a case in point, St. John's wort is publicized as having a beneficial effect in reducing depression. If a patient is on St. John's wort (and does not tell his or her physician about it) and then is prescribed an antidepressant for symptoms of depression and sleeplessness, the patient will be getting a "double dose" of a drug, resulting in potentially toxic levels (Eisenberg, 1997). Health care physicians, therefore, need to evaluate patients fully for their possible use of alternative medical therapies. Eisenberg has provided a comprehensive step-by-step strategy for conventionally trained medical providers to use with their patients to proactively discuss the use or avoidance of alternative therapies. This strategy involves the following:

- Have a detailed discussion with patients about their preferences and expectations concerning the use of alternative medical therapies.
- Review safety and efficacy issues related to alternative medical therapies. For example, the potential toxicity of herbal preparations, dietary regimens and supplements, and so on is important to review with patients. Request that patients maintain a symptom diary if they are using alternative medical therapies, which can be used to conduct a baseline assessment and follow-up evaluation of a subsequent alternative or conventional therapeutic intervention.
- For those patients who are utilizing alternative medical therapies, arrange for follow-up visits to monitor for potentially harmful side effects.

We know that the U.S. population includes a large number of users of alternative medical therapies. In the past, such therapies have been ignored by conventional medicine physicians. They can no longer be ignored. Therefore, careful monitoring of the use of such therapies is essential so as not to negatively affect some of the conventional medical procedures that may be prescribed. Obviously, this type of monitoring will require some additional evaluation and discussion between patient and physician. The clinical health psychologist can provide a valuable resource by filling this need and by evaluating medical outcomes.

EVALUATION OF MEDICAL OUTCOMES

As Mayer, Gatchel, and Polatin (2000) have noted, health care costs are continuing to increase at an alarming rate in the United States. Consequently, changes in health care policy and demands for improved allocations of health resources have recently placed great pressure on health care professionals to provide the most cost-effective treatment for these disorders and to validate treatment efficacy. As a result, treatment-outcome monitoring has gained new importance in medicine. Physicians are now being monitored to determine the effectiveness of the treatments they provide, as well as patient satisfaction with their treatment. Often, a "score card" is maintained by third-party payers to monitor practitioners' efficacy. Physicians need to monitor such outcomes for quality assurance purposes. Data are also needed that can provide third-party payers with demonstrations of treatment efficacy.

Unfortunately, most physicians do not have a background in conducting program or treatment evaluations, because the experimental methodology and statistical tools needed for such evaluations were never taught to them in medical schools. However, clinical health psychologists have these requisite skills and, hence, are in an ideal situation to provide such services to primary care physicians. They can set up a database with appropriate psychometrically sound measures to use at baseline and follow-up evaluations. They can also be utilized to collect such data and statistically analyze outcomes. It is now quite common for clinical health psychologists to serve as consultants for medical specialists who need to document treatment outcomes. Thus, besides the assessment and treatment skills that they can offer in the primary care setting, clinical health psychologists also have the added marketing value of being able to conduct such treatment and program evaluations. Indeed, this is a strong marketing strategy to use to become an integral part of primary care practices.

Primary care physicians also need to be prompted to use data on outcomes-based clinical research. A recent survey found that primary care physicians appear to select a treatment option based on their own experience, expert consensus, or patient and public expectations, and *not* on evidenced-based medical outcome studies ("Survey shows," 2001). They are not relying on such studies because they are usually not aware of them or do not appear to have easy access to them. Again, this is an opportunity for health psychologists to help educate primary care physicians in this area.

CONCLUSIONS

There are few settings in which attention to behavior, and its consequences, is more relevant than in the primary care office. Behavioral lifestyle factors, such as tobacco use, inactivity, a high-fat diet, and high-stress careers, have now been recognized as major contributors to various medical disorders for which individuals commonly seek medical care. Primary care physicians are at the front line for treating such behavioral and emotional concomitants of these medical disorders. As noted in chapter 1, a focused assessment of patients is often needed to identify problems and make recommendations. Indeed, the prevalence of mental health problems in the general medical population, and the comorbidity of mental health problems and physical symptoms (especially when the symptoms are chronic) for which patients seek medical care, is substantial (Gatchel, 1999). Any model of health care delivery should, therefore, include psychosocial screening. This has resulted in the development of brief structured psychosocial interviews for the primary care physician (e.g., Staab & Evans, 2001).

Many physicians, moreover, have not been suitably trained in psychosocial treatment, thus leaving a vacuum in the comprehensive care of patients. It is this vacuum that can be filled by an appropriately trained clinical health psychologist. Such behavioral health integration into primary care can also ease the workload burden on physicians, can improve health outcomes, and can enhance patients' satisfaction with care. Clinical health psychologists can also help constrain the costs of medical care by providing more efficient education and follow-up evaluations of patients.

Many of the major trends and future needs that have been discussed throughout this book have been summarized in the annual report of the Center for the Advancement of Health (2001). In the introduction to the annual report, the center emphasizes that "We all understand that health and illness are much more than simple matters of biology. They are products of individual behavior—how we think, breathe, eat, drink, handle stress, live and work in a community. . . . [T]he Center for the Advancement of Health has . . . a stake in the successful transition of a health system once dominated by acute disease but now facing an aging population trying to manage chronic disease" (p. 3). A summary of its recommendations for the future of health care is presented in Exhibit 14.2. As can be seen, health psychologists can play an essential role in implementing these recommendations.

Throughout this text, we have discussed the various roles that a clinical health psychologist can play in dealing with various disorders. We have also discussed the requirements such professionals need if they are to be embraced by the medical milieu and asked to provide such services. We briefly review these requirements next.

Clinical health psychologists should become experienced in the medical culture, so that they are knowledgeable about medical conditions and

EXHIBIT 14.2
Summary of Recommendations for the Future of Health Care

- Increase the quality of health care by reducing morbidity, mortality, and cost and by increasing patient satisfaction.
- Develop well-designed, effective, and widely available behavior change services.
- Help clinicians working in health care delivery systems to "accommodate the full range of individual counseling needs of patients through a brief office-based encounter. A range of high-quality resources should be readily available to which clinicians can refer patients for more tailored support to reduce risk, to improve adherence, and to manage chronic illness."
- Include as part of standard primary health care the services required to support and encourage individuals and families to stay as healthy as possible. Individuals should learn to "act for themselves and their families to avoid health risks and better manage chronic conditions."

Note. Source is Center for the Advancement of Health (2001).

procedures and conversant in the medical vernacular of the primary care setting. Simply reading books or didactic instruction is not sufficient to become competent. Actual experience in medical settings is essential. Our suggestion would be that anyone interested in pursuing this career should be encouraged to do some postdoctoral training in an actual medical environment. Attempting to go into a medical environment "blind" will usually not be successful, because the medical staff will question your basic medical knowledge. Also, MD Consult provides online information sites that serve the clinical content needs of physicians and other health care professionals (http://www.mdconsult.com). In addition, the Cochrane Collaboration provides an up-to-date review of relevant clinical studies evaluating the efficacy of various treatment procedures (http://www.cochrane.org).

Clinical health psychologists should be prepared to present clinical research data indicating that health psychology interventions can significantly improve medical treatment outcomes, enhance treatment adherence, decrease long-term complications of a disease, and decrease medical over-utilization.

To be successful and accepted, clinical health psychologists must integrate into the primary care setting by adapting their practice to that of the primary care culture. This may mean adapting to the fact that 1-hour sessions with patients are not feasible in such settings; instead, psychologists must be able to work in a more a time-delineated fashion, with 15- to 30-minute appointments being the norm. This will also require making decisions based on less data than one is necessarily accustomed to and then making recommendations to physicians that can be processed within brief 5-minute frameworks. These types of skills are usually not taught in graduate psychology training. One must become further educated to adopt this new method of assessment, treatment, and feedback.

The clinical health psychologist can also provide valuable research services to primary care physicians by conducting treatment-outcome evaluations for quality assurance and treatment documentation purposes. Most primary care physicians do not have the requisite skills to conduct such evaluations. Demands by the government and third-party payers to document efficacy and patient satisfaction are increasing, and the clinical health psychologist can provide the tools to meet these demands.

The clinical health psychologist needs to become conversant with different models of primary care delivery systems, such as staff model health maintenance organizations, multiple-specialty physician networks, rural public health clinics, and Veterans Administration hospitals (Bruns & Johnson, 1999). The type of setting will dictate the kind of practice a health psychologist can reasonably be expected to conduct. Relatedly, becoming knowledgeable in billing issues is extremely important. Many insurance carriers will not pay for mental health services when dealing with primary care patients. Becoming familiar with current procedural terminology (CPT) codes and other diagnostic entities that can be reimbursed under the general rubric of medical services is important. Knowing about issues such as preauthorization and precertification is also extremely important.

The potential rewards for a successful clinical health psychology practice within a primary care setting can be quite gratifying. Moreover, this is increasingly becoming a "growth industry" because one current major trend is to require better primary care services to prevent the development of chronic disorders. This is especially true in a society, like the United States, in which the older population is growing and has to be treated for chronic disorders over time.

Finally, the type of comprehensive, biopsychosocial care emphasized throughout this book will also lead to more compassionate care for patients. This is because patients will be treated as "whole" people whose medical, as well as emotional, needs will be met. Indeed, based on a comprehensive review of the literature, Di Blasi, Harkness, Ernst, Georgiou, and Kleijnen (2001) concluded that physicians who adopt a warm, friendly, and reassuring manner are much more effective with patients than those who keep consultations formal and do not offer reassurance. Thus, "good bedside manner" is still very important. This reaffirms the earliest doctrine of medicine to ensure the general welfare of all patients:

> No physician insofar as he is a physician, considers his own good in what he prescribes, but the good of his patient. . . .
>
> Plato (427–347 B.C.), *The Republic*

SUMMARY

In this chapter, we reviewed the many historical changes that have occurred in medicine during the past centuries. Replacing an outdated *biomedical reductionism* approach, a more comprehensive *biopsychosocial model* of illness was proposed early in the 20th century that emphasized the unique interaction among biological, physiological, and psychosocial factors that needs to be taken into account to better understand health and illness. One of the main reasons for this heightened acceptance of such a model has been the increase in prevalence of chronic medical disorders in this country, which can be expected to continue to rise. The medical community is now poised to give health psychology a higher profile in the education of new physicians in this country. Indeed, clinical health psychologists are poised to assume this role because they have developed numerous techniques to promote healthy lifestyles to prevent the onset of disease. One particular area that shows great promise, especially in terms of cost containment, is the use of psychoeducational programs in integrated primary care.

We also discussed the emergence of recent alternative or complementary medicine approaches that are being widely utilized by the general population. Health care providers need to be aware of such alternative therapies when dealing with their patients. Finally, we noted that the evaluation of medical outcomes is now an important endeavor because of the changes in health care policies; the demands for improved allocations of resources have placed great pressure on health care professionals to provide the most cost-effective treatment available for these diseases and also to validate treatment efficacy. As a consequence, treatment-outcome monitoring has gained new importance in medicine. Clinical health psychologists have the requisite skills to conduct such outcomes monitoring and are in an ideal situation to provide such services for primary care physicians. Finally, we discussed the important requirements that clinical health psychologists will need to have if they are to be embraced by medical colleagues and asked to provide important services in primary care settings.

RECOMMENDED READINGS

Bruns, D., & Johnson, R. (1999, Winter). Understanding the opportunities of integrated primary care. *The Health Psychologist, 21,* 14–19.

Center for the Advancement of Health. (2001). *2001 annual report: Putting the pieces together.* Washington, DC: Author.

REFERENCES

Bruns, D., & Johnson, R. (1999, Winter). Understanding the opportunities of integrated primary care. *The Health Psychologist, 21*, 14–19.

Carpenter, S. (2001, November). Curriculum overhaul gives behavioral medicine a higher profile. *Monitor on Psychology*, pp. 78–79.

Center for the Advancement of Health. (2001). *2001 annual report: Putting the pieces together.* Washington, DC: Author.

Committee on Education and Training, Division 38. (1999, Spring). What a health psychologist does and how to become one. *The Health Psychologist, 21*, 16–17.

Cummings, N. A. (2000). The behavioral health practitioner of the future: The efficacy of psychoeducational programs in integrated primary care. In J. L. Thomas & J. L. Cummings (Eds.), *The collected papers of Nicolas A. Cummings: The value of psychological treatment* (pp. 406–422). Phoenix: Zeig, Tucker & Co.

Di Blasi, Z., Harkness, E., Ernst, E., Georgiou, A., & Kleijnen, J. (2001). Influence of context effects on health outcomes: A systematic review. *Lancet, 357*, 757–762.

Eisenberg, D. M. (1997). Advising patients who seek alternative medical therapies. *Annals of Internal Medicine, 127*, 61–69.

Eisenberg, D. M., Kessler, R. C., Foster, C., Norlock, F. E., Calkins, D. R., & Delbanco, T. L. (1993). Unconventional medicine in the United States: Prevalence, costs, and patterns of use. *New England Journal of Medicine, 328*, 246–252.

Gatchel, R. J. (1999). Perspectives on pain: A historical overview. In R. J. Gatchel & D. C. Turk (Eds.), *Psychosocial factors in pain: Critical perspectives* (pp. 3–17). New York: Guilford Press.

Mayer, T. G., Gatchel, R. J., & Polatin, P. B. (Eds.). (2000). *Occupational musculoskeletal disorders: Function, outcomes, and evidence.* Philadelphia: Lippincott, Williams & Wilkins.

Staab, J. P., & Evans, D. L. (2001). A streamlined method for diagnosing common psychiatric disorders in primary care. *Clinical Cornerstone, 3*, 1–9.

Survey shows MDs not relying on outcomes-based research. (2001) *HABIT, 4*(16). Retrieved December 18, 2001, from http://www.habit@cfah.org

U.S. Census Bureau. (2000). *Population projections in the United States by age, sex, race, Hispanic origin, and nativity: 1999 to 2100.* Washington, DC: Author.

U.S. Census Bureau. (2001). *The 65 years and over population: 2000.* Washington, DC: Author.

INDEX

with obesity, 150–151, 153–154
with pain disorders, 120–121
Wood, J. M., 138, 147
Woodwell, D., 69, 81
Wright, E., 211
Wu, A. W., 114
Wyatt, S., 45, 61
Wysocki, T., 53, 63

Yager, J., 185
Yanovski, S. Z., 155, 165
Yavagal, S. T., 94, 100

Zaleplon, 138
Zautra, A. J., 214, 232
Zolpidem, 138

ABOUT THE AUTHORS

Robert J. Gatchel, PhD, is currently the Elizabeth H. Penn Professor of Clinical Psychology and professor in the Departments of Psychiatry and Rehabilitation Science at the University of Texas Southwestern Medical Center at Dallas, where he is the director of graduate clinical research in the Division of Clinical Psychology. He is also the program director at the Eugene McDermott Center for Pain Management at the Medical Center. He is a diplomate of the American Board of Professional Psychology (Health Psychology) and is on the board of directors of the American Board of Clinical Health Psychology. He has conducted extensive clinical research, much of it supported by grants from the National Institutes of Health (NIH), on the psychophysiology of stress and emotion; the comorbidity of psychological and physical health disorders; and the etiology, assessment, and treatment of chronic stress and pain behavior. He is also the recipient of consecutive Research Scientist Development Awards from NIH. He has published more than 250 scientific articles and book chapters and has authored or edited 20 books, including *An Introduction to Health Psychology* (with A. Baum and D. Krantz), *Psychophysiological Disorders: Research and Clinical Applications* (with E. Blanchard), and *Psychological Approaches to Pain Management: A Practitioner's Handbook* (with D. Turk).

Mark S. Oordt, PhD, is a clinical health psychologist in San Antonio, Texas. He is a diplomate of the American Board of Professional Psychology (Health Psychology) and a fellow of the American Academy of Health Psychology. He has experience as a practicing primary care psychologist and in establishing new behavioral health services in medical settings. He also conducts training and supervision with behavioral health providers working in primary care clinics and provides consultation to established integrated care practices.